Paul Bartel

ALSO BY STEPHEN B. ARMSTRONG

Andrew V. McLaglen: The Life and Hollywood Career (McFarland, 2011)

Pictures About Extremes: The Films of John Frankenheimer (McFarland, 2008)

PAUL BARTEL
The Life and Films

STEPHEN B. ARMSTRONG

McFarland & Company, Inc., Publishers
Jefferson, North Carolina

ISBN (print) 978-0-7864-9915-1
ISBN (ebook) 978-1-4766-2767-0

LIBRARY OF CONGRESS CATALOGUING DATA ARE AVAILABLE

British Library cataloguing data are available

© 2017 Stephen B. Armstrong. All rights reserved

No part of this book may be reproduced or transmitted in any form or by any means, electronic or mechanical, including photocopying or recording, or by any information storage and retrieval system, without permission in writing from the publisher.

Front cover: Paul Bartel, 1989 (Cinecom Pictures/Photofest)

Printed in the United States of America

*McFarland & Company, Inc., Publishers
Box 611, Jefferson, North Carolina 28640
www.mcfarlandpub.com*

For Charlotte Millicent Armstrong

"All humor is subversive."—Bob Newhart[1]

"My comedy probably comes from always wanting to make people laugh because I always thought they'd like me if I made them laugh."—Paul Bartel[2]

Table of Contents

Acknowledgments — ix
Preface — 1
Introduction: The Discreet Charm of Paul Bartel — 4

PART ONE: THE LIFE OF PAUL BARTEL

1. Growing Up — 9
2. Early Experience — 14
3. The Cormans — 23
4. More Fun at New World — 37
5. Independent — 50
6. In Demand — 66
7. About Men and Women — 99

PART TWO: INTERVIEWS

Joe Dante — 125
Allan Arkush — 136
Roger Corman — 148
Richard Blackburn — 152
John Waters — 164

Table of Contents

PART THREE:
FILM AND TELEVISION WORK

An Excrescence of Style: Paul Bartel and the Grotesque	169
Directing Credits	178
Chapter Notes	183
Bibliography	192
Index	195

Acknowledgments

Writing a book is always dizzying, and this one would never have been completed without help from Roger Corman, John Waters, Joe Dante, Ed Begley, Jr., Allan Arkush, Bob Schulenberg, Barry Dennen, Jonas Mekas, David Blyth, Michael Schroeder, Alan Toomayan, Dick Blackburn, Paul Chihara, Jim Katz, Tina Hirsch, Susan Saiger, Denny Tedesco, O-Lan Jones, Jim Turner, Rob St. Mary, Andy Stein, Jon Davison, James D'Arc, Tab Hunter, Allan Glaser, Lucy Kizirian, Wendy Bartel, Adam Walderman, Julie LaRue, Robert Powell, William Nesbitt, Daniel Lopez, Hope Lopez, Bernie Bennett, Mike McGrath, Dianne Aldrich, Laura Mulvey, Adam Abraham, Art Fein, Joe McBride, Doug Fowler, Cynthia Brown, Susan Allenback, Alix Elias, Elinor Silverman, Randy Jasmine, Susan Ertel, Jim Haendiges and the Dixie State University Professional Development Committee, Laura Schnitker (University of Maryland Special Collections in Mass Media & Culture), Jane and Jay Hudiburg, Michael and Kaitlin Oliveri, Mike and Janet Oliveri, Barcelona Armstrong and Dean and Mimi Armstrong,

Kind thoughts and special thanks to Zane W. Levitt, a friend to animals and a great photographer, who in conversation referred to Bartel's "discreet charm" and gave me the title for the introduction.

Finally, I cannot express enough thanks to my wife, Katie Armstrong, for her indefatigable support and patience.

Preface

In my early teens I liked to watch MTV—this was the era when the network played music videos throughout the day and sometimes music-themed movies late at night. I remember heading down to the basement one weekend to catch *Rock 'n' Roll High School*, a low-budget comedy about kids who love the Ramones and blow up their school. What really got me as I watched was Mary Woronov, the film's villain, Miss Togar, a malcontent school principal. She was mean and ridiculous but weirdly appealing at the same time, as was her crony, a music teacher named Mr. McGree. Played sympathetically by Paul Bartel, Mr. McGree over the course of the picture transforms from a member of the high school's autocratic faculty into an evangelist for punk rock. Seeing the actor wearing a Ramones T-shirt in the climactic concert sequence was at once funny and absolutely credible. Other than Miss Togar, who in this sad and beautiful world *doesn't* enjoy the Ramones?

We got by with basic cable in our house, though now and then the provider would give us temporary access to premium channels like HBO and Cinemax, and we'd watch commercial-free versions of films that had been spared the censors' scissors. On a weekend afternoon when my parents were out, I was watching one of these channels, and *Eating Raoul* came on. It opened with a credits sequence that featured a springing jazz score and cartoon images of the film's stars: Mary Woronov and Paul Bartel. I recognized the actors' faces and names from *Rock 'n' Roll High School*, and so I decided to see what the movie would offer. The bizarre and stunning story that followed, about sex and murder and sinister aspects of American-variety capitalism, left me bewildered and a little scared. Here was material I'm sure my parents would not want me to see—and I liked it! When it sank in that the male lead, Paul Bartel, was also the director, I became an admirer, finding in him the same radical temperament that would eventually attract me to artist-entertainers like Lou Reed and Iggy Pop, the novelist Harry Crews and outré movie directors John Waters and Todd Solondz.

My next big encounter with a Paul Bartel movie came a few years later. I was nineteen years old, and I had gone to New York City to spend the summer studying in a program at NYU. My father stayed a few days with me before the term started, and we stayed in a midtown hotel. At night, we went to see movies on 52nd Street. We took in a double-feature dedicated to Cary Grant and watched *The Philadelphia Story* and *To Catch a Thief*. Another night we caught a road film comedy called *Cold Feet*, with Tom Waits, Sally Kirkland and Keith Carradine. The last picture we watched together was Bartel's *Scenes from the Class Struggle in Beverly Hills*. When it was over, my politically moderate and sometimes socially conservative father declared that it had to be the funniest movie he'd ever seen. To this day he remembers *Scenes* as a movie that rivals the early Inspector Clouseau movies and the best work of Mel Brooks for laughs.

At that point in my life, I wanted to be a writer, a novelist, which never happened. Instead I became a film history writer and started publishing articles and books about movie directors, especially ones the critical establishment has underrated or ignored, for instance, John Frankenheimer. In 2014, I felt the impulse to get started on a new project, and the idea came to me that I should write about Bartel. In the decades since I'd seen *Scenes*, I'd watched all his other films but *Shelf Life*. *Private Parts*, *Death Race 2000* and *Lust in the Dust* in particular had left me with that same strange, dazzled feeling that came over me when I first saw *Eating Raoul*.

I pitched the idea for a book on Bartel to McFarland and the response was favorable. I proceeded to contact and set up interviews with as many people as possible who knew the director. I took advantage of the extensive interlibrary resources made available to me by my employer, Dixie State University, and looked into holdings related to Bartel at the Academy of Motion Picture Arts and Science's Margaret Herrick Library. Bob Schulenberg, Barry Dennen and Alan Toomayan graciously shared with me their own *barteliana*.

I've learned over the last two decades that researching and writing about a favorite topic can wear down the affection that prompted the effort in the first place. "Yet each man kills the things he loves," warned

Oscar Wilde—one of Bartel's favorite writers. But such is not the case here. I'm more convinced now than I was at the start that Paul Bartel is one of the great independent filmmakers, who used comedy and sometimes horror to question and challenge the rituals, beliefs, mores and laws that bind Americans together.

Introduction
The Discreet Charm of Paul Bartel

From 1970 to 1983, Roger Corman held the reins at New World Pictures, a low-budget independent production-distribution company that released dozens of remarkable movies onto the grindhouse circuit, among them *The Hot Box* (1972), *Caged Heat* (1974), *Jackson County Jail* (1976) and *Piranha* (1978).[1] Although he often paid the people who worked for him paltry wages, Corman attracted talent to an extraordinary degree, giving early roles to future stars Pam Grier, Sylvester Stallone and Tommy Lee Jones. David Carradine, who played the lead in several Corman productions, including *Thunder and Lightning* (1978) and *Deathsport* (1978), speculated, "It's almost as though you can't have a career in this business without having passed through Roger's hands for at least a moment."[2]

New World also served as a magnet for young directors eager to gain experience on the set, including Jonathan Kaplan, Joe Dante, Allan Arkush, Ron Howard and Penelope Spheeris. Paul Bartel (1938–2000) passed through New World, too. He served first as a second unit director on one of the company's best-remembered films, *Big Bad Mama* (1974), and later directed *Death Race 2000* (1975), a satirical poke at American's appetite for ultra-violent entertainment.

From Corman, Bartel learned to make commercially viable films on the cheap, using non-union casts, independent sources of financing and extensive location shooting to tell stories that combined action, sex and humor while coating them with "a patina of social conscience."[3] After moving on from New World, Bartel had tremendous success

Introduction 5

exploiting this formula with *Eating Raoul* (1982), a black comedy about murder, swingers and cannibalism that he wrote, produced and directed—and in which he also played one of the leads. Independently financed for $700,000, the movie went on to yield $10 million at the box office, drew favorable attention from critics and led to a lucrative period in the eighties for Bartel as a freelancer, during which he worked, most notably, on Steven Spielberg's *Amazing Stories* television series.[4] Several opportunities to make features came in, too, and in quick succession Bartel directed *Not for Publication* (1984), *Lust in the Dust* (1985) and *The Longshot* (1986). Although these pictures failed to connect with general audiences, *Lust in the Dust*, a send-up of westerns starring Tab Hunter, Divine and Lainie Kazan, found support in the gay community, which it retains today. As Kazan explains: "Well, it's a real cult classic. I mean, there is not a gay man in Los Angeles, New York or Chicago who does not come up to me and say, 'I saw *Lust in the Dust*.'"[5]

Bartel was himself gay, and he used his films to explore the conflicts and paradoxes that can arise between gay and straight people in settings where heteronormative codes abound. In his first commercial feature, *Private Parts* (1972), an impotent serial killer who preys on women and tries to penetrate them with a syringe turns out to be a woman. In *Eating Raoul*, repressed Mary Bland and her closeted husband, Paul, endure and even prevail as a married couple in part because they

Bartel, summer 1989 (photograph by Rick Kendzierski, *Cleveland Plain Dealer*).

are not attracted to one another sexually. *Lust in the Dust* features the male actor Divine looking astonishingly female—at times even beautiful—in his role as a dancehall girl. And the undersung *Scenes from the Class Struggle in Beverly Hills* (1989) climaxes with a pair of housemen, one bisexual, the other straight, consummating a physical relationship.

The frequency with which Bartel addressed transgressive subject matter is a hallmark of his style, along with his affection for ribald comedy. For Bartel, bawdy stories told well carried the potential to disorient viewers and prompt them to reconsider inherited notions about morality, mortality, crime, sex, business and family, even aesthetics. While promoting *Scenes from the Class Struggle in Beverly Hills*, for example, he admitted to reporter Terry Kelleher that the movie certainly exhibited "bad taste," but for him, bad taste, a bit like cholesterol, comes in bad and good varieties. "If you wish you hadn't seen [the film], it's bad bad taste.... If you feel you were brought dangerously close to the edge, but at the end you were made to laugh or learn something, then it's good bad taste."[6] In an interview he gave to radio host Terry Gross, Bartel expanded upon this strategy of amusing people by making them uncomfortable: "[W]hat I try to accomplish is a kind of contradiction. I try to take subject matter that is likely to offend and upset people in the abstract and treat it as tactfully, as discreetly, as possible so that they are induced to laugh at it at the same time that they are gasping."[7]

Critics were often unwilling or unable to appreciate Bartel's satirical intentions and condemned his films for being offensive, even silly. An instance of the hostility he could arouse appears in a review the *Los Angeles Times*'s Sheila Benson wrote on *Lust in the Dust*. Because the film, she felt, was unable to parody the western genre effectively, "it falls back on dumb, sniggering sexual innuendo that is vulgar without being particularly funny, or on jokes that just don't work."[8] Hal Hinson, writing in the *Washington Post*, dismissed *Scenes from the Class Struggle* on the same grounds: "Desperate to shock, Bartel forgets a truism—that those who care about outraging an audience almost never do. As a result, he is crass and obvious when he tries to be perverse, leaden where he wants to be deft."[9]

Since the director's death, comedies produced in the United States have employed coarse humor with increasing regularity, and now the raunchier bits in his films probably seem less outlandish and distasteful than they did two or three decades ago. The sharpness of his satirical vision, however, has persisted, and a survey of his body of work reveals the consistency with which he used his films, as well his acting, to underscore the unseemly, ludicrous and occasionally dangerous aspects of American culture, e.g., the sadism that seeps through sports entertainment (*Death Race, Cannonball!*); the opportunistic sensationalism that pervades news media (*Not for Publication*); the appetite for sexual violence nurtured by popular entertainment (*Private Parts, Eating Raoul*); and the unending divisions between the gentry and the poor (*Scenes from the Class Struggle in Beverly Hills*). A seriousness of purpose permeates Bartel's work that few critics have recognized or explored.

Paul Bartel: The Life and Films surveys this underrated filmmaker's career in its entirety. The book starts with a comprehensive biography that considers the ways in which personal experiences influenced his work, providing production histories as well, and a good deal of hermeneutical commentary. A part comprised of interviews with people who knew and worked with Bartel follows. A final part catalogues the signature themes and technical features that characterize Bartel's work and a filmography.

My hope for this effort is two-fold: to bring attention to the strengths in the Bartel canon and to precipitate new discussion of him and his work. Though his output in the end was small, Bartel, like Jim Jarmusch and John Waters, embraced independent filmmaking and relished the creative liberties it allowed. "I've always been more interested in doing my own eccentric little films instead of being a studio director," he told Deirdre Kelly.[10] In all likelihood, Bartel's commitment to working in the American motion picture industry on his own terms cost him the chance to make more movies than he did. His friend Joe Dante thought as much: "Obviously all filmmakers need somebody's money. But Paul was very specific about the kind of film he wanted to make—and this sometimes led to conflict—but he managed to hew to his own design, and he produced a unique body of work."[11]

Indeed, the eleven films he did complete bear the distinctive, personal mark of an artist—an auteur—who unvaryingly invested his work with subversive ideas, weird characters, fey wit and a great sense of fun.

PART ONE: THE LIFE OF PAUL BARTEL

1

Growing Up

On May 13, 2000, a Saturday, Paul Bartel died in his New York apartment.[1] Although the popular press had largely ignored the director since the release of *Scenes from the Class Struggle in Beverly Hill* a decade earlier, a spate of eulogies quickly appeared, praising him for the manner in which he'd used sex and violence to ridicule the moral underpinnings of American culture. "The films ... portray an askew world," wrote the *Advocate*'s Alonso Duraide, "but one hilarious enough to keep audiences engaged.... Bartel will be remembered as a witty and keen-eyed observer of human behavior, and even his most outrageous films convey truths about people and society."[2]

Bartel's passing was the second misfortune his family experienced that spring. In April, his eighty-seven-year-old mother, Jesse, had died in Delray Beach, Florida, where she and Paul's father, Bill, owned a home.[3] As preparations were being made for the funeral, Paul began to feel great fatigue, his skin had a yellow hue and his eyes turned a greenish-yellow. Understandably worried, he headed to Manhattan to meet with his doctor, who recognized that he needed a specialist's attention. He was in fact very ill—cancer had infiltrated his liver ducts—and he was promptly scheduled for surgery in Boston, during which half his liver was taken out.

The prognosis following the eight-hour operation had been encouraging, *Variety*'s Todd McCarthy noted, and Paul "felt good, even leaving the hospital early."[4] He headed to Bay Head, New Jersey, a beach town, where his family owned another house. His sister Wendy, back from Florida, was then living there, and she was eager to help him as he recuperated. But when their father called to tell them that he was coming from Florida to stay at the house as well, Paul decided to leave for

Manhattan. Though Bill Bartel had supported his son's efforts as a director for decades, loaning him money, sometimes large sums, his distaste for gay men and gay culture had hurt Paul. "My father was never comfortable with Paul being gay," Wendy said. "He took masculinity to a ridiculous limit. He was smart enough to not be ugly to Paul about it or to ever embarrass him, but he wasn't capable of discussing it…. I think Paul was bitter about that."[5]

Paul's apartment, which he'd owned since the early eighties, wasn't particularly spacious, but its proximity to Central Park, Broadway, restaurants and cinemas gratified him, and during those final days, he'd enjoyed himself as well as he could, bringing up meals, watching movies, listening to music—all his favorite things.[6] He was confident that he would live and that he would return to work soon. But his heart, weakened by the stress of surgery and travel and grief, wouldn't allow it. What killed Paul on that cool May night was myocardial infarction—heart failure—not cancer.

His life began in New York, too—in Brooklyn, August 6, 1938. Bill Bartel at the time worked in Manhattan as a copywriter for an advertising concern, but a few months after Paul's birth, he and Jesse decided to move to Nutley, New Jersey, a prospering suburb twenty minutes from the city, where they had grown up and where their parents still lived. The Bartels stayed in Nutley for more than a decade, during which Paul's siblings—Lucy, Peter and Wendy—were born. Though Bill's temper could be scary, the Bartel kids led fairly happy lives. They were pushed to work hard in school—"Education was our religion," Wendy recalled in a 2015 interview—but they were also encouraged to pursue extracurricular interests: "Lucy's was horseback riding. Pete had a motorboat and I had a lot of friends," said Wendy. Paul's passion was fireworks: the lights and sounds fascinated him and gave him an opportunity to put on shows for audiences.[7] His fondness for acting surfaced, as well, during these years, and he began to perform in stage productions at the Nutley Little Theatre. "[Paul] knew from the time he was a very young person that he was going to be in theatre in some way or another," Wendy said.[8]

It was also in Nutley that Paul began to enjoy movies, often watching them in a place called the Franklyn Theater. "[T]here was a film club in town that showed 16mm prints of old silent films and classic foreign films; I used to spend a lot of time there."[9] To Michael Singer, he explained, "I used to go to the movies a lot, and my favorite films were animated films. I loved Saturday cartoon matinees, the UPA [United Productions of America] films."[10] The *Village Voice*'s Michael Goodwin traced Bartel's earliest interest in making movies to this revival house in Nutley. "He was an artistic kid, into painting, marionettes, and old movies, and when he saw Disney's *Pinocchio*, he decided to become an animator."[11]

Following Wendy's birth in 1951, the Bartels moved again, this time to nearby Montclair, New Jersey. By then, Bill had become a well-paid advertising executive, and he was able to purchase "a big, beautiful, six-bedroom house." In Montclair, the family "lived a pretty cushy life," Wendy said. "We were members of a country club where our parents played golf. We also had a house at the beach, about an hour away. Our summers were spent in Bay Head, New Jersey, swimming, boating and entertaining."[12]

Paul's interest in cartoons, as well as painting and drawing, only increased as he grew older. "[W]hen I was about eleven, I decided that what I really wanted to do was direct animation." Ambitious and self-assured, as a young teenager he approached UPA, the animation company responsible for the cartoon characters Mr. Magoo and Gerald McBoing Boing, and asked for a job. "My father worked in advertising, and through his contacts I made some friends at UPA's New York studio, which mostly produced TV commercials. They let me borrow prints of their theatrical shorts, and then when I was thirteen, I actually had a summer job there. I learned to run the animation crane and picked up the basics of animation."[13] The UPA visual style often straddled the popular and the avant-garde, a tendency that would characterize Bartel's own best work as a director. In *When Magoo Flew: The Rise and Fall of Animation Studio UPA*, Adam Abraham explains: "In the fifties, the artists of UPA moved beyond the rounded realism of the Walt Disney Studio and the crash-bang anarchy of Warner Bros. to create films that were innovative and graphically bold—the cartoon equivalent to modern art."[14]

When Paul pursued his first experience directing, he received assistance from classmates as well as family and teachers. "By the time he was a student at Montclair High School, [Bartel] had persuaded his father to buy him a 16mm German-made motion picture camera and, in the words of his father, 'proceeded to con' a teacher into allowing him to devote a semester to making an animated cartoon, doing the main drawings himself and using the class to do the 'in-betweens,' which required 3,000 cels, the transparent sheets on which the original drawings are traced or transferred."[15]

Though his intelligence and creativity attracted admirers, Paul was not altogether happy during his high school years because he felt that he had to keep secret a fundamental part of his personality—his sexual orientation. In 1998, he explained to film director Tommy O'Haver: "When I was growing up and wanted to be a filmmaker, I had to fight all the horrible social attitudes—and my parents' attitudes—toward being gay. I remember when I was fourteen, my father and I were in the car and somehow the subject of gay men came up. He said, 'I find that really disgusting, don't you?' A little bit of me died inside, but I said, 'Yeah, I really do. It's horrible.' Of course, I'd known since I was ten that I was gay."[16]

Following graduation in 1956, Paul left New Jersey to study in UCLA's prestigious Theater Arts department. "The place was a creative hotbed in the late fifties ... and so close to the heart of American film production," he said to Jim Pickrell, a reporter attached to UCLA's newspaper, the *Daily Bruin*. "It was an all-around experience where I learned design, camera, painting, acting, writing and got a chance to work in some big musicals. I played the French ambassador in *Of Thee I Sing*, and I played in *Finian's Rainbow*—all fond memories."[17] The courses he took and several students he met at the university led him away from his earlier interest in cartooning. "When I came out to California for the first time.... I thought I wanted to be an animation director. But the bottom was falling out of the market for good, ambitious, sophisticated animation. And also, I became a little more interested in theatre and acting, as well as writing and live-action films."[18]

At UCLA, Paul made friends with people with whom he would work again when he became a motion picture director, including Bob Schulenberg—a graduate student in the Theater Arts department's animation program—and singer-actor Barry Dennen.[19] Dennen was introduced to Paul by another student, Gail Lucas. Dennen recalled in a 2015 interview that Lucas had come up to him on campus and said, "'Have you met Paul Bartel?' I said, 'No. Who is he?' 'Well, come over, I'll introduce you. He looks like Oscar Wilde. He should be standing with his nose in a lily.' I thought, 'This I have to see.' So I went over, and there was Paul. We started to talk, and that was it. That was the beginning of our friendship." The pair began to collaborate creatively as both shared a love for stagecraft and acting. "I [wrote] some plays at UCLA," Dennen said. "Paul was ... in one of them along with Gail Lucas, a play that I wrote specifically for him titled 'Encore.' It was a one-act play. The gist of it was that the commedia dell'arte characters—Pierrot, Columbine, Punch and so forth—have been asleep. They've been away for a long time. They haven't been in the theatre. They wake up on stage and find themselves in fifties America. They react to the automobiles, which they pantomimed, that kind of stuff. It was a sweet little play, and Paul was very good in it as Pierrot."[20]

Paul's college experience, unfortunately, was interrupted as a result of a disclosure he made to his family during a visit to Montclair. "I think it was his second year he came home and announced that he was gay," said Wendy. "My parents, typical of their day and age, thought homosexuality was something that could be 'cured.' So they took him out of college and had him see a psychiatrist for a year before he was allowed to return to California. I don't know for sure, but maybe most of Paul's anger at my folks, and life in general, was about this issue of being gay when it still wasn't accepted or understood. Paul was a very strong, independent fellow. He didn't compromise himself. But after that, he did keep his homosexuality hidden from his family."[21]

As Paul would never have a lasting, committed relationship during his adult life, the harm wrought by conversion therapy and his parents' disapproval seems to have run deep. Bob Schulenberg suspects that "Paul had a lot of self-hatred probably instilled by his father not openly accepting his sexuality."[22] This is not to say that he led a chaste or celibate life. Wendy remembers her brother divulging (with a bit of a smile) that he'd had so much sex as a younger man that he could spend the rest of his later days without ever needing it again.[23]

2

Early Experience

Bartel minored in romance languages at UCLA, and he spoke French and Italian fluently by the time he graduated in 1961.[1] To pursue his training as a filmmaker further, he went to Italy on a Fulbright scholarship for a year and studied at the Centro Sperimentale di Cinematografia in the Cinecitta studio complex in Rome.[2] Among his peers were Bernardo Bertolucci and Marco Bellochio, who each experienced broadly successful careers in world cinema.[3] The exposure to new ideas about moviemaking and its potential use for socio-political criticism excited the young American. While promoting *Cannonball!* in the mid-seventies (one of his more conventional and commercial pictures), he recalled: "The Italian approach stirred me up a lot. Godard, Antonioni, Elio Petri and Nanni Loy were the favorites at the time, and the Marxist line was in the air."[4]

Bartel and Bellochio collaborated on a seventeen-minute experimental film titled *Progetti* (*Plans*), which they filmed "in Rome in 35mm."[5] The short was selected for screening at the 1962 Venice Film Festival.[6] To improve *Progetti*'s chances for exhibition in his own country, after Paul returned from Europe he connected with the Film-Makers' Cooperative, a collective founded by brothers Jonas and Adolfas Mekas in New York City that distributes the works of independent directors.[7] For the group's catalogue, he prepared the following statement:

> This film was made in Rome in the spring of 1962 during my Antonioni period. I was on a Fulbright at the time, studying directing at the famous Centro Sperimentale di Cinematografia, and I wanted to sum up in a film some of my observations as a cinema student in Rome. So I made a film about two aspiring actors studying at the Centro who wanted to come to the Actors Studio in New York and become movie stars overnight, and who actually believe that this is going to happen to

2. Early Experience

them. The point of the film is that these actors are really incapable of acting in either sense of the word. But they certainly know how to go through the motions and are beautiful to look at and to listen to, if you don't mind Italian(s). One of the actors is dubbed by Marco Bellochio, who has since become quite a director in his own right. This film is also notable for the mysterious performance of Astrid Weyman, the star of the Dutch feature, *Gangster Girl*, by Franz Weiss. When Oskar Werner saw *Progetti* in Paris in the fall of '62 he became very excited and [showed it] for Truffaut and Clouzot, who were also reportedly enthusiastic about the film.[8]

Bartel's freedom to pursue personal film projects was thwarted, however. He was drafted, and being in good health, he was called up to serve a two-year stint in the U.S. Army, a disappointment that was so great his "friends thought I was headed for a nervous breakdown."[9] His time in the pre–Vietnam-era Army nevertheless benefited him professionally as he managed to get assigned to the Signal Corps Pictorial Center in Long Island City, Queens, a motion picture production facility "where he performed a variety of jobs (including assistant director, script clerk, and occasionally, actor) on training films, covering topics like how to properly fire missles."[10] He was able to keep an apartment in "Gramercy Park and drive to the Army studio, which was the old New York Paramount lot, every day."[11]

Living in Manhattan gave Paul the opportunity in his free time to socialize with others who shared his interest in the movies. Among these people was Elinor Silverman, a publicist attached to the Film Society of Lincoln Center.[12] Silverman was a friend of Helen G. Scott, the "director of public relations" for the French Film Office, an operation committed to broadening the American public's appreciation for France by "expanding the market for its films."[13] Thanks to their acquaintance with Scott, Bartel and Silverman would watch movies made by *nouvelle vague* figures like Roger Vadim, Francois Truffaut and Jean-Luc Godard before their formal release into American cinemas. Barry Dennen lived in New York at this time, too, and he and Bartel together sought out older French films, Clair's *Le Millions* and *À nous la liberte*, for instance, and Carne's *Children of Paradise*.[14] Bartel also attended screenings of experimental films throughout the city. These "underground" movies— often confrontational, satirical and quasi-pornographic—were the subject of analysis and praise in Jonas Mekas's "Film Journal" column, which he wrote for the *Village Voice*, and they would guide Bartel as models later in the decade when he made his own independently-financed shorts, "The Secret Cinema" and "Naughty Nurse."

When his obligation to the Army was complete, Paul went to work as an assistant production manager at Rose-Magwood Productions, Inc., "a New York production company that made TV commercials." There, he worked "primarily as an assistant production manager—planning out budgets, hiring crews, etc.—but never allowed to direct."[15] He continued to visit movie houses with Elinor Silverman, volunteering to work on other people's movies, too, and occasionally landing paying jobs. He designed, for example, the titles for a full-length independent feature, *The Double-Barrelled Detective Story* (1965), which Adolfas Mekas directed.

Bartel was not content in his role at Rose-Magwood. "I was very frustrated. They would never let me direct, which in retrospect was probably a blessing. I decided at the urging of several of my friends to just make a movie however I could, by hook or by crook."[16] He crafted a script for a picture that would exploit the low-budget shooting techniques and anti-establishment themes of underground cinema as it simultaneously needled cinephiles (like him) who enjoyed movies of this type. Titled "The Secret Cinema," the story chronicled the experiences of a character named Jane whose life, unknown to her, is being filmed by a motion picture production and screened for the pleasure of a clandestine film society. In a 1985 piece he wrote for *American Film*, Bartel explained: "The story, which sprang from the darker reaches of my unconscious, concerned a young woman living alone in New York, who begins to suspect that everyone she knows, including her fiancé and her mother, is conspiring to film her life with hidden cameras and present it as a sort of comic serial."[17] To Mark Olsen, Bartel explained that the original concept was harsher than the film he wound up making. "[T]he first image from the story that occurred to me was the ending. I wanted to have the heroine, Jane, deceived and abandoned by everyone, alone in her apartment, stumbling into her bathroom to open her veins with a razor. And instead of being in her bathroom she finds herself on the stage of Radio City Music Hall with thousands of people cheering her and applauding. That was the first idea and the whole rest of the scenario followed. And as so often happens with first ideas, it was never realized."[18]

The movie was shot on location throughout the city in the spring of 1966. Bartel built his cast and crew with several friends: Bob Schulenberg—who was now living in New York and working at Bill Bartel's advertising firm—served as both producer and production designer;

the part of Jane went to Amy Vane, a UCLA Theater Arts alumna; and Barry Dennen, cast in a standout role, played a sinister psychiatrist figure. Made for just $5,000 and dependent on donated time from volunteers and loaned equipment, the production anticipated logistical problems Bartel would face on a larger scale fifteen years later when he made *Eating Raoul*.[19] "I was so naïve, I thought ["The Secret Cinema"] could be made in about four days, but as it turned out it took a number of weekends, I don't remember exactly how many.... I borrowed a camera and enlisted the aid of everybody I knew in the movie business in New York and made [it] on short ends that the commercials company [Rose-Magwood] gave me. I also used their editing facilities to put it together. In fact, the last scene of 'The Secret Cinema' was shot in their cutting room."[20] Dennen recalled that spare stock was supplied from another source as well: "Paul couldn't really afford to buy a roll of negative film, and he got the short ends, that is to say the film that was not exposed, from porn films. He would pick up what lengths of footage he could from the leftover film on the porn reels." More money was saved by shooting the movie silent, a technique still customary in Italy when Bartel studied there. "We dubbed it later on, supplied the voices," Dennen said, "which gave it that very rough quality that was so crazy and so *young*."[21]

Bartel and Schulenberg, with some help from Bill Bartel, also succeeded in shooting a portion of the film in New York's regal Plaza Hotel. Paul felt this opportunity was "an incredibly big deal." He said, "We shot all night and barely got everything done. I had a friend who was an AD working at Filmways at the time, and he was able to bring down a truckload full of lights and a bunch of electricians to plug them in. The Plaza gave us *carte blanche*, and we invited all our friends to be extras. The hotel donated all their leftover pastries from the day before."[22] Bartel's care with money sometimes prompted him to skirt the law. As he told *L.A. Weekly*'s Michael Dare, "I made a deal with a guy in a New York lab to process the film under the counter, and I always got my rushes in boxes marked 'CBS.' I met the guy in the men's room, and we exchanged cash—it was very New York. Each time we did it the price went up a few cents."[23]

When he started to show "The Secret Cinema" later in 1966, Bartel's refusal to abide by what Jonas Mekas condemned as the "high moral and esthetic standards" of mainstream filmmaking generated an enthusiastic response.[24] Aided by Elinor Silverman, he successfully submitted the movie to the 1966 London Film Festival and the 1967 New York Film Festival. A distribution group called Aries picked up the picture and booked it with a feature, *Murder à la Mod*, directed by Brian De Palma. "The only place we could find to open the films was Tambellini's Gate, a theater on Second Avenue at Tenth Street," Bartel said. "We had to make 16mm reduction prints of both films, for which I, as the one with the steady job, paid. But the film opened, found a responsive audience, got good reviews and launched Brian and me on our respective paths."[25] Incidentally, the night the "The Secret Cinema" and *Murder à la Mod* premiered at Tambellini's Gate—May 1, 1968—the Theatre of the Ridiculous, an avant-garde stage company, was booked to appear. A member of this ensemble was Bartel's friend—and future collaborator—Mary Woronov.[26]

"The Secret Cinema" anticipated character types and narrative scenarios Bartel would return to often. Gary Morris writes, "The film presaged the sardonic tone of most of his later work, though he would mostly abandon 'The Secret Cinema's' experimental aspects in favor of linear narratives with perverse touches."[27] Trapped, imperiled females like Jane show up in *Private Parts*, *Eating Raoul* and *Shelf Life*; surveillance and conspiracy factor into the plots of *Death Race 2000*, *Cannonball!*, and *Not for Publication*; and parodies of health professionals turn up in "Naughty Nurse," *Death Race 2000*, *Eating Raoul* and *Scenes from the Class Struggle in Beverly Hills*. Stylistically, the picture betrays the influence of German expressionist cinema, *film noir* and the satirical humor that works through pictures like Godard's *Bande à part* (1964) and Malle's *The Lovers* (1958)—a lobby poster for *The Lovers* actually hangs from the wall in Jane's apartment.

"The Secret Cinema" displays a willingness to explore sexual themes that in the second half of the sixties were far more marginal in the U.S. than they are today. The film upsets our ability to sort between the real and the invented, actuality and performance, gay and straight. For instance, Jane's boyfriend, Dick (Philip Carlson), explains early in the film that he no longer wishes to date her because "[l]ook, it's not just that you bore me, it's that, well, I don't really like ... girls in general." Later, Jane learns that Dick is apparently having a sexual relationship with an African American woman named Helen (Connie Ellison). The genuineness of these scenarios is unclear—is Dick acting when he intimates to Jane that he is gay? Is his relationship with Helen real—or an invention of Troppogrosso (Gordon Felio), the director overseeing the film being made of Jane's life? In short, the film is deconstructive and "queer," exploring as it does the ways in which "normative and nonnormative varieties of sexuality depend on, or interact with, one another."[28]

Bartel eventually left Rose-Magwood to work for Hearst Metrotone News, Inc., a newsreel service located in midtown Manhattan. His duties there included creating documentaries for one of the company's biggest clients, the U.S. Information Agency (USIA). Under the leadership of George Stevens, Jr. (son of the acclaimed Hollywood director), the USIA distributed theatrical films, news programs and radio shows for audiences in third world countries, where, it was hoped, they would enhance perceptions of American diplomatic initiatives.[29] The *New York Daily News*'s Frank Sanello explained: "[T]he aspiring auteur found himself ... making flattering documentaries about right-wing dictators from Asia and Latin America who happened to be visiting the White House. The U.S. government gave the documentaries to the dictators as personal souvenirs and for consumption at movie theaters in their home countries."[30] Bartel also oversaw production of a monthly Spanish-language USIA program called *Horizontes* for Latin American audiences. One of the films he made for the series was "Preludio Olimpico," a promotional overview of the 1968 Mexico City Olympics.[31]

During the three years he worked for Hearst Metrotone News, Bartel lived in Manhattan, and he continued to spend his free time with people who made films that subverted what they felt were this country's reactionary views on class, race and war—views that Bartel ironically upheld with the documentaries he was making. Among these filmmakers was writer-director Ted Gershuny, with whom Bartel collaborated on several unrealized comic scripts—including one titled *Queen Kong vs. the Devil Dykes*. Another was Charles Hirsch, who'd produced *Greetings* (1968), a comic anti–Vietnam feature starring Robert De Niro, which Brian De Palma had directed. With Hirsch, Bartel co-wrote a softcore comedy with the working title *Cornucopia Sexualis* (1969), which set out to provoke—and titillate—audiences with depictions of interracial sex, lesbianism and transsexuality. Directed by Hirsch and edited by his wife, Tina, the picture was shot in color on 16mm film and picked up for distribution with an X rating by an adult-content group called DistribPix, which re-titled it for release as *Does Size Really Count?* The picture marked the first time Bartel had a substantive on-screen role. He played, as he put it, a "demented psychiatrist who runs a group therapy session. And each of the members of my group tells the story of the experience that led to his or her sexual dysfunction. The climax of the film is a member of the group who is completely paralyzed and unable to speak, so her sexual adventure which has been pieced together by our researchers is acted out in front of her by other members of the group ... in the hope that the shock of seeing it reproduced will cure her. But instead she falls over dead. And there's a little epilogue in which I'm viewed in prison soliciting funds for my lawyer in order to carry on with my ... experimental psychiatric work."[32]

Though he enjoyed contributing to other directors' movies, Bartel still longed to make another self-financed short that he could show as a sample of his directing skills. In spite of the good notices that came to "The Secret Cinema," he had experienced difficulty getting the movie screened in theaters. "It was too short to play on its own and too long to play before most features."[33] The next film he made, he decided, would have an even shorter running time, and he proceeded to work up a brief, comic—and confrontational—scenario about a ménage a trois titled "Naughty Nurse," a satire of "pornography, involving rubber bands, paper clips, but no sex or nudity."[34]

Shot on location throughout New York with short ends and borrowed equipment, "Naughty Nurse"—which runs just around nine minutes—presents viewers with subject matter quite different from what Bartel had exploited previously, depicting sex between men, for instance, as something that could be playful and fun. Wayne M. Bryant in his *Bisexual Characters in Film* classifies "Naughty Nurse" as a "fine example of bi-situational humor." Of the film's plot, he writes: "A man and a woman are having rather kinky sex in a cheap hotel room when they hear a knock at the door. A sadistic cop walks in and threatens to arrest them for being so sick and perverted. Instead, the lovers undress him and pull him into their lovemaking. The joke is sprung in the next scene when we see the three standing at an operating table. One of the doctors is telling the nurse that she was very good. So good, in fact, that *she* can be the cop next time."[35]

Bryant fails to point out that the actor playing the cop-doctor, Chris St. John, is African American. The film, thus, is doubly subversive, not only presenting an idealized portrait of transgressive sex but also with its anti-racist inference that blacks and whites in both the workplace and the bed can enjoy one another's company as friends, colleagues and lovers. Notably, director-actor Robert Downey—who'd helmed *Putney Swope* (1969), a satirical diatribe against racism in corporate America—makes a cameo appearance in "Naughty Nurse," playing a clerk in the pay-by-the-hour hotel where the tryst takes place.

The desire to support himself as an independent filmmaker was such that Bartel quit his job at Hearst Metronome News in 1970. "I suddenly saw that these documentary films, fun as they were, were only going to lead to more of the same. I might as well have been a butcher as a documentary filmmaker trying to get into features."[36] Thereafter he committed himself exclusively to independent film projects: writing scenarios, pitching ideas to producers and securing deals with distributors for the two shorts he'd directed. He optioned "The Secret Cinema" to the Cinerama Releasing Corporation, and the film had an extended run at the 68th Street Playhouse in Manhattan, where it opened for Woody Allen's *Take the Money and Run* (1969). He also secured a deal with Grove Press, a book publisher that had moved into film distribution, to have "Naughty Nurse" included in a travelling movie program called Erotic Cinema Circus, which played arthouse and college theaters around the country.[37] Although Grove Press had a reputation for publishing challenging, acclaimed novels by the likes of Henry Miller, William S. Burroughs and Jean Genet, the company promoted "Naughty Nurse" as though its audiences were comprised of people who enjoyed *Screw* magazine. A tagline developed for the movie read: "Her leather fetish lunchtime fantasy frolics with the doctor get her through the trying day."

Grove Press also bundled "Naughty Nurse" with other short works on a series of videocassettes, each of which expressed an "erotic viewpoint." Distributed to members of a subscription service called the Evergreen Club, these "video magazines" were developed to "provide consistent wide exposure for less-than-feature length material. New filmmakers who find the shorter forms more realistic economically or better expressive of their immediate concerns, will have a ready forum for their work, and established talents can realize their more succinct ideas with the assurance that a responsive and financially viable outlet."[38] The tape on which "Naughty Nurse" appeared included an excerpt from Godard's documentary *British Sounds* (1969), no doubt boosting Bartel's confidence in himself and his work, as he'd counted the iconoclastic French director a model since his time in Italy.

Bartel continued to collaborate with his friend Chuck Hirsch, following up on *Does Size Really Count?* with a brief role in the opening credits sequence of *Hi, Mom!*, De Palma and Hirsch's sequel to *Greetings*. "I was in New York for a year writing films and working on different people's films. I appear in the title sequence of one of Brian De Palma's films."³⁹ An absurdist comedy in which a returned Vietnam vet (Robert De Niro) uses low-budget filmmaking techniques to shoot porno movies surreptitiously from New York City rooftops, the picture is a tongue-in-cheek homage to Hitchcock's *Rear Window* that doubles as a critique of modern urban life, indicting violence, poverty and racism. Wrapped up in a black coat—his character's name is Uncle Tom Wood—Bartel appears on the screen for no more than a second, shaking hands with actor Gerrit Graham—who in the film plays a protest kid committed to civic justice. Bartel would cast Graham a few years later as a goofy cowboy singer in *Cannonball!*

3

The Cormans

In Manhattan, Bartel watched new movies whenever possible, often visiting the Bleecker St. Cinema in Greenwich Village as well as keeping up with screenings at Lincoln Center.[1] An important discovery for him during this period was a motion picture by Spanish director Fernando Arrabal, *Viva La Muerte*, a fragmented, violent chronicle of a boy's efforts to reunite with his absent father, who may or may not be dead. Arrabal's readiness to blend bizarre imagery, profane humor and social criticism appealed to Bartel, whose work already displayed a similar aesthetic, though quieter and less abrasive than Arrabal's. Bartel, Elinor Silverman and an investor named Max L. Raab in turn pursued an arrangement with the film's French producer, Jacques Pollreneaud, to book *Viva La Muerte* for a run at St. Mark's Theatre in Lower Manhattan in the fall of 1971. The *New York Times*'s Roger Greenspun attended a screening and found himself both impressed and revolted by Arrabal's depictions of cruelty and suffering. "The imagery of *Viva La Muerte*—the defecation, self-mortification, strange and unusual punishment—reads like an illustrative footnote to some Surrealist manifesto. It is as if the famous razor across the eyeball that opens Buñuel's *Un Chien Andalou* had never lost its cutting edge, its sharp capacity to peel back fair surfaces and reveal the soft sources of corruption underneath."[2]

The influence Arrabal had on Bartel's subsequent work was significant. In the creative films he'd directed in the sixties, he'd approached taboo subject matter in an oblique manner—we never actually see the sex act in "Naughty Nurse," only the *préliminaires*—but in the first film he made after seeing *Viva La Muerte*, *Private Parts*, Bartel replaced narrative subtlety and indirection with fanciful renderings of perversion, crime and mental illness. A "kinky horror film with lots of original stuff in it," as he described it, *Private Parts* began much as "The Secret Cinema" had, as an independent collaboration between friends.³ Chuck Hirsch had "brought me a script which he thought would make an interesting low-budget horror film. It turned out to have been written by two friends of mine [Les Rendelstein and Phil Kearney], from UCLA, where I had studied theater, whom I hadn't seen in almost ten years. So I contacted them, and we had this discussion about the script, and I optioned it from them. I rewrote it and was trying to put together a $60,000, 16mm production of it in New York."⁴ Without Bartel's permission, his agent passed the script onto Roger Corman's brother, Gene, an independent producer who was scouting for "very low-budget, nonunion" projects to develop for Metro-Goldwyn-Mayer.⁵ Gene Corman "liked the script," Bartel said, "and came to New York to see my short films, and we made a deal. About six weeks later I was in Los Angeles making my first feature."⁶

Originally titled *Blood Relations*, a pun on the incest theme that runs through the story, *Private Parts* focuses on a teenaged thief, Cheryl (Ayn Ruymen), who enjoys watching, but never herself engaging in, sexual activity. The story opens with Cheryl (whom the other characters address as Chair-ill) watching her roommate, Judy (Ann Gibbs), as she has intercourse with a boyfriend. Disgusted, Judy tosses her out of the beach apartment the pair share, and Cheryl moves into an "exquisitely seedy downtown L.A. hotel" managed by her Aunt Martha (Lucille Benson).⁷ There, Cheryl becomes acquainted with and tantalizes her aunt's fashion photographer son, George (John Ventantonio), an impotent maniac, who, Bartel reveals late in the film, is actually female. As the love affair between the cousins progresses, a mysterious figure—presumably George—murders several of the hotel's eccentric occupants.

Featuring nudity, explicit violence and a cast of talented, but far from famous, actors, *Private Parts* in many ways resembles an exploitation movie, especially the sort that Roger Corman had begun releasing through New World Pictures—films like *The Student Nurses*, *Beast of the Yellow Night* and *Women in Cages*. Simultaneously, though, a subtle, contradictory disdain for exploitation pictures and their conventions permeates this picture. While Bartel concedes to the grindhouse audience's expectation for softcore content, for instance giving us footage of Cheryl sitting topless in a bathtub, he does so in a manner that inculpates the audience, attacking it in Hitchcockian fashion for having—and indulging—its own voyeuristic desires, "the guilty relationship," Dave Kehr finds, "between the American audience and the spectacles we choose to see on the screen."[8]

Staring at Cheryl with us is the unsettlingly weird George, who peers at his cousin through a peephole. Even more disquieting, Cheryl, whose eyes are covered by a sexy black mask, turns her face toward her cousin, bidding him to join her in the filthy bathroom where she sits. Bizarre, ironic, beautiful even, the scene rather obviously alludes to the first part of the famous shower scene in Hitchcock's *Psycho*, during which Norman Bates ogles Marion Crane through a wall. But while the Marion character is an unknowing—and absolutely vulnerable—participant in a voyeur's fantasy, Cheryl, a voyeur herself, delights in the experience of being watched.

While *Private Parts* was in production, it came to the attention of Roger Corman, who sensed market potential in the film's creepy mixture of violence, sex and comedy. Bartel recalled that "Gene had his offices then at New World, so I was around Roger a lot. Although for the first few months he looked right through me as if I were invisible, but gradually we got to know each other, and he was rather interested in *Private Parts*. In fact, when it was finished, the guy who was his sales manager then [Frank Moreno] suggested to Roger that since MGM didn't seem to know what to do with *Private Parts* that he, Roger, buy it away from them and distribute it through New World. But MGM having gone through several financial manipulations on the picture was not interested in selling it."

Nor was MGM interested in promoting the movie, and *Private Parts* died at the box office when it had its release in early 1973. "I outsmarted myself by making the film so kinky and offbeat, MGM didn't know what to do with it and decided it wasn't worth marketing," Bartel lamented.[9] The few notices the picture received were mixed, such as the review that Roger Greenspun—who'd appreciated the subversive qualities of *Viva La Muerte*—wrote: "Bartel succeeds in some details and fails in others. But the attempt, even when it isn't quite working, is a good deal more interesting than most. With Ayn Ruymen as the beautiful Cheryl and Lucille Benson as her protective aunt ... he has been fortunate in getting good performances from perfect types. Not all the film's nonsense is under imaginative control, but most of it is. *Private Parts* is at least a hopeful occasion for those of us who love intellectual cinema and at the same time care for the menacing staircase, for the ominous shadow, for empty rooms shuttered against the light of the afternoon."[10]

Likewise, Jay Cocks at *Time* wrote:

> At its best, *Private Parts* is a smooth parody of hellhouse horror melodramas, with an unsparing musical score by Hugo Friedhofer that furnishes a crescendo every five bars. The cast, however—except for Lucille Benson, who is gruff and quite good—seems to consist mostly of rejects from Central Casting, and the villain (John Ventantonio) looks like someone who spends most of his time in the balcony of all-night movies.
>
> Bartel, making his feature debut, exhibits a great deal of somewhat perverse and not necessarily admirable skill. *Private Parts* tends to be short on horror and long on kinky grue, like a gross animated cartoon. Its most outrageous scene is one between a lovesick voyeur and an inflatable plastic dummy. The distributors, MGM, are keeping quiet about *Private Parts*. One can appreciate their apprehension.[11]

Bartel deflected blame for the poor commercial performance of *Private Parts* from its disturbing content and its then-audacious treatment of gay and transgender themes. Instead, he faulted MGM and the studio's president, James Aubrey. "[W]hen it was finished and turned over to MGM, the marketing people didn't know what to do with it. Mr. Aubrey personally changed the title from *Blood Relations* to *Private Parts*, which, in 1971 [sic], was unprintable in major newspapers. In Chicago, the film was advertised as *Private Arts*; in Boston it was advertised as *Private Party*."[12] Bartel had been so annoyed by Aubrey's decision, in fact, that he approached the executive in person and told him that the picture "should be called *Cocks and Cunts*."[13] Stanley Livingston, a supporting actor in the film, reached a similar conclusion about the damage caused by the title's change. "You know what killed the movie? ... [T]here was a point in time in America where there were actually porno movie theaters, and there was a real push at that time to not let them advertise. They would grey out the ads. You'd look through the paper to where the movies were playing, and when you got to the porno theaters it looked like they didn't use any ink. It looked like a light grey color. I guess MGM, because the title *Private Parts* offended people, ended up advertising it on the porno page."[14]

Through the latter half of 1973, Bartel tried on his own to promote *Private Parts* with little success. He found himself unemployed, too: the film's poor reception—proving Marie Dressler's axiom that in Hollywood "you're only as a good as your last picture"—thwarted his ability to land a follow-up directing assignment. And after more than a year without a job, in the spring of 1974 he used his association with Gene Corman to meet with Roger Corman about working for New World Pictures. "I crawled the length of Sunset Boulevard up to Roger's desk on my hands and knees and begged to be forgiven for my indiscretion of having worked for his brother and made this awful picture."[15]

Bartel had hoped Corman would give him his own movie to direct, but instead he was told he would work under director Steve Carver on *Big Bad Mama*, a Depression-era gangster feature starring Angie Dickinson, Tom Skerritt and William Shatner. Overseeing a second unit crew, Bartel handled himself well, shooting in then-rural Temecula, California. The footage he produced pleased Carver, Corman and the film's associate producer, Jon Davison. As Davison remembers, "They shot some nice scenic shots, drive-bys, a bit of the action."[16] Following the picture's premiere in the summer of 1974, *Big Bad Mama* earned $4 million for New World, at that point the highest yielding release in the company's history. Critics generally liked the picture, though a few conservative reviewers expressed disappointment that Dickinson, an actress of some repute, had chosen to bare her breasts in sex scenes with co-stars Skerritt and Shatner. "The best that can be said for this shocker is that it is a tasteless and cheap rip-off on *Bonnie and Clyde* that's hardly in keeping with Angie's image," lamented Dorothy Manners.[17]

Bartel's contributions were such that Corman, now confident in his talent, gave him his own film to direct. "*Big Bad Mama* (or *Big B.M.* as it was affectionately referred to in the cutting room) was a big hit for Corman," Bartel explained in a 1978 essay he wrote for *Take One*. "I was tapped by Roger to direct his next 'big' picture: New World Picture Production no. 144, *Death Race 2000*."[18]

Planned as a science fiction movie in which the heroes wouldn't pilot spaceships but rather racecars, *Death Race 2000* had been greenlighted by Corman after United Artists in mid–1974 announced that it was going to make *Rollerball*, a futuristic story about professional athletes who try to kill one another on a roller derby track. "*Death Race 2000* was dreamed up as a quickie rival to *Rollerball*, and it was apparently Corman himself who had the idea of exploiting United Artists' lumbering multi-million-dollar project by producing a cut-price, low-budget alternative," explain Chris Petit and Tony Rayns.[19] An adaptation of a short story by Ib Melchior titled "The Racer," the

New World film would feature a transcontinental race in which participants scored points by killing pedestrians with their cars.

When Bartel joined the production, he was told that he would need to cast, shoot and cut the movie in less than a year—and for his efforts he would receive $5,000. His desire to direct again was such that he accepted these provisos, though he emphatically rejected the script Corman presented him, which had been written by Robert Thom. "It was extremely unpleasant, very bizarre. The violence was not leavened by much humor and what little humor there was … seemed to be rather forced. And most of the characters were transvestites or were very kinky." His concern over the inclusion of transvestites in the story was, perhaps, driven by his suspicion that the crossdressing killer in *Private Parts* had contributed to that film's poor commercial performance.

Corman agreed to a rewrite and gave the script to Charles B. Griffith—who'd written a pair of successful comic horror films Corman himself directed, *A Bucket of Blood* and *The Little Shop of Horrors*. "Chuck added a human touch, and a lot of humor, which was also my principal interest," Bartel said. "His version was very long, so I then cut it down. I guess I did most of the simplification, rewrote some of the dialogue, put in some of my own ideas."[20] With Corman's apparent approval, Bartel tried—in an effort to soften the narrative's violence with satire—to make the film's characters and their approaches to killing pedestrians at once absurd and funny. He and Griffith also worked up a subplot in which a band of resistance fighters headed by an elderly woman named Thomasina Paine strives to disrupt the race in order to undermine the totalitarian government that controls the United States of the future.

"[T]he whole idea of inflicting death more or less capriciously seemed to me a good basis for comedy," Bartel explained to Michael Singer. "The premise of the movie was so grim that the only way I could deal with it was to exaggerate it outrageously, artificialize it and not take it seriously."[21] To do this, he made sure that both the film's protagonists and their vehicles resembled nothing any viewer had seen before in the racecar movie genre, a camp approach that owed more in terms of style and content to Hanna-Barbera's Saturday morning cartoon *Wacky Races* than films like Blake Edwards's *The Great Race* (1965), John Frankenheimer's *Grand Prix* (1966), Lee H. Katzin's *Le Mans* (1971) and even Roger Corman's 1954 production *The Fast and the Furious*.

Poster for *Death Race 2000* (New World Pictures, 1975), the director's first hit movie.

Bartel and costumer Jane Ruhm dressed many of the movie's drivers in get-ups that caricatured familiar character types: a mobster, a Nazi, a gladiator, a gunfighter. The one exception was Frankenstein, the film's central character, whose body is a composite of artificial parts thanks to the numerous wrecks and accidents he's experienced on the road. Bartel and Ruhm had their hero wear a skintight outfit with a mask and a cape, creating a look that evoked the costumes worn by comic book superheroes *and* the leather gear associated with bondage and SM subculture. The automobiles, designed by Dean Jeffries and James Powers, were correspondingly fantastic: the mobster character's car was given a machine gun that protruded from its front; bull horns and a nose ring replaced the gunfighter-driver's front bumper; Frankenstein's car resembled a dragon with teeth and scales; the Nazi's car was given a camouflage-style paint job, evoking Rommel's panzers, along with an enormous tank gun mounted to its roof.

Bartel cast the film with mostly unknown actors who came from television, independent film, even pornography. He gave parts to friends, too, including Mary Woronov, a very tall and very beautiful acquaintance from his days in New York, who played Calamity Jane, the gunfighter. Bartel and Woronov had known once another since the mid-sixties. "Paul was very good friends in New York with my husband [Ted Gershuny] way before he thought of doing a movie in Los Angeles. They both did short films."[22] A one-time art student at Cornell University, Woronov had joined Andy Warhol's Exploding Plastic Inevitable, an art ensemble that hosted movie screenings and avant-garde rock shows around the city. Though she'd never aspired to be an actress, Woronov had appeared in Warhol's film, *Chelsea Girls* (1966), and also performed for the earlier-mentioned Theatre of the Ridiculous. She starred in a pair of low-budget independent films Gershuny directed, too, *Sugar Cookies* (1973) and *Silent Night, Bloody Night* (1974).[23] When Bartel called her from Los Angeles and "said he could get Corman to hire me for *Death Race 2000*," she responded with interest. "[Paul] said, 'I can get you in on this movie, and I need you.' I said, 'Fine, I'd *love* to drop everything I'm doing in New York.' I'd just finished a play, *In the Boom Boom Room*, and I was doing a soap opera, of all things, to make money. So I said, 'Yeah, I'll go out.' And then he said, 'I'll just introduce you to Corman—he'll look at your legs, so wear something that shows your legs off—and he'll hire you.'" Corman hired her.[24]

For the part of Frankenstein, Corman had wanted Peter Fonda, the star of two films Corman directed in the late sixties, *The Wild Angels* and *The Trip*. But Fonda declined, worried that he might get typecast as an action movie actor, having recently appeared in a string of exploitation flicks that included *Dirty Mary, Crazy Larry* and *Open Season*. "[H]e wasn't about to commit himself to a movie in which people were deliberately run over."[25] Lee Majors was also offered the part but declined presumably for similar reasons. David Carradine, however, the star of the *Kung Fu* television series, expressed interest. After three years playing Kwai Chang Caine, a peace-seeking nomadic master of the martial arts, Carradine wanted new material and new roles to explore. In his autobiography *Endless Highway*, he explained: "Two weeks after I left the series, I went right into *Death Race 2000* for Roger Corman in a deliberate mood to kill the image of Caine and launch a movie career."[26]

The cast was filled out with several people who would soon experience extensive success in TV and film. Fred Grandy, the navigator for the Nazi-inspired driver Matilda the Hun (Roberta Collins), went on to play the part of Gopher, the purser character in the late seventies TV hit *The Love Boat*. And Sylvester Stallone, the mobster driver Machine Gun Joe Viterbo, went on to become one of Hollywood's biggest stars ever. Stallone, whose first film role had been in a porno called *The Party at Kitty and Stud's*, asked permission from Corman and Bartel to re-write his own lines in *Death Race 2000*, making them, he hoped, funnier and more appropriate for a gangster. He wrote the insult, for example, that his character directs at his "moll" companion: "You know, Myra [Louisa Moritz], some people might think you're cute. But me, I think you're one very large baked potato." When Stallone wasn't on set, he spent his time writing for another character he hoped to eventually play. Woronov recalls: "You know who was really sweet on that film? Stallone. Not only was he sweet, but he told me that he was writing this script about a boxer. At the time, he was living in someone's closet on a narrow mattress. That's where he wrote *Rocky!*"[27]

Director John Landis, who played a mechanic in *Death Race 2000*, would soon score box office hits with *Animal House* and *The Blues Brothers*. He recalled: "My friend Paul Bartel directed *Death Race 2000*, and he hired me as a stunt guy. He gave me a line, actually. I'm one of the mechanics pushing Sylvester Stallone's car to the starting line. Stallone's character had been in a fight with David Carradine the night before and had a black eye. So I make a crack about his black eye. When they start the race, everyone zooms forward but Sly, who goes backward and kills me—throws me into the wall. So I'm a victim in *Death Race 2000*."[28]

Despite the opportunity to work with friends, *Death Race 2000* was far from pleasant for Bartel as he and Corman squabbled over the tone and content of the film all the way up to its release in April 1975. "As the script passed from the hands of Robert Thom to mine, to Chuck Griffith's and back to me, Corman several times threatened to abandon the project altogether (always changing his mind, however, when reminded that he had already *invested more than $5,000* in it!)"

Bartel found himself at odds with Carradine as well. "He didn't like the fabric from which his costume had been made (although he had OK'd a swatch of it). So he simply ripped the costume up. He didn't like the shape of the helmet we had specially designed and molded to his head. So it had to be done over in a hurry at a tremendous cost." Carradine wanted to challenge Bartel's status as director and would laugh in his face when he told the star what he wanted from his performance. The conflict was such that Bartel went to Corman and asked for Carradine to be replaced, which, in turn, prompted the actor to send a telegram with the following apology: "DEAR PAUL, I KNOW HOW YOU ARE FEELING. IT IS TRUE THAT I HAVE BEEN ARROGANT AND NASTY. I HUMBLY BEG YOUR FORGIVENESS PLEASE DON'T KICK ME OUT OF THIS MOVIE." Bartel accepted the apology, and the two got on well for the remainder of the production.

The vehicles used in the film's racing sequences presented numerous problems, too. Corman had decided to spend no more than $5,000 dollars on what Bartel referred to as the "Death Cars": "To save money, Corman had ordered them built without roll bars. It was only when I pointed out that the stuntmen (let alone Carradine) would refuse to drive them without these safety devices that he relented and agreed to spend the extra $50 per car. According to the script, the cars were supposed to go hundreds of miles per hour—but they were really nothing but fiberglass bodies mounted on junker Volkswagen chassis, and nobody could goose them up over forty-five mph. We made endless tests, undercranking the camera at 20, 18, 16 frames per second to increase the apparent speed of the cars. This undercranking lent a cartoon-like quality to the film," which Bartel, the animation aficionado, was not unhappy with.[29]

Rainy weather also threatened the safety of the drivers. Carradine remembers that "it rained almost every day. There were some near tragedies. The cars looked great but were a joke as far as the mechanics went. Mine was the fastest at a brisk fifty-four mph. Stallone's could do forty-eight. Even so, with the chances we took on the wet mountain roads [outside Los Angeles], there were some close calls."[30] Bartel confirmed this, telling journalists: "In the picture we actually use the footage of what came closest to being a fatal accident. Very early in the film when the cars have just left New York and are on the freeway one of the them, the [Nazi] buzz bomb car tries to pass the machine gun car, and it misjudged the distance because of the little fake machine guns on the side and went into a swerve and the machine gun car went off the road. The machine guns broke off."[31]

Corman for the most part stayed away from the seventeen-day shoot. "[He] showed up on the set just once to make certain there was enough nudity in the steamy scene between Simone [Griffith, Frankenstein's navigator] and me. When he couldn't see her breasts, his eyes turned black with anger," Carradine said. "We fixed it, and his eyes turned blue again. The next time I looked up, he was gone."[32] Carradine's memory may be a bit off—reputedly Corman got behind the wheel of a Death Car at one point when a hired driver became unavailable.

At New World's offices on Sunset Boulevard, Corman would review dailies from the production. Bartel's farcical treatment of the subject matter struck him as inappropriate, and once principal photography was complete, he asked for several scenes to be removed or re-shot. Bartel and the picture's editor, Tina Hirsch (a friend from his New York days), tried to work around Corman's decisions but with little success. In a 2014 interview, Hirsch said: "The truth is, Roger thought it was a silly film, which he didn't like. He cut out several things that were very funny, that, frankly, we tried to get back in a couple times, but he wouldn't hear of it."[33]

Joe Dante, then a cutter in New World's trailer department, had a close-up view of Corman's intervention. "Paul really couldn't take the film's premise too seriously. The finished film was pretty satirical. Roger re-cut it to make it more of an action film. A lot of the humor was excised because Roger felt it would alienate the audience. There are whole scenes in this movie that led up to jokes that have been cut out of the film. The movie came out and made a lot of money. Roger was justified. Many of us, however, felt that the film would have made just as much money with the comedy left in. Who can argue?"[34]

Corman also had Chuck Griffith shoot "violent inserts" for the movie, including presentations of injured pedestrians and drivers and what Bartel described as close-up shots of "crushed heads and splattering blood."[35] Griffith recalled: "I was not involved in the first unit production, but I led the second unit. And there was considerable action work done after the picture was finished ... for instance ... the scene where Stan Ross the stuntman was sitting on the edge of the broken-away bridge. I had to go back in the second unit ... and have the car chase him up the creek and run over him and put a blood bag under the rear tires, so it would foam up red. Paul had soft-pedalled [the movie] a bit. And we hardened it up."[36]

Corman, however, granted Bartel freedom over the use of music on the soundtrack. The film's composer, Paul Chihara, observed that "Paul Bartel had a very unusual way of working—if he'd hear something that he liked, he'd say, 'I can use that!' and then he'd put it where ever he wanted. For example, Paul used my Bach fugue over all of the final chase, the climactic chase of the movie. I didn't intend that—I don't know what I wrote the fugue for. But he stuck it over that chase, and it was brilliant. I wrote what I thought was appropriate, but Paul Bartel, in his lunatic genius way, put the music wherever he wanted to." Chihara, incidentally, regards *Death Race*, despite its comic ambitions, as a response to then-current problems arising from American domestic and foreign policy: "[I]t was ... the time of the Vietnam War, which lives in all our movies and mythologies. For those of us who lived through that time, and we were very young, it was a terrible reality because we all had friends who literally were with us one day and dead the next. It was not just a chic political stance that we took—we were really concerned about many, many serious things."[37]

While promoting *Death Race* in Cannes in May 1975, Bartel expressed his discontent with Corman, despite the admiration the film had been generating in critical circles since its release a few weeks earlier. He explained to a New Zealand TV crew covering the film festival: "My biggest problem on the film really was not anything to do with the danger of shooting in the cars but probably the producer. In this film I felt it was more appropriate to go heavily into comedy, but the producer didn't want to, and as a result when the film was all shot and ... we put it together, the producer started to tamper with it and ... take out large chunks of comedy, and for a while he confused action with really unpleasant violence ... and there were inserted into the film scenes of excruciating gore, which he felt that the audience would enjoy. But as it turned out after one screening, with the gore it was obviously obscene, and it was taken out."[38]

Bartel himself was eventually able to look back on the film favorably, even conceding that Corman's interventions probably strengthened it. To Kevin Thomas he said, "We worked under terrible pressure. Roger and I had an essential disagreement over comedy. He took out a lot of the comedy scenes. He may have been right and was probably more objective. It's grossed over $8 million and cost $530,000 to make."[39] He also revealed to Michael Singer that he was pleased that he managed to get in "a certain thing that I wanted" into the film, and wasn't resentful that he hadn't been able get in more. "The finished film is very much a synthesis of his vision and mine. And people seem to enjoy the film, so I'm not unhappy with it."[40] *Death Race* eventually yielded $12 million, the company's highest grossing production. Carradine noted, "Roger told me after the picture was released, he said, 'What I had in mind was an action-message-comedy and what Paul gave me was a comedy-action-message. But you can't argue with these grosses.'"[41]

As with *Private Parts*, the reviews were mixed for *Death Race*. Several critics responded with distaste to the picture's sensationalism, its gore and, in Woronov's words, its "tits-and-ass and blood-and-guts and ... lots of driving around."[42] An unnamed critic at the *New York Times* snorted:

> *Death Race 2000* ... is an Orwellian vision of the American future, if you believe that Orwell was afflicted with blurred perception and an inclination toward the adolescent in satire.... [It] has a good time belaboring the easy, targets—spectators, sportscasters, victims and the sort of clergy who have a benediction for anything.
> When it comes to political satire, however, *Death Race 2000* finds the going tougher. In the end, it reveals itself to have nothing to say beyond the superficial about government or rebellion. And in the absence of such a statement, it becomes what it seems to have mocked—a spectacle glorifying the car as an instrument of violence.[43]

Dave Kehr writing for *Film Comment* in 1977, however, argued that with *Death Race 2000*, Bartel delivered an expressionist tour de force in which the movie's visual aspects, its political themes and its ability to arouse the audience's emotions were expertly realized. "Within ten minutes of the start of the film, Bartel has done what Norman Jewison couldn't do with the whole of *Rollerball*: bring us to a sickening realization of how strongly death figures in our entertainment. *Death Race* is a first-class piece of agitprop, done up in a bright, flat, comic-book style, that effectively forces the critical viewer to make hard, personal decisions about what is and what is not acceptable as 'catharsis.'"[44]

4

More Fun at New World

As a New World regular in the mid-seventies, Bartel made frequent appearances in colleagues' movies, something he quite enjoyed. He explained to the *Boston Globe*'s Bruce McCabe: "Although I consider myself a director, acting is my addiction."[1] But though he'd given himself cameos in *Private Parts* (as a flasher) and *Death Race* (as a surgeon), he had not had an onscreen part of any substance since *Does Size Really Count?* This changed when he was asked by producer Jon Davison, who was then "New World's director of advertising, publicity and promotion," and two friends from New World's trailer department, Allan Arkush and Joe Dante, to play an important supporting part, a kooky movie director, in a film they were planning.

The production had arisen from a wager that Davison had made with Corman. Eager to play a larger role developing new properties, he "told Roger I'd like to make a bet with him that I could produce a film fifty percent cheaper than any that had been done at New World since he founded it in 1970. I said, 'Your average picture takes fifteen days to shoot, right? I'll do mine in ten days.' I saw a funny self-satisfied look come over his face, and he said, 'O.K., you've got a bet. In order to win it, you'll have to do the picture for $80,000, but I'm only going to give you $60,000.' I groaned and went away to discuss my problem with two other young guys who work in the Corman office, Allan Arkush from NYU and Joe Dante from the Philadelphia College of Art. They were going to be my directors, and it would be *their* first picture, too."

To minimize their costs, Davison, Arkush and Dante decided early on "to take a lot of footage from former Corman schlock epics—mob scenes, revolutions, car chases and such—and do a picture about four actresses working in similar schlock for a fictitious movie studio."[2] Instead of putting together a movie solely with new material, the filmmakers would blend new material with odds and ends culled from New World's archive. Once they'd decided on this approach, Dante, Davison and Arkush commenced with writer Danny Opatoshu to hash together a story about a screen actress who murders anyone she thinks may stand between her and a part. The picture—ultimately given the title *Hollywood Boulevard*—would double as a critique of Corman and the manner in which he made features. As Dante said, "*Hollywood Boulevard* was about a movie company that was somewhat like New World Pictures—perhaps a little too much like New World for Roger's tastes."[3] The actress-characters whose deaths are the focal points of the film's storyline all work for Miracle Pictures, a grade-Z operation that specializes in exploitation fare. The company's ironically candid slogan declares: "If it's a good picture it's a MIRACLE."

Among the members of the cast were several actors who'd previously worked for Corman and New World (Dick Miller, Candice Rialson), screenwriters (Chuck Griffith, Opatoshu), editors (Lewis Teague, Tina Hirsch) and directors (Jonathan Kaplan, Paul Bartel). Davison recalled that the wages for everyone involved with the production were meager. "The cameraman was the highest paid, he got $200 for the film. The directors, Joe Dante and Alan Arkush, were paid $100 each."[4] Shooting was rushed, too, with two units working simultaneously over ten days in October 1975.[5] A record for New World was set when the crew organized eighty-two set-ups in a single day. Woronov recalled that Arkush and Dante "were so busy, I almost didn't see them. They were so busy doing stuff and putting it together. They were wonderful, though…. But on this one, they were running around like chickens without heads. They had to do *everything*!" The two also cut the final version of the film, following through on their plan to maintain continuity between the new material they shot with outtakes from New World productions *Big Bad Mama*, *Caged Heat*, *Women in Cages* and *Death Race 2000*.

Dante and Arkush often didn't have the time to explain to their actors how the scenes they filmed would fit into the finished movie. Woronov told Will Harris: "[T]here's a scene where I have two dogs—it was filmed in Canoga Park—and I'm looking at the camera and everything else, and they told me, 'Okay, now pretend there are two dogs there, little Chihuahuas.' So I'm going, 'Coochi, coochi, coochi….' Then when I see the movie, they have these giant fucking Rin Tin Tin dogs. Everything was like that. They used other movies from Corman to fill in. They shot a movie in a week.... I mean, I would shoot a gun, and then there'd be a scene of all these agents falling out of the palm trees, dead."⁶

Bartel was given the part of Eric von Leppe, the director at Miracle Pictures whose actors are methodically getting killed. As he helms movies with titles like *Machete Maidens of Mora Tau* and *Atomic War Bride*, the impassioned, autocratic von Leppe spoofs the egocentric and dictatorial mannerisms of such bygone Hollywood directors as Otto Preminger, Fritz Lang and Erich von Stroheim. His characterization is all the more ridiculous because he fancies himself an auteur of the *Cahiers du Cinema* variety, whose personality is strong enough to invest his work with artistic merit and a distinct worldview. To one of his actresses, a busty, nearly naked brunette (Rita George) who presses a machete to a man's neck, he portentously declares: "Now, Bobbi, this is your big moment. You have the line that sums up the entire inner meaning, the core, the essence of the entire film. Are you ready? All right. Action!" (Bobbi proceeds to tell her companion: "Now get it up, or I'll cut it off!") To another actor wearing a Godzilla suit (Jonathan Demme), von Leppe cries out: "Your motivation in this scene is to step on as many people as possible." And to a reporter visiting the set, he declares: "What we're trying to do here is combine the legend of Romeo and Juliet with high-speed action and a sincere plea for international atomic controls in our time."

The strategies Davison used for promoting and distributing *Hollywood Boulevard* proved to be lucrative. He sold the film's rights in Spain for $50,000—a sum that nearly matched the production's final cost of $53,000, and thus the picture went into the black quickly after its release.⁷ "The film made money—it couldn't help it, as it was so inexpensive—money mostly from drive-ins."⁸ The reviews that came in were often favorable, too. *Variety* declared that "New World Pictures has done as good a satire job on itself as anyone could in *Hollywood Boulevard*, a loving-hands-at-home tribute to the philosophy that a good piece of action footage deserves more than one usage."⁹

Outside of the five days he worked on *Hollywood Boulevard*, Bartel's schedule in the wake of *Death Race* was largely open, enabling him to turn his creative attention to a pair of independent projects he wanted to develop. The first was a science fiction comedy called *Frankencar* on which he collaborated with writer Richard Blackburn. A graduate of UCLA's film and theatre program, Blackburn shared with Bartel an interest in suspense and horror and had directed a vampire picture, *Lemora: A Child's Tale of the Supernatural* (1973), that featured a young female character in distress, not unlike the protagonist Cheryl in *Private Parts*.[10]

The pair worked up *Frankencar* to exploit Bartel's growing reputation as a car film specialist. They would combine comedy and violence in the same fashion as *Death Race 2000*, while introducing plot elements that bring to mind Franju's *Eyes Without a Face*, Disney's *Pinocchio* and *The Six Million Dollar Man* TV show. "The premise is that a young racecar driver has his neurosurgeon father develop a car that responds directly to his brain," Bartel told James Verniere. "It simply does what he thinks. But it's sabotaged by a financier who's trying to get control of the invention. The driver is burned and loses his arms and legs and part of his face. His father announces that he has died but smuggles his still living body out of the hospital. He then rebuilds the car with the kid in it, so that it becomes a living being—part-man, part-car. The rest of the film is revenge time."[11] The pair had a script completed late in 1976 and were confident the film would proceed. But their hopes were frustrated. "United Artists agreed to produce a script of mine called *Frankencar*, and it dragged on and on for months. Just before we were supposed to start pre-production, they pulled the plug because their new man in charge of productions didn't believe that anyone could make a film for less than $3 million, and my budget was just under $3 million. It was one of those ridiculous things. This guy had only worked on James Bond films, and he didn't know low-budget pictures. He just happened to be there the weekend were making the final decision to go or not."[12]

The second independent project Bartel pursued during this period made its way out of development hell. Though he was an epicure who enjoyed delicacies like veal and foie gras, Bartel was not averse to taking meals and drinking coffee at Schwab's Pharmacy on Sunset Boulevard. And in early May 1975, just days *Death Race*'s release, he was approached at the lunch counter by Don Simpson. An unemployed writer—and an acquaintance of Martin Scorsese—Simpson threw out an idea to Bartel for an action-adventure film—a fictionalized treatment of an illegal transcontinental race called the Cannonball Baker Sea-to-Shining-Sea Memorial Trophy Dash—which Simpson had read about in a magazine that day at the drugstore.

4. More Fun at New World

Bartel sensed the commercial potential in Simpson's concept immediately: "[A]lthough I had all kinds of ideas for films, I could only get people interested in financing another car action movie. Also, at that time the notion of a film about the Cannonball Baker race was in the air around Hollywood."[13] His finances factored in as well. "I wanted to do another comedy. I had several ideas but nobody would talk to me about anything but another car movie. Since I needed money desperately—I had been working for Roger for a year for a grand total of $5,000—I gave in."[14]

That day in Schwab's, Simpson had probably been reading *Time*, which profiled the race in its May 5, 1975, issue:

> One sunny morning last week, 2,890 miles, 35 hr. 53 min., and one $250 traffic ticket away from East Side Manhattan's Red Ball Garage, Rick Cline and Jack May parked their pockmarked white Ferrari Dino in front of the Portofino Inn in Southern California's Redondo Beach. Having shaved one minute from the previous transcontinental record, the partners became undisputed holders of the 1975 Cannonball Baker Sea-to-Shining-Sea Memorial Trophy Dash.
>
> The Cannonball what? Unsponsored, illicit, and carrying no prize money, the Cannonball car race does not exactly compete in the public imagination with the Indy 500 or Le Mans. Yet, among dedicated speed freaks, the nontelevised nonspectacular has become something of a legend in the five tenuous years of its existence.
>
> There are no rules in the Cannonball. Anyone is eligible to compete, in any land-based vehicle of any shape or size, at any speed. "God," sighs Brock Yates, senior editor of *Car and Driver* and one of Cannonball's founders, "the anarchistic barbarity of it all!"[15]

Bartel went with Simpson's idea to independent producer Samuel Gelfman, whom he knew through Corman; Gelfman had worked for an investment company called Artists Entertainment Complex that had co-produced the New World movies *Caged Heat* and *Cockfighter*. Gelfman, now on his own, liked the illegal road race concept—a lot—and said he'd buy the rights to the story. Warner Bros. had recently announced that it would produce a movie, *The Gumball Rally*, also based on the Cannonball Baker Sea-to-Shining-Sea Memorial Trophy Dash, and Gelfman probably felt that a low-budget treatment of the same theme had a good chance for box office success. The quick turnaround Bartel had facilitated amazed Simpson: "Within forty-eight hours of pitching, I had $6,250 in my jeans! ... I thought, 'This is it, I'm a star.'"[16]

As Simpson and Bartel drafted a script, Gelfman pursued investors both in the States and abroad. When a deal with Fox fell through, he arranged lines of support from a pair of international production companies, Shaw Brothers and Harbor Productions, and later Corman's New World Pictures, which may have worried Bartel at first, given the problems the two had experienced working on *Death Race 2000*. But, as David Everitt asserted, this "time around, since the picture was independently financed and Corman was only the distributor ... [Bartel] had little trouble in controlling the project."[17]

Whatever tensions still remained between Bartel and Corman, in fact, seem to have dissipated by the time shooting on *Cannonball!* started as Bartel put Corman into the movie, having him play a district attorney who tells a subordinate—played by Don Simpson—that law enforcement needs to shut down the race before it even starts. Bartel loaded the film's cast with other friends and acquaintances from New World, too. "I wrote parts for all [of them]," he told Michael Dare.[18] David Carradine played the film's hero, Coy "Cannonball" Buckman. Mary Woronov was given the role of a quasi-feminist driver who crosses the country in a van, joined by a pair of beautiful navigators she steals away from their jobs as waitresses. New World editors Allan Arkush and Joe Dante appeared as a pair of mechanics who give Coy a car that allows him to complete the race after his own ride is sabotaged. Sylvester Stallone adopted an underworld persona for a short scene in which he eats from a bucket of Kentucky Fried Chicken. Dick Miller is Coy's brother, Bennie, a gambler who orchestrates the deaths of several drivers in order to improve his chances of collecting on a bet he's made with a mobster named Lester Marks that his brother will win the race. Bartel cast himself in the role of this mobster. He gave small parts to other directors, too, including Jonathan Kaplan, Carl Gottlieb and Martin Scorsese.

Cannonball! was filmed primarily in southern California over four weeks in the spring of 1976 with twice the budget Bartel had for *Death Race*. Carradine writes in his memoir *Endless Highway*, "The picture's about an automobile race from L.A. to New York. We never left L.A.; highways all look the same."[19] Actually, some footage that didn't feature the actor was shot in Manhattan, which Bartel had editor Mort Tubor cut into the film's closing sequence.

To meet the conventions of the auto race genre and to satisfy audience expectations, Bartel included exploding cars, topless women, fist fights and other sensationalistic elements, none of which he found to be exciting himself. "I really wasn't very interested in the premise of the movie at all," he confessed to Michael Singer.[20] Despite good faith

4. More Fun at New World 43

Mobster Lester Marks (Bartel, center) and some pals (Martin Scorsese, left; Sylvester Stallone) devour fried chicken in *Cannonball!* (Cross-County Productions, Shaw Brothers, Harbor Productions, 1976).

efforts to make *Cannonball!* conventional and commercial, he did manage to slip in several moments of subversive comedy, most notably the scenes in which he appears as crime lord Lester Marks. Bartel's appearance—bald, stocky, bearded, fair—is blatantly at odds with the popular depiction of gangster characters in films and TV. In addition, Marks is an egoist who fancies himself a composer, an imitator of Cole Porter, and sings and plays the piano in a hammy, exaggerated manner. The scene in which Bartel as Marks sits and eats with Stallone and Scorsese in the sitting room of an affluent West L.A. home is likewise campy: the principals wear overblown haute couture suit wear and drink from crystal glassware as they gnaw on chicken. These sham grandees have bad taste, the scene infers, but the ultimate target and purpose of Bartel's satire is unclear. Is he parodying rich people in general or members of the nouveau riche who've come into wealth in a less than scrupulous way?

Hostile reviews met *Cannonball!* upon its release in September

1976. Kirk Honeycutt, writing for the *Valley News*, argued that the movie had been created for "the intellectually unendowed": "It is a critic's nightmare to sit through a lousy movie he's seen already. I saw *Cannonball!* which is about an illegal L.A. to New York car race. Now isn't that the same plot as *Gumball Rally* and *Death Race 2000*? In fact, didn't director Paul Bartel and actor David Carradine make both *Death Race* and *Cannonball!* for New World Pictures [sic]—what the hell's going on—is some hack film crew crisscrossing the country shooting enough racing scenes and car wrecks for two and three movies?"[21] Roger Ebert was even harsher. The film differs, he argued, from other "race-and-crash movies chiefly in its pretensions; we're supposed to know that Bartel's 'really' an ambitious director who's just turning out this stuff with his left hand—after all, doesn't the movie costar Bartel himself and six fellow directors (including Corman, Martin Scorsese and Joe Dante?) If you can't be an auteur, at least get one in your movie."[22]

Cannonball! was nevertheless selected by the 1976 Edinburgh Film Festival's organizers to open that year's program "as part of a mini-retrospective of [Bartel's] work."[23] Peter Biskind passed on an interesting remark Bartel made about his experience at the festival and Don Simpson, with whom he "shared a hotel room": "'My one real regret was that I didn't have sex with him when I had the opportunity,' says Bartel. 'Don told me he had had homosexual experiences in jail when he was sixteen or so. He and a friend had stolen a giant spool of copper cable from the telephone company, melted it down to sell it, and got caught. My impression of him was that although he was basically heterosexual he was open to all kinds of sexual experiences.'"[24]

Cannonball! also yielded a decent profit for its investors, and this success led to a series of paying jobs for Bartel, none of which, however, advanced to completion. "After *Cannonball!* was released," he told Terry Gross, "I went through a period of five years where I worked on projects that never quite made it to the screen.... I was hired to write scripts, to supervise other people writing scripts., which I was supposed to eventually direct, but none of them were fully financed or could be cast to the satisfaction of the studio."[25] One of the pictures he worked on was *Underground Aces*, a comedy about valet attendants.[26] He was also hired to compile "a complete history of New World Pictures in trailers."[27]

To ease his frustration, Bartel read a lot—and became a collector of signed first-edition books—a hobby he would pursue the rest of his life. "I find reading and book collecting are great ways to redirect my energy during the endless waiting periods that infect the movie business."[28] Many of the writers he collected, by the way, shared his jaundiced view of America and his fondness for rough language and grotesque humor: Harry Crews, David Mamet, Norman Mailer.

Bartel also kept busy playing small parts in low-budget films, for example Ron Howard's debut feature, *Grand Theft Auto*, and *Mr. Billion*, which Jonathan Kaplan, a friend from New World, directed for 20th Century–Fox. And in Joe Dante's brilliant *Piranha*, released in July 1978, he played an officious camp director who reveals in the film's final moments that he possesses a surprising degree of courage, saving children from the teeth of the titular monsters. *Piranha* was produced for New World by Jon Davison, who, with cheeky candor, acknowledged the movie's resemblance to Steven Spielberg's blockbuster about homicidal marine life. "We're not denying that *Piranha* is a rip-off of *Jaws*," he said, "but we'd much rather think of it as a rip-off of *The Creature from the Black Lagoon*."[29]

For Arkush's *Rock 'n' Roll High School*, another New World production, Bartel introduced a degree of amiable sweetness into his role as a music teacher named Mr. McGree, who becomes a fan of the punk rock band the Ramones. Filmed in early 1979, *Rock 'n' Rock High School* had been in various stages of development. Initially, Roger Corman had proposed an idea for a film he wanted called *Girls' Gym*, which he asked Arkush and Dante to turn into a script. After hashing out a sixty-page draft, the pair passed the story onto more experienced scenarists—first Chuck Griffith, then "film historian and former *Variety* film critic" Joseph McBride and finally a pair of TV writers, Russ Dvonch and Richard Whitley.[30]

The storyline that emerged from this collective effort shared several traits with earlier New World productions—especially *Big Bad Mama*, *Death Race 2000* and *Eat My Dust!*—as it followed characters who undermine authority figures that misuse their positions of power. In this instance, the narrative focuses on a rock music buff named Riff Randle (P.J. Soles) and her conflict with her school's autocratic principal, Miss Togar, who does what she can to stop the students at Riff's school, Vince Lombardi High, from having fun. Togar's stridency in due course undoes her, prompting the disgruntled students to grow violent—and blow up the school.

Cast in the role of Miss Togar, Mary Woronov initially planned to play the principal as a sweet and quick-witted character reminiscent of Eve Arden's character in the *Our Miss Brooks* TV show, but her approach changed spontaneously once shooting commenced. She recalled that the producers "brought us to this ghetto, and they had all of these kids and they were like rats. Then they put my outfit on and that was really stiff. When I stepped out of the dressing room, everything that I told Allan I would do, I didn't do. I became Miss Togar. I swear I never thought about her until I stepped out of the dressing room with the makeup and costume on. She just happened, man. I don't know where she came from, but she's endeared me to the hearts of many."[31]

Filmed over twenty days with a $280,000 budget, *Rock 'n' Roll High School* was shot principally on location throughout Los Angeles, and had its release in the spring of 1979. Despite the picture's confrontational attitudes—and music—it opened in the conservative Southwest and the Great Plains, a decision that exasperated Arkush: "To open a punk rock movie in Texas and Oklahoma ... showed so little understanding of what the film was about."[32] The movie as a result stumbled at the box office, but it entertained reviewers (and also subverted their expectations), among them the *Los Angeles Times*'s Kevin Thomas: "*Rock 'n' Roll High School* is a rambunctious drive-in movie designed to show off East Coast New Wave rockers, the Ramones. It marks the sol directorial debut of Roger Corman protégé Allan Arkush, who displays plenty of energy and humor.... It's the same old formula of rock-crazy kids in collision with a kill-joy principal. Of course, the film is a fantasy not to be taken seriously, but because it is precisely that, it is all the more distributing for suggesting that it's perfectly OK for students to burn down their school when they don't get their way."[33]

Rock 'n' Roll High School directs much of its satire to Hollywood musicals and dramas produced in the fifties and sixties that focused on the adventures of teenagers and hoodlums. The film is filled with familiar character types from the period, including moonstruck teen lovers and a hard-nosed police officer who doesn't like young people very much. Arkush and his writers also built their narrative upon the fissures between teachers and students that materialize in such earlier movies as *Blackboard Jungle* and *To Sir, with Love*. While Riff, her classmates and the Ramones fight for their freedom to enjoy life on their terms, Miss Togar and her allies—a committee of goofy school administrators, police figures, a pair of brown-shirted school monitors—exert as much control and force as they can to stop them.

With the opposing sides set from the start, the conflict that arises between the two groups shapes the bulk of the story, and little occurs in terms of character development. Bartel's amiable Mr. McGree, however, is one of the few dynamic characters in the film, as he transforms from a fuddy-duddy music teacher who favors Beethoven to the Ramones' most ardent adult supporter. "It was of course a satirical role. I tried to play him more realistic in the beginning so he wouldn't come off as a complete caricature. The transition the character makes is more amusing that way, I think: You have this square, bookish professor and lover of classical music who in the end evolves into a sort of punk dilettante. The last scene of the picture, I'm rocking out in the high school ... holding drums and cymbals. I enjoyed the role and the chance to work with people I like. It was great fun.... I never danced so much in my life." And how was it working with the Ramones? Bartel joked that it was like "a breath of fresh amyl nitrite. Fresh, intoxicating and full of life."[34]

In the film Bartel is marvelous—he manages to make McGree memorable, matching, even surpassing, the outsized performances of Woronov and Miller, while contrasting and complementing the surreal weirdness of the Ramones. In a picture loaded with bizarre images and non sequiturs, he dominates the screen when he tears off his clothing to reveal a T-shirt that has the band's name written on front as punkers, jocks, even a giant mouse mosh on the dance floor.

The recollection from the production that aroused the most affection for him, though, had nothing to do with the band:

> There's a scene in Arkush's film ... in which I, in the role of a stuffy music teacher, receive a note from principal Mary Woronov in the form of a paper airplane. This airplane is launched down the hall from her office and sails all over the school, outdoors, in windows, finally coming to rest in my ear—prompting the dumbest one-liner I have ever been asked to deliver: "Ear Mail!" I get a kick every time I see this scene, and it isn't the clever cutting or the special effects. It's the memory of the excruciating pain the scene caused me, take after take.
>
> This paper airplane was really fairly heavy *cardboard* airplane. And it wasn't sailing through the air, but sliding along a piece of invisible monofilament, one end of which was anchored to a plug which had been *glued* into my right ear. This caused a painful and potentially dangerous vacuum/concussion effect, like having your ears boxed over and over. In take after take that rotten plane would be launched by the prop man from a platform outside the classroom window, only to

Poster for New World's *Rock 'n' Roll High School*. Bartel's character, Mr. McGree, waves from atop a trash can (New World Pictures, 1979).

stop short a few inches from my ear or, worse, to hit my ear with a painful blumph and bounce away again, ruining the shot.

What could be dumber than risking an ear for New World Pictures? The take in which it finally hit my ear and stuck was, I had promised myself, absolutely the last take I was going to permit.

What gives me pleasure when I look at the scene now is the fact the gag plays so nicely. The monofilament doesn't show, and the music teacher betrays no anticipation of the pain he knows so well is coming.[35]

5

Independent

Bartel and Blackburn continued their creative partnership through the late seventies, pitching *Frankencar* to potential investors without success while developing new ideas for films to make together. The initial concept for what eventually became *Eating Raoul* emerged from this experience.

"In the winter of 1979, having worked on several projects that failed to reach the screen, I was fed up," Bartel said. "I wanted to do something personal and outrageous. A 'fun' picture that could be made quickly, easily and cheaply, and that would give me an opportunity to work with a bunch of my friends."[1] He and Blackburn got together in Schwab's and started "to sketch out a little story about a married couple as detectives in Florida." Blackburn felt, though, "that married detectives in Florida didn't stand a chance of selling."[2] He argued, Bartel remembered, "'Oh, that's too conventional, that's been done. Let's be a little more daring and make them the murderers instead.'" The couple instead would "murder for money, much like the protagonists in *The Honeymoon Killers*. Comedy could be worked into the script … just as it had into Alexander Mackendrick's *Kind Hearts and Coronets*."[3] Bartel was attracted to this take on the couple, imagining himself playing the story's male lead, with Mary Woronov as his wife. "There's something about the way Mary and I, together, perceive the world and relate to it that just seems naturally funny," he told David Chute. "One of the things Mary and I have in common is a great deal of suppressed anger."[4]

Along with what he made from acting and developing movies, Bartel drew income participating in panels at international conferences and serving as a judge at festivals. According to John Landis, "He made a career out of going to film festivals for a while all around the world."[5]

5. Independent

Before Bartel and Blackburn had begun to explore their new script idea, he'd accepted an offer to serve on the jury at the 1979 Berlin Film Festival. Unwilling to set either the Berlin commitment or the new project with Blackburn aside, he brought Blackburn to Germany with him. "[T]the festival sent me a pair of tickets—one for me and one for my wife. I didn't have a wife.... So I took Blackburn and we stayed in this elegant Berlin hotel."[6] As Bartel fulfilled his judging duties, Blackburn worked in his room, crafting a story about a married couple—Mary and Paul Bland—who devise a plan to lure "unsuspecting sexual swingers to their home, murder them, steal their money and then sell them to a creep who grinds them into dog food."[7] The Blands knock off their prey with an iron skillet, and the money they steal goes toward a $20,000 down payment for a restaurant they hope to open—Paul and Mary's Country Kitchen.

Back in the States, Bartel and Blackburn fleshed out the narrative and their characters. One plotline they developed further involved a Chicano thief who learns about the Blands' murder-for-money scheme, extorts them to get in on it, seduces Mary and futilely attempts to persuade her to help him kill Paul. Another character, a young mom who works as a dominatrix, also materialized. The part had been inspired by an article in *Village Voice*. "The subject of the piece was a real dominatrix who was fifteen years old and had been trained by her mother," Bartel told Diane Jacobs. "The reporter found her at home with her baby, talking about the predilections of her customers—who were mostly businessmen—in a very matter-of-fact way, as if she were in the crocheting business."[8]

By June, Bartel and Blackburn had a going script, which they submitted to both mainline studios and independent operations with the deliberately ambiguous title *Eating Raoul*. Bartel and Blackburn reasoned that they needed a peculiar title that brought attention to itself and intrigued potential viewers. "It's provocative, suggesting sex or possibly cannibalism," Bartel said. "We needed a title people will remember and grow curious about, since the movie has no famous stars and doesn't come from a famous novel." All the same, their early efforts at selling their story were spurned. "The major criterion in financing a low-budget picture is that it relates to something that's been successful in the marketplace in recent years," Bartel explained. "When we were making *Raoul*, 'splatter' films were considered the safest bet. But comedies—nobody knows what's funny. You can't tell from reading a script. They're hard to export, since what's funny in one country may not be in another. And they generally require a famous name to sell."[9]

Neither he nor Woronov had a famous name, and their physical appearances flouted potential investors' expectations for how the leads in a commercial film should look: "[N]obody would give us a penny. They said, 'Audiences aren't interested in black comedy, and starring who? You and Mary?'" One producer considered financing the movie, but the deal failed to materialize because of a disagreement over casting. "Michael White, who produced *The Rocky Horror Picture Show*, liked the script and said he'd produce it if I'd direct and somebody else played the leads. But then I remembered how Sylvester Stallone had been offered money to let somebody else play *Rocky* in his script and I said no. The project had been devised as a lark for Mary and me, and that was the way I wanted to keep it."[10]

Early on, Bartel had been hopeful about persuading Roger Corman to back the movie. With Blackburn he had purposefully included thematic material Corman liked to see in the movies he backed—sex, action, humor, with slivers of social criticism. "I thought that if I could come up with a funny idea that was based on the elements of sex and violence, which were the two cornerstones of the Corman empire, I could probably get Roger to back the project."[11] But New World's chief was reluctant to offer financing. "He didn't like the idea of our starring in the movie. Where was the TV sale with us as the lead actors?"[12] Corman didn't reject the project outright, however. Instead, he offered to cover 50 percent of the budget—an impossible task at that point. "Roger ... always offered us exactly half of what we needed. When I needed $600,000, he offered me $300,000; when I needed $300,000, he offered me $150,000."[13]

The inability to secure financing forced the still-hopeful filmmakers to change their sales strategy. "Given the subject matter, and that Mary and I were the leads, I felt that if anything was to happen, people would really have to see some of it [the movie], to see what I had in mind."[14] In November 1980, Bartel and Blackburn proceeded to start up the production. "[W]e decided to shoot some scenes in the Blands' apartment, over a weekend, hoping that we could impress a big studio and get them to finance the rest of the film."[15]

Just as he had when he made "The Secret Cinema," Bartel used short ends that were given to him and covered other costs out of pocket. "The film stock was a gift," he told *Variety*, "the location was donated, everything was done on spec, just to get a few minutes of films as a sample. This is a tactic that people have tried over and over and which almost never works, but after the first weekend of shooting ... we had ten minutes finished."[16] One of the people who supplied Bartel with footage was John Landis: "I was doing some big studio picture. I don't remember which it was. But I wound up giving him a lot of film. Not just ... outs and trims, but we would order several thousand feet extra and give it to Paul because we figured Orion or Universal or Paramount or whatever it was could afford it."[17] Joe Dante and Mike Finnell, who had moved on from New World and were making *The Howling* for AVCO, also supplied the production with scraps of film.

Through his friendship with Dante and Finnell, by the way, Bartel met Alan Toomayan—a young assistant editor who'd been volunteering on *The Howling* in order to gain practical experience in the cutting room. "Toward the end of the production," Toomayan said, "Paul was hired by Joe Dante to be the interpreter for Pino Donaggio," an Italian composer with limited English, who'd been contracted to score the movie. Dante had been unable to communicate with Donaggio about what he needed from him in terms of music for this end-of-the-seventies take on the werewolf genre. "Paul spoke fluent Italian, as well as a few other languages.... So he acted as the translator for Pino and Joe. And that's how I got to meet him." Bartel eventually brought Toomayan on as the editor for *Eating Raoul*, and the pair would team up again for *Not for Publication*, *Lust in the Dust*, *The Longshot* and *Scenes from The Class Struggle in Beverly Hills*.[18]

Much of the early sample footage compiled for *Eating Raoul* was shot in a Hollywood apartment made available by the apartment's tenant, Art Fein, a friend of Blackburn. Fein remembered, "My place was decorated fifties, which was very 'out.' The stuff was cheap, and plentiful. They [Blackburn and Bartel] thought it would be perfect for the Blands."[19] Bartel explained his reasoning for using Fein's apartment to Ira H. Gallen: "When I saw the apartment with its fifties furniture and fifties decor it occurred to me that this was a perfect visual metaphor for the idea that the Blands are stuck in the fifties both emotionally, socially, sexually: all their attitudes that are out of date."[20]

Bartel and Blackburn reassembled cast and crew for a second weekend and shot more material in a hospital in nearby Duarte, where Woronov's character works as a dietician, yielding another ten minutes.

They proceeded to show the sample reel, but outside financing continued to elude them. And then bad news hit. "[W]e learned that the [apartment] building we'd used as the set was going to be torn down. I had to either shoot the whole film in the building before they tore it down; build a new set for the shooting of the rest of the film or scrap what I had and start over."[21] The problem was acute because the filmmakers had now nearly exhausted their finances.

Paul turned to his parents for assistance. Fortuitously, Bill and Jesse Bartel had recently sold the house in Montclair, which enabled them—along with some money Jesse had earned in the stock market—to cover the production's most pressing costs. "[T]hey gave me the money to shoot all the apartment scenes. Ultimately, it was savings from acting in and directing other people's movies and the money my parents got from selling their house ... that paid for the film."[22] The Bartels lent their son approximately $300,000, freeing him at that point to relinquish his role as producer and turn his attention more fully to his performance and the film's direction. The investment would turn out to be a shrewd one: "[S]ince my family ended up giving me the money," Bartel said in 1989, long after the production had gone in the black, "we owned it one hundred percent, and we got all the profits from it."[23]

Freed from the need to chase financing, Bartel decided to hire on someone to replace him as the film's producer. "A friend suggested I meet Anne Kimmel, who had just produced an ambitious short, 'Greatheart,' with her husband Kevin Hynes."[24] He approached Kimmel about the job, and she accepted without hesitation: "[W]hen I saw the first weekend's footage he had shot to help fundraising, I knew I wanted to produce it. I just loved Paul and Mary's bizarre perceptions of reality, outrageous but with taste."[25] Bartel quickly recognized that he had a made a good decision. "[H]er contributions were invaluable, making crew deals, obtaining locations at very reasonable rates and keeping me organized."[26] He elaborated for *Rolling Stone*'s Paul Scanlon, "She did all the line production functions; she made the deals with the crews. She bought raw film stock for the lowest possible price from underground dealers. She got the lab to develop and print for half its normal price. She saved us a fortune."[27] Bartel said that Kimmel, in fact, took the negative "to a cheapo porn movie shop to get our print. It was a scuzz parlor, and they couldn't insure anything. So we just crossed out fingers."[28]

5. Independent 55

The filmmakers' attempts to save money sometimes took a comic turn. For one of the picture's pivotal sequences, Paul and Mary Bland decide to advertise in a publication promoting the services of a pair of dominatrices, Naughty Nancy and Cruel Carla, whom they have invented to help them lure swingers to their apartment. Bartel told Terry Gross that "we went to some sex stores, and we looked at some sex papers, because there's a whole plot element that involved running an ad in one of the Los Angeles sex papers. Unfortunately our budget was so low we didn't have enough money to be able to afford to print prop paper, so we went to one of the real sex papers [*Hollywood Press*], and we offered to mention their name several times in the film, and in exchange we asked them to run our ad one week in their paper. And we got some very curious answers." One of the letters they received came from a man in Germany who was certain he'd procured Cruel Carla's services previously and "hoped she would remember his specialty and still be willing to engage in it."[29]

A second letter came from the film's crew itself. Production designer Bob Schulenberg and his set dresser, Denny Tedesco, were behind the prank. Tedesco recalled: "We actually put a letter into the *Hollywood Press*. [Property master] Loma Lee Brookbank, Bob and I actually waited after everybody left one night. We got ourselves in get-up. I had my back against the wall in underwear. You couldn't see my face, and I had this hand come across with a whip across my back. We sent it in and wrote this long nasty letter to Paul and Mary. When they finally got the letter, they read it at lunch. And everybody had their theories. 'Oh, my God, that arm is a man's arm.' 'It's two men.'"[30]

The production stretched off-and-on for eighteen months, with filming often scheduled over weekends.[31] Though the bulk of Bartel's attention was given to *Eating Raoul*, he continued to line up other work opportunities for himself. *Frankencar* was given new life when foreign backers optioned the script, though this deal fell through as earlier ones had. "It got too expensive, I guess," Bartel told David Chute. "A Japanese firm was supposed to do it, got involved in other things, and backed out. As simple as that."[32] Bartel also accepted an offer to appear in director Sam Fuller's *White Dog* (1982), a drama about the efforts of a white woman (Kristy McNichol) and an African American animal trainer (Paul Winfield) to help a German Shepherd that has been conditioned "from birth to hate anyone with black skin."[33] Bartel's friend Jon Davison served as the film's producer. Bartel played a cameraman in a short scene—filmed in spring 1981—who sets up shooting equipment while the film's principals chat with a TV director played by Marshall Thompson. Thompson was a character actor who had appeared in dozens of television programs and low-budget features. "Originally we tried to get Rouben Mamoulian for the part of the director," Davison remembered. "He would occasionally show up at Paramount where I was working, and I thought maybe he'd do it for Sam but he declined. Then I asked [screenwriter] Curtis Hanson, with Sam's blessing, to try to get Joseph H. Lewis. I believe he was living on his boat, and Curtis was friendly with him, but he also turned us down. By then we were running out of time, and I hired Marshall Thompson. Paul, on the other hand, never turned down a role (or a roll)."[34] Despite good reviews, Paramount dumped *White Dog* after booking it in a handful of theaters, and the picture more or less vanished until Criterion released it to general audiences as a DVD in 2008.

The willingness of *Eating Raoul*'s cast and crew to work for little pay helped Bartel and Kimmel considerably as the film progressed. Bartel explained: "The performers took deferred payments and points ... and the technicians we finally got took base wages."[35] Much of the cast was comprised of people recruited from the crew and friends. Soundman Ben Haller played a hospital orderly who gives an enema to a sex-obsessed patient at Mary's hospital. Denny Tedesco was a busboy in a restaurant where Anne Kimmel is a diner. Dick Blackburn is James, the real estate agent who tells the Blands that if they can come up with $20,000 in two weeks, they can put a down payment on the restaurant they want to open far away from the city.

Several contacts from New World also appeared in the movie: Joe Dante as a waiter; Jon Davison as a guest at an orgy hosted by Don Steele; and John Landis as a goofy bank customer. The director also put his sister Wendy in the picture. In the finished film's opening sequence, the camera captures various down-and-outers who cling to the sides of Hollywood Boulevard. Wendy stands on a corner, trying to provoke interest from johns with her skimpy clothes and heavy makeup.

Writer-actor-director Buck Henry agreed to appear in the movie, too, as "a lecherous banker" who tries to fondle Mary Bland when she applies for a loan.[36] Henry had met Bartel "when they served together on the Selection Committee for the Los Angeles International Film Exhibition (Filmex)," Bartel explained in press materials prepared for the film. "But before he would agree to be in the picture we screened a rough cut of the two-thirds of the picture we had already shot. He liked it and was happy to participate."[37]

The decision to cast the film's third lead, the titular Raoul, came about after shooting commenced, once the money from the sale of the Bartels' home in New Jersey was assured. The part went to Robert Beltran, a young stage actor from central California, whose previous screen experience had been limited to a small role in a film directed by Luis Valdez called *Zoot Suit*. The casting director from *Zoot Suit*, Gene Blythe, was an acquaintance of Bartel. Blythe sensed that Beltran would be good as the suave crook who learns about the Blands' scheme and later seduces Mary. A call came a few weeks later from Bartel to the actor's mother's house in Bakersfield, where Beltran was living. "One day I got a call from Paul.... He said, 'Well, I'm really interested in you for my film, *Eating Raoul*.' And I said, 'What? ... No, man. I don't do those kinds of films. I'm not interested.' He goes, 'No, no, no. It's completely legitimate.' And I said, 'Okay, well, what else have you done?' I

Mary (Mary Woronov), Paul (Bartel) and a dead swinger in *Eating Raoul* (Bartel Film, 1982).

was rather cheeky in those days. 'Well, you might have seen "The Secret Cinema" or—'And I said, 'No.' 'You might have seen—' He mentioned another one. I said, 'Ugh, no.' And finally he says, 'Well, maybe you saw *Death Race 2000*.' And I said, 'Oh, man! You did *Death Race 2000*?' He says, 'Yes, that was me.' And I said, 'Okay. Where do I go to meet you?'" A few nights earlier, Beltran had watched *Death Race* in a drive-in on a date, and the film had amused and impressed him. "I had to see it twice because I was with this girl. We didn't see very much of it at the first showing. But it seemed really interesting enough to stick around for the second showing, right? And I just laughed. It was so funny."[38]

Beltran took the job, a decision that pleased not only Bartel but Blackburn, Kimmel and Woronov. "We were so tickled, so excited, when we met him," Bartel said. "We saw how funny he was, how good-looking and how soulful. I was unbelievably lucky to find him. He has, within his own personality, so may attractive qualities, which he brought to the part."[39]

For the role of Doris the Dominatrix, Bartel went with another talented actor who was starting her career, Susan Saiger. Originally, Bartel had given the part to Betty Thomas—one of the stars of the *Hill Street Blues* TV series—but shooting commitments for the show ultimately forced her to quit on him. Saiger subsequently came to Bartel's attention—she performed improv at the Comedy Store on Sunset Boulevard—and had the ability to play a wide range of character types effectively. As he had with Beltran, Bartel reached out to Saiger by telephone. She recollected, "Paul called me, and he said, 'I am the director of this movie, *Eating Raoul*. My assistant director said he knows you and says that he saw you the other night at the Comedy Store. He says you're really funny. Would you be interested in reading for the role of Doris the Dominatrix?' And I was just like, 'Excuse me?' It's not your normal request, right? He just said, 'I know you do improv, that you do a lot of character work. She [Doris] has to pose as several people in disguise, and I'd love to have you come read.' I said, 'Okay. Where should I go?' 'My apartment.' First I'm reading for a dominatrix, then it's at some dude's apartment. Two things, you know, you're told as a young novice actor don't do.'"[40]

Throughout the production, Bartel invited suggestions and creative contributions from the people working around him. Blackburn often stood in as director when Bartel needed to play his part as Paul

Bland, for instance. "The points of view of an actor and director are too different, and having to jump back and forth between them is too confusing, too hard, I had to depend on Dick Blackburn, who actually collaborated with me in directing the scenes I was in."[41] Woronov as well was given great leeway with her performance as Mary Bland. "I had just played Miss Togar [in *Rock 'n' Roll High School*], who was this reeling bitch, and I was afraid that I would be pushed into that kind of role forever. When *Eating Raoul* came along, I was supposed to be that same kind of angry person, and I said no, I wanted to be this sweet person. Besides, I could never be angry with Paul—I really liked him, and I was always considerate with him because he was a great person. That is what happened–we became this loving couple, but then I thought that people were going to think that I was married to him. From that, I thought that we had to have separate beds and absolutely hate sex—that way, people would buy that we were this loving couple that was strange because we didn't like sex. I just thought that was great."[42]

The extemporized fashion in which much of *Eating Raoul* was made prompted Bartel to share with David Chute an illuminating statement about his view of the moviemaking process—an admission that despite his deep investment in the production as director, writer, financier, casting director and actor, he was never fully in control: "Good films and even good sequences are imagined visually and then carefully executed. But even so, you never end up with the movie that was in your mind when you wrote or read the script. Movies inevitably change as you make them and become something else. You have to keep reconceiving them and accepting and rejecting ideas within the context of what you actually have, not what you started out to get. The challenge is to perfect what they are *becoming*, rather than what they started out to be."[43]

Several people who worked closely with Bartel during the production were grateful for his refusal to take a star turn or demand adherence to his singular vision for the film. Woronov told *Pyschotronic*: "Working with Paul is great. He's not the kind of director that screams and yells at you. At first you think he doesn't know what he wants, but he does."[44] Beltran was likewise appreciative for Bartel's supportive manner after petitioning him about making changes to his part: "I changed some of the dialogue to get the street slang right. Raoul is no wetback. He's a native American citizen, a Chicano, and I tried to authenticate the part however I could."⁴⁵ Bartel's receptivity to new ideas crossed over off the set as well. Editor Alan Toomayan said, "Paul would just bang out something [with the cast], and we'd fix it in the editing room. When there's little or no budget you have to be creative and fast. Or at least fast. Sometimes things suffer for it, but sometimes the spontaneity brings out something unplanned and wonderful."⁴⁶

As the film neared completion, Bartel was curious about how audiences would respond to it, and he scheduled previews at USC, UCLA and the Pacific Film Archive at the University of California. The comment cards that came back were generally promising, and Bartel and Blackburn began to suspect that their movie could be a hit. But finding an interested distribution company remained a challenge. "The material was too offbeat, too risky," Bartel said. "They kept saying 'Who's in it? Who's going to come [to see it]?' The rule of thumb in Hollywood is that to sell comedy you need a name, somebody like Steve Martin, Woody Allen or Mel Brooks."⁴⁷

Then fortune smiled on the filmmakers. Thanks to the assistance of Tom Luddy, a contact Bartel had at Francis Ford Coppola's Zoetrope Studios in San Francisco, the Europa Films group offered him $60,000 in exchange for future rights to distribute *Eating Raoul* in Scandinavia, a deal that "helped financially not only in terms of finishing the film but also acted as a considerable vote of confidence for the project."⁴⁸ More good news followed when *Eating Raoul*, still a work-in-progress, was selected for inclusion in the 1982 Los Angeles International Film Exposition. "When the film was shown the audience went wild," Bartel declared after the film's first screening on March 23. "Word of mouth spread fast, and the movie attracted sell-out crowds."⁴⁹

That May, *Eating Raoul* also played at the Cannes Film Festival. Blackburn recalled that he and Bartel booked the picture in the smallest theater in the city, and afterwards vigorously promoted it. Interest grew, and Bartel responded by booking the second largest theater in town. Now people began to fight to get in to see the picture. For the film's third screening, an even larger theater was booked, and again people couldn't get in, which aroused more interest and enthusiasm.⁵⁰ Following the third screening, Bartel was approached by critic Richard Roud, who then commanded great power in film circles as a regular contributor to *Sight & Sound*. Roud had seen *Eating Raoul*, liked it and wanted to feature it at the 1982 New York Film Festival, over which he served as director. Bartel told Lawrence Van Gelder, "I was sitting on the terrace of the Carlton Hotel in Cannes, sipping a $7 coffee [when Roud] came strolling down the Croisette, casually glanced in my direction and turned thumbs up." Bartel well understood the implications of this acceptance: further attention in the press, additional bookings and increased revenues. "I felt enormous elation and relief."[51]

The favorable response the film generated eventually led to a stateside distribution deal. In the early eighties, at the same time as *Eating Raoul* was filming, several commercial studios had begun to operate boutique "classics" divisions that looked for art films to buy and then book in metropolitan areas and later release on videocassette. In June 1982, 20th Century–Fox International Classics let Bartel know it wanted *Eating Raoul* and offered him a $400,000 "advance against profits." The outcome understandably pleased the director: "The lurking muscle of Fox gives me access to better theaters."[52] Anne Kimmel was of course happy, too: "We would screen [the movie] in various states and try to raise money or sell TV rights. And then when it was just about finished, I think we were still on two reels—we hadn't locked or mixed it yet—we took it to the Seattle Film Festival. That's where we got interest from Fox Classics. Fox Classics picked it up."[53] Quartet/Films, Inc., an independent distribution company owned by New York City businessmen Meyer Ackerman and Julian Schlossberg, also came on to assist with booking the movie in independently-owned theatres throughout North America.[54]

A rollout plan was quickly developed after the arrangement with Fox Classics came to be. Following the movie's September screening at the New York Film Festival, Fox and Quartet would release the picture nationally. In the interim, Bartel would develop and execute a marketing plan. Traditional measures would be employed—a trailer was cut, for instance. Alternative tactics were planned, too. Jane Alsobrook, Fox International Classics's marketing director, hired people to advertise the film "with sandwich boards at rock concerts."[55] And instead of producing a novelization of the film to sell in stores, a comic book adaptation was commissioned. Bartel, the cartoon enthusiast, had been a longtime admirer of underground comics—independently published satirical magazines loaded with graphic art, especially anthropomorphic characters. He told *L.A. Weekly*, "I did the comic book, which cost me about $10,000, as a promotional item, and because I love underground comics. Fox wanted it as a promotion, and then they wouldn't pay us."[56]

For the adaptation, Bartel engaged alternative cartoonist Kim Deitch, who welcomed the job and assembled a team of graphic artists to help him, among them Carol Lay. In 2015, Lay recalled:

> Kim and I were new friends when he brought me in to work on an underground comic version of the soon-to-be released film, *Eating Raoul*.
> As a teenager, Paul Bartel had worked at UPA and knew and admired Kim's father, Gene Deitch, a cartoonist at the studio. I forget how we transposed the movie into a thirty-six-page comics plot—I remember watching the film many times, but I forget who did the breakdowns, or if we did them collaboratively. (Kim probably got a shooting script, translated it into a comics script, and then we moved along to page layouts.) We worked closely on the layouts and pencils. Bartel wanted the comic to be ready for a film premier, and we had a month to get it done.
> Kim drew the Pauls, and I drew the Marys, and we traded off other drawing duties as well. I tried to draw as close to Kim's style as possible, as he was the cartoonist Bartel wanted. Sometimes when artists draw characters some of their own features sneak into it—Bartel's character resembles Kim in a way, and the way I drew Woronov had perhaps too much of my long face.
> We worked out of the living room of my apartment on New Hampshire Street in L.A. One month to do the book from scratch was tight—adapt the movie to comic book-length and plot it to fit the page count, character designs, layout, pencils, lettering, inks, and so on.... We met the deadline. Sometime during all that we met Mary Woronov, the actor who played Raoul, and a few of Bartel's Hollywood friends. One memorable night we went to Bartel's apartment on Fountain [Avenue] where he showed some of Gene Deitch's vintage animations.[57]

Amidst all this advance work, Bartel agreed to appear in his friend Allan Arkush's second "rock 'n' roll" musical comedy, *Get Crazy*, which started shooting in August 1982. Set in Los Angeles on New Year's Eve, the movie tracks a concert hall manager who stymies a seamy businessman's efforts to destroy his theater. As hijinks proceed, several musical acts perform on stage, including punker Lee Ving, Flo & Eddie's Howard Kaylan and, finally, Lou Reed. Bartel appears on the screen for only a moment as a doctor who is called in when the theatre's owner falls ill and fears his death is imminent. The patient is actually suffering from food poisoning brought on by a heaping serving of egg foo young. Several actors from *Eating Raoul* have parts in the movie, too—Mary Woronov, Ed Begley, Jr., Susan Saiger—as well as New World veterans Dick Miller and Danny Opatoshu.

On September 25, *Eating Raoul* had its first of two screenings at the New York Film Festival in the Film Society of Lincoln Center's Alice Tully Hall. The attention the movie drew from critics was again favorable. Vincent Canby declared that "one has to be careful not to overstate the case when praising *Eating Raoul*. Like Paul and Mary [Bland], it is sensitive. One mustn't blunt its pleasures by calling it a laff riot. It is full of smiles, punctuated here and there by marvelously unseemly guffaws, but most of the time it works its little wonders quietly. The comic style is purposely flat, plain and ordinary, like a piece of Pop art."[58] *Time*'s Richard Corliss sensed that the movie's excellence—and its commercial potential—would lead to more directing opportunities for Bartel: "With his bow tie, manicured beard, debaucher's lips and a forehead that recedes in disapproving furrows almost to the collar line, Paul Bartel looks like the last surviving member of the Preston Sturges Repertory Company. Sturges, whose spitball farces (*The Lady Eve*, *The Miracle of Morgan's Creek*) sped moviegoers giddily through World War II, might appreciate Bartel's continuance of that tradition, as actor and writer-director, in high-camp style."[59]

Eating Raoul opened on October 1 at the 68th Street Playhouse in Uptown Manhattan—one of several movie theatres owned by Quartet/Films's Meyer Ackerman—where "Naughty Nurse" had played with *Take the Money and Run* in 1969. The picture was then booked up and down the eastern seaboard, drawing favorable notices in many of the cities where it played. Bruce McCabe was impressed by the allusive aspects of the picture, for instance its parody of "the dramatic and theatrical conventions of Hollywood moviemaking to an almost sublime degree by exaggerating them to unbelievable proportions and then playing them with the kind of poker-faced aplomb once endemic to drawing-room comedies."[60] *Eating Raoul* also reminded several reviewers of past comedies about murderers. Desmond Ryan gathered (correctly) that "Bartel's inspiration seems to be those classic English comedies like *The Ladykillers*, *Kind Hearts and Coronets* and *The Naked Truth*. Those movies slyly upend the expectations and sympathies of the viewer and place the audience on the side of the murderer. Much of their humor stems from making people laugh at something that isn't funny."[61] And *Newsweek*'s Jack Kroll drolly noted: "Remember Charlie Chaplin's classic updating of the Bluebeard story, *Monsieur Verdoux*? *Eating Raoul* is a kind of Mr. and Mrs. Verdoux. Paul and Mary Bland are quiet, respectable folk. They abhor the swanning set that infests their comfy neighborhood, and they go about their business of swingercide with the faintly squeamish determination of the householders setting up a Roach Motel."[62]

Not everything written about the film was glowing, though. Several conservative critics regarded *Eating Raoul* as nothing more than an inappropriate joke. Others, in contrast, faulted Bartel and Blackburn for hedging on their efforts to ridicule the middleclass values espoused by the Blands as they purge Los Angeles of its "sexual freaks." *New York* magazine's David Denby complained: "Who cares about the triumph of the Blands? They're hardly alive. The movie seems to be saying that sexual drives make people so disgusting that they might as well be murdered. But disgust with sex is not a satiric point of view; it's an unhappy mood, not all that different from a sour stomach. In the end, *Eating Raoul* is almost as fussy as Paul Bland, a man who dreams in perfect sentences."[63] And the *Los Angeles Times*'s Sheila Benson, grumbled, "*Raoul* is fey and agreeable; what it lacks is the vitality to be really outrageous. It *almost* makes you yearn for the honest tackiness of a John Waters.... In crucial ways, Bartel is playing it safe, the bland leading the Blands."[64]

The buzz the film generated was such that journalists throughout the country approached Bartel for interviews. He would often use these conversations to have fun at the reporters' expense, telling them that he and Mary Woronov were real-life spouses. Woronov confirmed this, explaining to *People* after Bartel's death: "When we were on our press tour, he'd pretend we were married. Once I told him, 'You've got to stop that!' So in our next interview, when the reporter asked if we were married, he looked sad and said, 'No, we're divorced.'"[65]

On occasion Bartel was asked if *Eating Raoul* was in any way a political film, if he and Blackburn had intended for the Blands and their predatory business practices to underscore shortcomings in contemporary American culture. Bartel was inconsistent in his responses to these queries. To Diane Jacobs, he explained: "If you look at John Waters's work or the late Andy Warhol ... you see that beneath the surface humor there's a pessimistic attitude. Any good work of art is resonant. While *Eating Raoul* is meant to be entertainment, it's not a message film by any means."[66] To John Barron, however, he allowed for the possibility that the film had some political import, but only, perhaps, by accident: "The movie touches on many things: the perversion of middle-class values, the resurgence of Nixonism, Latin machismo vs. WASP fastidiousness, *film noir*. I don't really mean to be didactic, however. These are all afterthoughts."[67] Yet in promotional materials prepared for the movie, he presented himself as a director who purposefully worked social commentary into the movie. "Paul and Mary's approach to dealing with the swingers is just like President Reagan's solution to the problems in El Salvador or Nicaragua. The current administration is just accelerating the trend of insularity and intolerance, with everyone selfishly pursuing their narrow interests at the expense of anyone else. I wanted to make a film about two greedy, uptight people who are at the same time not too unlike you and me and Nancy and Ronnie [Reagan], to keep it funny and yet communicate something about the perversity of these values."[68]

This perversity, he felt, bared itself particularly in repressive attitudes about sex embraced by bourgeois America. "The Blands are awful, but they're also nice. They're naïve and innocent, but they're also criminally insane. The joke is that something as basic and human as sexuality discomfits them, but something as antisocial and as inhuman as murder for profit doesn't faze them at all. They dehumanize the swingers: Mary at one point says, 'He *was* a man, honey. Now he's just a bag of garbage.' And without wanting to make an ostensible 'message picture,' that is the underlying idea, and it's something funny about our culture."[69] To Gene Siskel he explained that the Blands' ideas about sex "belong to the fifties," adding that the movie "is a protest against the sexual lies of the fifties, that sex isn't nice and that nice people aren't overtly sexual."[70]

6

In Demand

Bartel savored the accolades that followed *Eating Raoul*'s release and his new status as a quasi-celebrity. A favorite anecdote he shared during this time went as follows:

> I was walking down Central Park West the other day, and this couple came running up to me. They said, "Don't we know you from some place? Aren't you *Eating Raoul*?"
> "Not at the moment."[1]

Directing offers now poured in, many of them bizarre, including an invitation to work on a musical about serial killer Ted Bundy.[2] He was approached, too, about adapting a play "about a woman who is raped by a friend of her uncle, and in the second act she gets revenge by serving them a meal, the remains of the aborted fetus."[3]

As *Eating Raoul* played at festivals and in cinemas around the world, Dick Blackburn was also approached about working on new projects. In an essay titled "Digesting Raoul," he recalled a telephone conversation from this period:

> "Hey, Dick—Charlie. You're back! I hear you hit a lotta festivals."
> "You're not kidding! Dallas was great. They loved the film. In Cannes we had three screenings. Each one was packed. In Toronto we had a limousine at our disposal. Mary liked it so much that when it drove us to the airport she wouldn't get out. It was kind of embarrassing. In New York, [film director] Joan Micklin Silver gave me a party. She wants to work with me on something. I met the novelist Robert Stone at another party. It's great to meet people whose work you admire."
> "What else has been happening?"
> "I get letters from people I don't know. My agent sometimes calls *me*. There are a lot more little bullshit projects, so I have more excuses to keep from finishing the novel."
> "Yeah, but has anything really changed?"
> "I don't know. Every time I wake up I still see the same old wall."[4]

Bartel began to talk to interviewers, too, about the next film he wanted to develop, which he'd given the working title *Scenes from the Class Struggle in Beverly Hills*. The storyline, he said, would draw on *The Marriage of Figaro*, Beaumarchais's eighteenth century stage comedy about the carnal intrigues of aristocrats and their servants.[5] In November 1982, he told *Rolling Stone* that he was "writing [the picture] with a fellow named David Columbia."[6] He imagined casting Peter Falk and Jeff Bridges as the male leads, giving Mary Woronov a major part, too.[7] Bartel's ambitions for *Scenes*, would again be arthouse, as he planned, Woronov said, "to make it like an Eric Rohmer movie—a very elegant look. The background music will be Chopin."[8]

Bartel and Blackburn also went to work planning a sequel to *Eating Raoul* that would have Bartel and Woronov reprise their roles as the Blands. Blackburn took the lead on writing the script, an account of the couple's lives after they open their restaurant. Titled *Bland Ambition*, the story was conceived as a political satire. "Paul and Mary Bland run for governor of California—jointly," Bartel told Lawrence Van

Paul (Bartel) and Mary Bland (Mary Woronov) with their lethal skillet in *Eating Raoul* (Bartel Film, 1982).

Gelder.⁹ "They have their own little TV show, a combination of sitcom and political commercial. In order to improve their family image, they adopt a little girl from an orphanage run by John Waters and pretend she is their biological child. The little girl turns out to be just to the right of *The Bad Seed*. She manipulates Paul and Mary and makes more and more outrageous demands, threatening to make public her orphanage background. So they decide she will have to meet with a tragic accident on election eve to generate sympathy for them ... but she gets wind of it and runs away and joins the opposition."¹⁰

For the role of the child, Bartel and Blackburn wanted to use Aileen Quinn, the star of John Huston's *Annie*.¹¹ This time out, though, Bartel would produce the movie, and Blackburn would direct. As Bartel explained to a reporter, "I'm not crazy about directing and playing the lead.... I will enjoy the luxury of just acting."¹²

But once again financing eluded them, and Bartel and Blackburn open themselves to other projects. A re-make of *Kind Hearts and Coronets* was proposed, with Robin Williams to play one of the leads. *Frankencar* was briefly resurrected, too; Bartel even approached William Friedkin to direct it—Friedkin had explored the horrific in *The Exorcist* and worked a spectacular car chase into *The French Connection*—but the director politely passed.

Bartel also gave some thought to launching his own production company out of his house on Fareholm Drive, a "Spanish home, built in 1924, in the Hollywood Hills" that he'd purchased, along with an apartment in New York's Upper West Side, with money from *Eating Raoul*.¹³ This operation, he hoped, would enter into "an arrangement with some company that is not otherwise involved with movies—an oil company, a steel company, a computer company, maybe some big conglomerate. Some company that has lots of capital to play with and wants to diversify. They would put up $10 million, to cover the cost of producing one $4 million picture and two $3 million pictures. What I'm hoping to do is cross-collateralize for the investor. The $4 million would be the umbrella film, the one obviously commercial exploitation film. It's called *Frankencar*, a car-chase picture and revenge melodrama with a lot of eccentric comic ideas in it. The other ... films will be modestly enough priced that there's little likelihood of losing money on them—and they will be covered by *Frankencar* in any case."¹⁴

As financial support from family, friends and strangers had made *Eating Raoul* possible, Bartel experienced a sense of obligation to help

6. In Demand 69

young filmmakers—now that he was prospering—in similar fashion. One of his early beneficiaries was Jim Jarmusch, a fledgling director based in New York City, who'd served for a time as Nicholas Ray's assistant. From German director Wim Wenders—whom he'd gotten to know when Wenders was shooting an experimental documentary about Ray titled *Lightning over Water*—Jarmusch had borrowed forty minutes of undeveloped film, which he'd subsequently used to shoot a thirty-minute short titled "The New World." Jarmusch had started to screen his film at festivals throughout Europe, hoping to attract investors who would help him turn his "deadpan comedy about the adventures of a couple of slummy deadbeats from New York and a visiting teenage girl from Hungary" into a feature-length release. He also needed money to pay off Wenders for the film that had been provided to him.[15]

In October 1982, Jarmusch screened "The New World" in southeast Germany at the International Hof Film Festival. Bartel was at Hof, too. Jarmusch recollected for Peter Belsito that Bartel was there "showing *Eating Raoul* and saw the first part of my film. Then he read my script, and he just was really excited, and he said that he had spent so much time fighting to work independently that now, since he had a little money from *Eating Raoul*, he wanted to turn around and help someone else." Bartel, for whom the title "The New World" may have had symbolic resonance, "actually wanted to try to produce [Jarmusch's movie] as a feature, too, but he wasn't able to come up with enough money either. So he loaned me the money, as a friend, to pay [Wenders] back, for no percentage, no interest, nothing. He loaned me $15,000 just like that."[16] Nearly a year would follow before Jarmusch was able to resume shooting, but in May 1984, he managed to screen *Stranger Than Paradise*, as the expanded film was re-titled, at Cannes, where it won the Camera d'Or, a prize for best first feature film.[17]

In 1984, Bartel also made the acquaintance of another talented young director, Tim Burton, who approached him by letter with an invitation to appear in a black & white short titled *Frankenweenie*, which Disney was financing. Bartel accepted the offer and wound up playing "a science teacher who uses electricity and dead frogs to inspire one of his students (Barret Oliver) to revive a pet dog who was killed in an accident."[18]

Paul eventually secured a new independent project for himself, too, but it was not, as he'd hoped, *Scenes from the Class Struggle in Beverly Hills*. Rather, he got started on *Not for Publication*, "a light comedy about yellow journalism and political corruption in New York."[19] British production company Thorn EMI optioned the story in 1983, giving Bartel $2.5 million for a budget. "They sought me out and let me make whatever I wanted."[20] He had written the script for the picture several years earlier in New York with a friend, a composer named John Meyer, whom he'd first met in the early sixties through a mutual acquaintance, Barry Dennen.

Bartel and Meyer's friendship had initially blossomed thanks to a shared taste for Hollywood musicals. In 2015, Meyer recalled: "Paul and I bonded immediately over our love of shows and films; like me he'd been exposed to both forms from childhood and knew the work of masters like Lubitsch and René Clair, not to mention Busby Berkeley. We were always watching *42nd St.* or the *Golddigger* films or *Footlight Parade* or *Love Me Tonight*–all the classics, plus the obscurities like *Moonlight and Pretzels.* We agreed that Harry Warren and Al Dubin were our favorite songsmiths."

They had written the first draft of their script before Bartel left New York for Los Angeles to make *Private Parts.* "We wrote the script for *Not for Publication* in the apartment of [singer] Margaret Whiting, with whom I was living at the time. I typed it on a Smith-Corona electric portable. I'd sit typing, like Charles Brackett, while Paul lounged about the room, like Billy Wilder." They "decided to write a screenplay that was a kind of homage to the Frank Capra comedies of the thirties, where Jean Arthur played a manipulative reporter who dupes—and then falls in love with—an innocent male. *Mr. Deeds* is an example, also *Nothing Sacred.*" Meyer added, "My job was constructing a plausible narrative, keeping the [principals] straight, and not letting the situations veer into the totally nonsensical" while Bartel concentrated "on the bizarre and the satirical." As a result of these contradictory aspirations, the script the two worked up featured a fairly conventional "screwball" protagonist—who is by turns nervy, tough and warm-hearted—but who finds herself facing off against peculiar, visually arresting characters, including a masturbating politician.

Initially, Bartel and Meyer hoped Bernadette Peters would play the film's female lead, a well-heeled journalist who divides her time writing copy for a semi-pornographic tabloid and developing publicity for a mayor who wants to purge porno magazines from the newsstands of New York. "We began casting," Meyer said, "and couldn't find the right leading lady; we should've gone with Bernadette Peters or maybe even Ruth Buzzi, but they weren't available. Paul finally became frustrated and impatient and EMI was getting antsy so we cast it."[21] For the role of Lois Thornedyke, the reporter, Nancy Allen was selected—Allen had won acclaim for her performances in several films directed by Brian De Palma, including *Carrie* and *Dressed to Kill*. David Naughton was given the part of her love interest, a nerdy photographer named Barry Denver—Naughton had played the lead in *An American Werewolf in London*, which Bartel's close friend John Landis directed. Laurence Luckinbill was cast as the crusading mayor, who also happens to be a crook. Bartel and Meyer filled out their cast with friends and former colleagues, several of whom had worked with Bartel previously, including Barry Dennen ("The Secret Cinema") and Richard Paul (*Eating Raoul*), along with Richard Blackburn and Anne Kimmel.

Surprisingly, Bartel declined to give Mary Woronov a part, wasting the opportunity to exploit the celebrity that had come to her thanks to *Eating Raoul*. Woronov disclosed to *A.V. Club* that although she would have had little trouble playing the Lois character, Bartel "just dropped me," telling her that he was now making "real movies" and as such was only interested in "working with real actors." Still bitter three decades later, she concluded, "I hated him for that. You know, Paul was a little misconceived."[22]

While the story for *Not for Publication* takes place in and around New York City, most of the picture was shot in Dallas, where Bartel worked out of the Melrose Hotel, an elegant red brick midrise located in the city's gay-friendly Oak Lawn neighborhood. In December 1983, toward the end of shooting, the *Dallas Morning News*'s Philip Wunitch visited Bartel at the hotel. "Call sheets, shooting schedules and production budgets can be found on almost every available surface," Wunitch noted in his profile. "Even to the most unwitting outsider, it's obvious an entire wing of the floor is being used as production offices for a movie." During a break, Bartel told Wunitch that he "chose Dallas because of the city's talent pool, locations that match New York and Texas's right-to-work status." This right-to-work status, allowing Bartel to use a non-union crew, spared him from paying his workers scale. "We looked at Atlanta. We even considered shooting the entire film in New York. But we finally decided on Dallas…. Any snags that we hit were because of that week in New York. We lost time in New York and gained time in Dallas."[23]

Time was lost in New York, Kimmel explained, as a result of rainy weather and troubles with a local chapter of the Teamsters union that imposed itself on the production. She remembered that "we owned Time Square for about eight hours, which was a pretty heady experience. Paul totally loved that. We were shooting, and we had to lock up equipment. We had a Teamster guy in charge of locking up our equipment. And some of our equipment disappeared that night. And we were talking to Teamsters about it. 'Hey, what's the story?' A camera had gotten lost. Cameras don't get lost. It turns out the guy that was guarding our stuff had recently been let out of jail for robbery! I said, 'This isn't going to do. We actually need people who are watching our things, who don't steal them!'"[24]

In the Melrose Hotel, the cast and crew shot the film's funniest bit, a wild sequence in which Barry Dennen, playing a vampy pimp named Woparico, discovers that several of his treasures—an electrified El Greco painting, for instance—have been stolen. Another standout sequence featured Allen and Naughton dressed up, respectively, as a lamb and a chicken, singing together at a swingers club named the Bestiary. The routine was actually shot at an east Dallas nightclub called Tango. Meyer, whom Bartel had asked to score the film, wrote the music and collaborated with Bartel on the lyrics for this song and was on set for Allen and Naughton's performance. "My fondest memory of the shoot was walking into the discotheque in Dallas … at 9:00 a.m. and seeing the camera on its tracks before the stage on a six-foot-high platform that ran the width of the room. It was all set to film the number I'd written—'You Bring out the Beast in Me.' I burst into tears."[25]

Once shooting wrapped, Bartel announced to reporters that he expected the film to open sometime in spring 1984. The Samuel Goldwyn Company, an independent distributor (which also handled the American release of Jarmusch's *Stranger than Paradise*), had secured rights from Thorn EMI to release the picture in the United States and ultimately released the picture in November that year. The reviews that came in, sadly, were almost universally hostile, with several critics expressing disappointment that Bartel had made a movie that lacked the understated perverseness that characterized his previous features. Vincent Canby, for example, complained: "Like all of Mr. Bartel's films, *Not for Publication* has a comic conceits that more often prompt knowing smiles than knee slapping laughter. Unlike the very funny *Eating Raoul*, which was so laid back it was upside down, *Not for Publication* seems to be trying too hard to be comic."[26]

The *Los Angeles Times*'s Patrick Goldstein was annoyed for the

Advertisement for *Not for Publication* (Thorn EMI, 1984), a film reviled by critics but adored by Bartel.

same reasons: "Operating on the low-budget outer limits of Hollywood, Paul Bartel has always been a wayward minstrel, a director perhaps too intelligent and audacious for his own good. Nearly all of his films offer a delightfully bleak comic vision, whether it's for the guilty pleasures of *Private Parts*, the black humor of *Death Race 2000* or the sly, caustic wit of his 1982 feature *Eating Raoul*. Which makes it all the more disappointing to see Bartel at the helm of *Not for Publication*, a wan, dishearteningly dull clinker that one is tempted to nickname *Not Quite Ready for Release*. A failed attempt to re-create some of the brash, brittle energy of a thirties screwball comedy, the film wastes its talented cast, botches its best comic premises and never figures out a way to sustain its zany, comic book situations."[27]

Paul, however, thought he'd done some of his best work with *Not for Publication*. As he told Michael Dare, "[P]eople are expecting more *Eating Raoul*. There's a certain percentage who are disappointed that my new film is in a different genre. I'm actually every bit as fond of *Not for Publication* as I am of *Eating Raoul*. It reflects a younger me, but as a confection—as an entertainment—I love looking at it. It's daring in a different way, and I hope that word of mouth will build an audience for it."[28] His confidence in the movie was such that he chose to screen it at the United States Film Festival in Park City, Utah (the forerunner of the Sundance Film Festival), after he was invited to sit on a panel titled *Roger Corman and His Prodigies* with directors Joe Dante, Jonathan Demme and Corman himself.

Eating Raoul's notoriety—enhanced by high videocassette sales—continued to yield new work opportunities for Bartel. Early in 1984, he was approached about directing *Lust in the Dust*, a parody of westerns in the vein of Mel Brooks's *Blazing Saddles*, that actor Tab Hunter had conceived and in which he would star. For the first time in his career as a feature director, Bartel was being asked to helm a movie without having to spend months laboring over the construction of a workable shooting script, an opportunity that excited him. "I thought the chance of doing a balls-out, raucous western parody, especially a western in the widescreen format, was the chance of a lifetime."[29] To Michael Dare he elaborated, "*Lust in the Dust* was entirely put together before I had anything to do with it. Tab Hunter was producing, and he had cast it, the script was ready, and the sets were being built. I was just finishing *Not for Publication*, and I wanted to just jump into another movie. It was heaven sent."[30] Making a movie on somebody else's terms—which he hadn't done since *Death Race 2000*—also appealed to him. "I believe it is beneficial to alternate between working on your own projects and putting your talents at the disposal of someone else, that is, trying to achieve somebody else's aims. This helps you stretch and grow—and keeps your ego in line."[31]

6. In Demand

Blessed with striking looks and a good singing voice, Tab Hunter had enjoyed popularity in both the movies and on the music charts in the fifties and even had his own TV show. By the late seventies, however, he was a regular on the dinner theater circuit performing in productions like *Bye Bye Birdie* and *Under the Yum Yum Tree*. He told Pat H. Broeske, "I'm one of the pioneers of dinner theater. I've probably performed in every theater in America at least once—probably two or three times."[32] He found himself crisscrossing the United States for long stretches of time, often staying in strange motel rooms in uneventful towns. To relieve boredom, he began to write out a script for a parody of Hollywood westerns that he gave the title *The Reverend and Rosie*.[33] Hunter was quite familiar with the western genre, having appeared in pictures like *Gunman's Walk* and *The Burning Hills*.

The script chronicled a search for treasure by rival parties, including a pair of sisters who despise one another, in a wide space in the road called Chili Verde. Hunter had hoped to cast his friend Rosey Grier as one of the leads. "I wanted to do it on television with [him]— that's where the name Rosie comes from."[34] He was unable initially,

Abel Wood (Tab Hunter) confiding to Father Garcia (Cesar Romero) in *Lust in the Dust* (Fox Run Productions, 1985).

though, to muster interest from investors and continued to act in dinner theater productions as well as taking occasional roles in American TV shows like *The Love Boat* and *Charlie's Angels*.

In 1980, independent director John Waters had asked Hunter if he'd appear in *Polyester*, a parody of fifties women's dramas, which would have Hunter play the love interest of Divine, a 300-pound female impersonator star who'd starred in earlier Waters ventures like *Pink Flamingos* and *Female Trouble*. Hunter was game, and he headed to Baltimore to shoot the picture. During a break from shooting, the actor had an epiphany. "Divine got such a huge charge out of working with a Hollywood star" like him, he explained in his autobiography, *Tab Hunter Confidential*. "But I got something even more valuable from our collaboration: a whole new take on my treatment of *The Reverend and Rosie*—what if Divine played Rosie?"[35]

Divine was also enthusiastic about pairing up with Hunter for a second time and agreed to play the role of Rosie if and when the movie got financing. "[Tab] enjoyed working with me, more than he did any of his previous leading 'ladies.' He thought I was easy to work with, I didn't give him any attitude—there was no sort of 'star trip.' We had a wonderful working relationship."[36] Though the film would be an independent production with a moderate budget, Divine felt that it could help him achieve recognition as a viable mainstream actor, demonstrating to casting directors he could carry a picture that had not been made by his friend John Waters.

Years would pass, however, before shooting on Hunter's dream film got underway. Working with a young producer named Allan Glaser, he created an independent production company, Fox Run Productions, and eventually secured around $4 million in financing. He was able to attract the experienced producer and former studio executive Jim Katz to the project, too. Upon the recommendation of another producer, Allan Carr, Hunter and Glaser changed the screenplay's title from *The Reverend and Rosie* to *Lust in the Dust*, "the name Gregory Peck had jokingly given his overheated 1947 western melodrama *Duel in the Sun*."[37] As the project progressed, a TV writer, Philip John Taylor, was brought on to re-work the original script, which Hunter now insisted would balance broad comedy with the "gutty feel" of a Sam Peckinpah film, especially *The Wild Bunch*.[38] Supporting roles were cast, too, with several character actors familiar from westerns, such as Woody Strode (*Sgt. Rutledge*), Cesar Romero (*Vera Cruz*), Geoffrey Lewis (*High Plains*

Drifter) and Gonzalez Gonzales (*Rio Bravo*), along with cabaret singer Lainie Kazan, who was asked to play Divine's nemesis, a madam named Marguerita.

The filmmakers decided shooting would commence on location just south of Santa Fe, New Mexico, in the spring of 1984. Their decision about who would direct the picture, though, came fairly late. Bartel was not a first choice. Hunter had hoped for Joan Rivers and also John Waters, for whom he'd developed a great deal of affection and respect during the shooting of *Polyester*.[39] In a 2014 interview he explained: "John's like your friendly undertaker. He's like Adolphe Menjou with that little moustache of his. He's just a delight…. But John only does his own stuff."[40]

Acting on a suggestion from Jim Katz, Hunter and Glaser approached Bartel about coming on. "I wasn't familiar with Paul, so we went and saw *Eating Raoul*. I thought that was interesting," Hunter explained. Meeting Bartel, however, was an underwhelming experience. "He didn't bowl you over with his personality, but he did agree with our vision for the film…. An agreement was quietly struck, since our start date was rapidly approaching." Hunter however began to lose confidence in his director almost immediately. "After the deal was signed, Paul invited us to a screening of his work in progress, a film called *Not for Publication*. The movie was not for public consumption. Allan and I were stunned. 'This might be the worst movie ever made,' Allan whispered to me. We convinced ourselves it was the story, not the director, that was to blame."[41]

Bartel had his own early reservations about working with Hunter and Glaser. "I hesitated [before accepting] a little because Divine and Tab had both worked for John Waters, and I thought the project might be perceived as a John Waters film without John Waters. And I didn't want to do something that was seen as a rip off." He was particularly concerned over a casting decision: the producers' plan to have character actor Edith Massey (a grotesque, even hideous-looking, regular in several Waters films) play the role of Big Ed, a hooker who works in Chili Verde's brothel. "When *Lust in the Dust* was first brought to me, Edith Massey had already been cast as the old prostitute. I said I was happy to work with Divine and Tab because I thought I could get from them different performances from those that had been done in Waters's *Polyester*. I thought this film would have a basically different feel to it. But Edie Massey had worked only for John and was very closely identified with him. Edie was not really an actress but simply an eccentric person who 'behaved' on film. I told the producer I wasn't doing a John Waters picture without John Waters."[42] The producers accepted his request, and Massey was replaced by Nedra Volz.

Since *Eating Raoul*'s release, Bartel had found his work increasingly compared to Waters's, with critics noting that both men excelled outside of the mainstream Hollywood system, working on low-budget productions with garish characters and violent, albeit comic, content. Bartel himself was conscious of parallels, but he was careful in interviews to emphasize the manner in which his work differed from Waters's. He told Gene Siskel: "There are certain similarities in our approach to humor, but in John's films, I find an underlying pessimism that simply isn't in my films. I think my films are basically optimistic because the audience develops a positive investment in my characters, as opposed to John' characters, who are always acting in protest of the human condition."[43] He felt that his lighter approach to marginal subject matter was characteristic of his own, distinct directing style. "I enjoy both Morrissey and Waters films. I think they are a watershed of personal and original ideas, probably the outer limits of what is socially acceptable in the realm of comedy. For myself, I am interested at this stage in making a conscious effort to pull back from some of the extremes."[44]

When Bartel came out to Santa Fe in late April, his spirits were high. The meticulousness with which Glaser and Hunter had prepared cast and crew impressed him. "My happiest surprise was the excellence of the sets and costumes. I didn't see them until just before we started shooting, and everything is better than I had a right to expect—very rich in detail."[45] To handle the production's makeup needs—for example, helping Divine look as beautiful and feminine as possible—the producers hired Hollywood veteran George Masters, who'd "won critical acclaim for doing Dustin Hoffman in *Tootsie*," Sydney Pollack's comedy about a male actor who finds work as a female character on a TV soap opera. Masters told Cree McCree as the film was shooting: "Divine is a lot easier to do than Dustin. With Dustin, I used lifts on his face to mouth out the smile lines, and the whole process took about three hours. Divine doesn't have a heavy beard, and he doesn't need heavy makeup."[46] Working with Divine could be difficult, however. The actor, according to Jim Katz, suffered from narcolepsy, and as a result, Masters and his assistants needed to use a sling that supported his chin "so even when he fell asleep his head was still up and they were still able to do his makeup."[47]

Bartel and Divine got on easily throughout the production. Bernard Jay in his biography of the actor claims that Divine "was pleased with the choice of Paul Bartel to direct, having seen *Eating Raoul* ... and feeling certain that they would share a similar sense of humor and approach to the script. Indeed, Paul and [Divine] hit it off wonderfully from the first moment they met."[48] The actor luxuriated in the new experiences the production provided: "I have my own trailer with my name written on it. I never had anything like that before. Every time I walk onto the set five people attack me from different directions—hair and makeup—and I think, 'What is going on?' When I was making films before, I would walk right across the room into the scenes, and nobody would pay any attention to me. They've really spoiled me now."[49]

Tensions surfaced between Bartel and Hunter, however, as shooting got underway, primarily over the manner in which the actors were asked by Bartel to perform. The director recalled for *L.A. Weekly*'s Anne Thompson:

> Tab is a gentleman—kind, generous, and very serious about his work. But occasionally he would talk to other actors and explain to them who their characters really were and how they should play the scenes. The actors would then come to me and say: "What's wrong with Tab? He's being a 'green room director.'" I had to ask him several times not to do this.
>
> I realized, however, that his was a project that Tab had been developing for seven years and that while Tab was not a director, *Lust* was his baby and he had preconceptions of how it should be played. It was turning into something else, of course, as every movie does. The characters that he had in mind were not the characters that were actually being played by the actors.
>
> I asked him not to interfere. He stopped, then he started doing it again, and I would speak to him again. He would apologize, then he would do it again. He couldn't resist.[50]

The source of Hunter's frustration was what he felt was Bartel's overly safe approach to directing. "I told Paul when we started the film, 'I want you to think of Divine in a Sam Peckinpah film. That's how I want *Lust in the Dust* to be, which I think was a very clever idea. But we never got that far.'" For Hunter Bartel's approach was simply too conservative. "[H]e toned down things that should have been ... outrageous. He directed like a den mother, reigning in our enthusiasm when he should have been inspiring it."[51]

For Glaser, the differences between the director and the producer were real, but their impact on the production was not in the end destructive. "There was tension because Paul may not have been the perfect person to direct *Lust in the Dust*.... Tab had one vision of the movie, and Paul had another.... But it ended up being a good film. I remember having a good time on the set. Even Tab when he's asked about it says it's one of the more pleasurable experiences he's had making a movie. So the [tension] couldn't have been that bad, though it was there."[52]

Lust in the Dust was picked up for distribution by New World Pictures—though Roger Corman had nothing to do with the deal, having sold off his interest in the company in 1983. Glaser remembered: "We shot the movie in May and June. We posted it in July and August. And by September we held the first screening at the DGA for industry people. We were looking for a distributor. We couldn't give this film away originally in concept, but after the screening we had all these calls from places wanting to take it."[53]

Lust in the Dust premiered in February 1985 at the United States Film Festival in Park City. A month later, New World gave the film its national release, and it performed fairly well. It enjoyed immediate popularity with gay audiences, scoring "extended engagements in New York and San Francisco, where it set a box office record at the Castro Theatre." *Lust in the Dust*, opened the Berlin Film Festival that year, too.[54]

Writer Quentin Crisp was present the night *Lust in the Dust* opened in the Castro: "When I was last in San Francisco, preaching to the perverted, on one enchanted evening I found myself with my hosts in front of a cinema.... Searchlights caressed the façade of the movie house; photographers took innumerable pictures; televisionaries asked countless questions; crowds of fans stood staring or were herded this way and that by amazingly indulgent policemen. The day of the locusts had obviously arrived. As soon as we joined the swarm, the cinema manager darted into the street, crying, 'Don't just stand there; come inside.' In the lobby, we were introduced to Mr. Divine, disguised as himself. That is to say that he was dressed in a navy blue suit, white shirt and dark tie. He looked rather like a Catholic priest on his night off."[55]

The critical response to *Lust in the Dust* was by and large negative, however, often panning Bartel for mishandling his material and his stars, echoing Hunter's earlier complaints on the set. For example, Vincent Canby groused: "One of the distinguishing features of *Eating Raoul*, in which Mr. Bartel, the director, also starred, was its earnest innocence. The actors didn't appear to know that they were being funny. With the exception of Mr. Hunter, everybody in *Lust in the Dust* seems to believe that he/she is hilarious, but the jokes remain witless."[56] Several critics also disdained Bartel for delivering a pallid John Waters imitation, which must have been particularly galling. Jay Scott, for instance, cracked that "the best thing about *Lust in the Dust* is the cast list," adding, "the parody is supposed to combine the rambunctiousness of *Blazing Saddles* with the outrageousness of the films of John Waters ... but the picture is too dumb to be raunchy and too inept to be offensive."[57]

Reviewers neglected to remark on or were unable to recognize the numerous parallels between *Lust in the Dust* and another revisionist western, Nicholas Ray's *Johnny Guitar* (1954). In Ray's picture, the eponymous hero (played by Sterling Hayden), blond and handsome like Hunter's character, Abel Wood, arrives in a dusty town and finds himself quickly caught up in feud between two women, a saloon owner, Vienna (Joan Crawford), and a rancher, Emma (Mercedes McCambridge). Ray's characters hate one another much as Bartel and Hunter's do. But while Marguerita and Rosie present a grotesque portrait of female sensuality, thanks to their exaggerated curves, their extravagant makeup and their manes of black hair, Vienna and Emma keep their hair cut short and wear shirts that obscure their breasts, muting their gender. The four women in these films all claim to be heterosexual as well: Marguerita and Rosie as prostitutes vigorously enjoy sleeping with male clients; Ray's female protagonists likewise express their desire for men, yet they fixate on and hate one another obsessively. Roger Ebert felt that the fanatical resentment Vienna and Emma direct at each one another is, paradoxically, the expression of their stifled mutual attraction and that an implicit "bisexualism" permeates their story. Does an implicit bisexualism also distinguish *Lust in the Dust*?[58]

Bartel had been challenging audiences' expectations about the sexual identities of his characters as far back as "The Secret Cinema" and "Naughty Nurse." With *Private Parts*, he'd introduced a transgender antagonist. He exploited Mary Woronov's at-times androgynous facial features in *Death Race 2000*, hiding her long, beautiful hair with a crash helmet, while outfitting her car as a bull with a pair of phallic

Sisters Rosie (Divine, left) and Marguerita (Lainie Kazan) scheming in Chili Verde in *Lust from the Dust* (Fox Run Productions, 1985).

horns poking out from the front. Paul Bland, uninterested in sharing a bed with his wife, sleeps with a plush wine bottle pillow that rather resembles a penis.

Bartel played with the disjunction between outward appearance and underlying reality in his next project as well, a re-make of "The Secret Cinema," which he directed for NBC's *Amazing Stories* television program. The brainchild of director Steven Spielberg, *Amazing Stories* had been developed as an anthology series comprised of one-off tales of fantasy, suspense and horror. In July 1984, when the network announced

6. In Demand

its decision to feature the show in its 1985–1986 season, NBC Entertainment's president Brandon Tartikoff explained that *Amazing Stories* would "be a show with a lot of fun, great adventure and imagination, with nice touches of comedy where called for. It will be sort of a throwback, in some senses, to the great anthologies that were on television in the fifties, like *Alfred Hitchcock Presents* and *The Twilight Zone*."

Although he was still fairly young, Spielberg wielded enormous power in Hollywood in the mid-eighties due to the commercial and critical success of *Raiders of the Lost Ark* (1981) and *E.T.* (1982), which he'd directed, and Joe Dante's *Gremlins* (1984), which he'd produced. His reputation helped him secure a two-year minimum run for *Amazing Stories*, which ensured the production of forty-four episodes. As executive producer, Spielberg would have creative control over the program—many of the ideas that were developed into scripts were his. He also negotiated for substantial shooting budgets that ranged between $500,000 and $1 million per episode, an enormous amount by contemporary standards for directors working with five-day television shooting schedules. "I am hopeful that *Amazing Stories*, besides being entertaining, will also serve as a forum for the introduction of new talent, directors and film makers," Spielberg proclaimed before shooting for the first season commenced.[59] In several instances, he handpicked talent, especially directors, inviting acquaintances and friends to helm episodes, including Martin Scorsese, Joe Dante and Robert Zemeckis. He alone had final say over who would write and direct the shows, though he claimed in statements to the press that directors would be given the "freedom to cast" the actors they wanted.[60]

Bartel came to Spielberg's attention thanks to his acquaintance with Brian De Palma. In November 1984, De Palma called Bartel on the telephone, surprising him, as the two had "seen very little" of one another since his appearance in *Hi, Mom!* Bartel recalled in "My Amazing Story," an essay he wrote for *American Film*, that De Palma "had been chatting with *Steven* about his new television series for NBC…. Brian had told him the plot of 'The Secret Cinema' and *Steven* was interested in talking to me about remaking it for television." Bartel agreed to meet with Spielberg, whom he knew casually, "but certainly did not count among my close friends." Bartel's admission to the Motion Picture Academy of Arts & Sciences earlier that year, which had been sponsored by his close friend John Landis—a Spielberg associate—may have also helped bring him to Spielberg's attention.

After meeting with the producer to discuss the project, Bartel proceeded to re-craft the original script for "The Secret Cinema" to make it more accessible for general TV audiences. As before, a beleaguered female protagonist named Jane would find herself surrounded by conspirators who covertly film and later screen bizarre segments from her life for the enjoyment of a secret cinéclub. A new ending was written, giving Jane an opportunity to exact revenge: turned into a star by her movies—rather than destroyed—she arranges for a garbage truck to unload its contents on the director who has been filming her as well as his abettor, a treacherous actress.

Barry Dennen helped Bartel re-work and update the script. "As a writer, I've always worked best with a partner," Bartel admitted. "Although I received solo screen credit, a great deal of what is good and funny in the new script is Barry's." It took just about a week for the pair to ready and submit a script to Spielberg and his readers for approval. To signify that this revisited version of Jane's story was something different from the original, they dropped the article "The" from the black & white film's title, naming the new work "Secret Cinema." The project was quickly greenlighted, with shooting scheduled to begin at the end of March and wrap during the second week of April 1985. Bartel was told his budget would be "nearly a million dollars ... more than two hundred times the budget of the original."

Much of his time in advance of the start date was given to preparing sets, the most elaborate of which was the movie theater where the cinéclub watches Jane and her adventures. "It unfolds, like a child's pop-up book, out of a plain brick wall. The marquee slides out from inside as the ticket booth comes hissing up from underground." Fireworks—his boyhood passion—blasted out of the marquee, an allusion, Bartel revealed, to a surreal musical sequence in Vincente Minelli's *The Band Wagon* (1954) in which Fred Astaire dances near a penny arcade machine that lets out orgasmic vents of steam from a series of pipes lining its sides.[61] The name of the arcade in the film, incidentally, is The Gayest Music Box.

Contrary to Mary Woronov's claim that Bartel shirked her after *Eating Raoul*, he gave her a prominent part as the actress who schemes to push the Jane character into embarrassing situations. With Bartel casting himself as the director, the pair in essence were reprising or at least referencing their roles in *Hollywood Boulevard*. The Woronov and Bartel characters have a protean quality in "Secret Cinema," taking on new roles and appearances as the updated story of Jane progresses. At one point visually recalling her role as a hospital dietician in *Eating Raoul*, Woronov's character poses as a nurse; in another, she dresses as a male waiter, with her breasts flattened, hair smoothed back, and a heavy moustache glued to her lip. Bartel likewise takes on a secondary role as a disingenuous psychiatrist. He gave roles to other friends, too. Dennen, the psychiatrist in the first film, now played a blind news vendor. Alix Elias ("Naughty Nurse") and Gary Goodrow (*Eating Raoul*) showed up, too.

Yet Bartel's freedom to cast the program was not absolute, despite Spielberg's claims otherwise. For the role of Dick, Jane's slippery boyfriend, the show's producers insisted on Griffin Dunne (another actor from Landis's *An American Werewolf in London*). For the role of Jane, Penny Peyser was used, a decision forced on him by Amblin, Spielberg's production company. Bartel had hoped for Susan Saiger in the role.[62]

The production's generous budget allowed him the liberty to rehearse his actors and to work out shots with crew and run through the various special effects and lighting tricks that he, production designer Rick Carter and director of photography Robert Stevens concocted. Most of the shots were done in one take thanks to this preparation. A setback arose, however, when footage of Woronov, Peyser and Eve Arden (the initial inspiration for Woronov's Miss Togar character in *Rock 'n' Roll High School*) interacting in a restaurant "was scratched in the camera." Otherwise, the production went smoothly. Bartel, though, was prevented from supervising the cutting of the show immediately after filming wrapped; the editor assigned to the "Secret Cinema" episode, Joe Ann Fogel, had been sent to New York to work with Martin Scorsese on the episode he'd directed ("Mirror, Mirror") for the series.

It was then the middle of April 1985, and Bartel, eager to start on new projects, found himself sorting through several potential television assignments, among them a job on a resurrected version of *The Twilight Zone*, and a job with yet another anthology series, *George Burns Comedy Week*. But he was led to understand that accepting TV work while he was attached to *Amazing Stories* would hurt his relationship with Spielberg, and so he passed on all these offers. He was still free to make movies, however, and that same spring, he agreed to meet with director-producer Mike Nichols about helming a horseracing comedy titled *The Longshot*, which had been written by and would star Tim Conway.⁶³

Best known as an actor who specialized "in the humor of the familiar gone berserk," Conway had experienced considerable success in television, having played supporting roles in programs like *McHale's Navy* and *The Carol Burnett Show*.⁶⁴ But he also wrote or co-wrote (and starred in) several comedy features that primarily targeted family audiences, including *The Billion Dollar Hobo* (1977), *The Prize Fighter* (1979), and *The Private Eyes* (1980). *The Longshot*, in contrast, was written to appeal to seasoned audiences, especially viewers who liked gags about toilets, private parts and beer.

The story Conway came up with focused, in particular, on four compulsive, working-class friends who each dream about the easy living that might be theirs if they had the chance to put big money on a horse that actually crosses the finish line first. When a crooked trainer tells them he can turn an unlikely horse into a winner with the help of illegal drugs, the friends convince themselves that this longshot is truly a sure thing, and they scheme to put together a wager that is so big that if their horse indeed comes in, they will make themselves rich. But the trainer, they learn too late, has no intent of drugging any horse, and because the source of their money is a mobster, they must make sure their horse wins if they want to stay alive, let alone live like Croesus.

Conway had grown up around thoroughbreds—his father was a horse trainer. And as an adult, he was a regular at the track, getting to know the broken dreamers who collect there, learning their stories and sharing with them the desire to have a better life as the result of a well-placed bet. "I've really been gathering the material all of my life," Conway said. "All of the characters and most of the situations I've taken from real life—they're all my friends from the track." His script, he felt, tells "the story not only of four guys, but of everybody who has ever gone to the horse races looking for the big one. It's the story of four guys who have no business making more than a $10 or $20 bet ... deciding to borrow $10,000 to make this big bet because this is the big one."⁶⁵ The narrative came to him quickly, taking, he claimed, a single day in July 1984. "I just got up and felt like doing it." Conway hoped the film would not only make people laugh but charm them, too, with its sad but sympathetic personalities. "It's a strange, fascinating group that hangs around a track," he said, speaking of the real-life people who served as models for his characters. "It's not like any other sport—there are no fistfights, nobody throws their beer. There's a lot of compassion here because everybody knows we're all losers. I don't know of a winner at the track."

Conway sat on the script for several months before passing it on to his friend, actor Harvey Korman. "I thought it was the best thing Tim had ever written," Korman said, and he persuaded Conway to reach out to director-producer Mike Nichols, whom Korman had known since the fifties, having appeared with him in a Chicago production of *Waiting for Godot*. "I said, 'Let's send it to Nichols and get an appraisal; see what's there.'"

Nichols responded with interest. "When I read the script, I got very excited," he said. A horse fancier who bred Arabian horses, he liked the story's racing theme. The possibility of working with "two of my favorite funny people" was appealing, too. He was also "drawn to the human part of the story more than the equine part. It's very, very funny, and it's also very serious. It's about little guys who rarely have a chance at anything.... There are very few pictures now about real working guys, and Tim somehow plugged into that thing we all loved so much about *The Honeymooners*."

Nichols was not available to direct the picture, having previously committed himself to *Heartburn*, a comedy he was preparing with Jack Nicholson and Meryl Streep. He agreed instead to serve as executive producer and "was involved in everything from script changes to casting to approving the director." The project got another boost when Lang Elliott, who'd come on to *The Longshot* as a producer, secured $6 million in financing from Orion Pictures. Orion, in turn, encouraged the filmmakers to ask Bartel if he would direct, an idea that Nichols favored. "I liked *Eating Raoul* a lot," he said. "Bartel is very swift, very incisive in his style." Bartel agreed to direct the film because of the opportunity it presented him of working with Nichols—the director of *Who's Afraid of Virginia Woolf* and *The Graduate*. Yet Bartel had little actual contact with Nichols, who remained in New York readying *Heartburn* as principal photography on *The Longshot* got underway in June 1985.

Bartel, Nichols and Conway each felt that Conway, Korman, Jack Weston and Ted Wass—the actors cast to play the film's down-on-their-luck bettors—would need to have their exuberant onscreen personalities reined in by Bartel for *The Longshot* to have narrative coherence. In an interview he gave toward the end of filming, Bartel told Jack Matthews: "This is the first film where I'm functioning exclusively as a director. It's very much a Tim Conway film. Nichols and I both felt it had to be made as real as possible within the confines of the comedy. When they [the actors] get going, they get looser and looser and sillier and sillier. I'm trying to suppress the silliness and keep it moving." Just as he had on *Lust*, Bartel was managing and subduing his actors' performances.

The production proceeded with relative ease, although footage had to be sent "in batches to Nichols in New York." Bartel, despite his claims of "functioning exclusively as a director," was able to bring on several people with whom he enjoyed working: editor Alan Toomayan, production designer Bob Schulenberg and Michael Schroeder, his assistant director on *Lust in the Dust*. Wanting as ever to help younger filmmakers, Bartel had Schroeder shoot race footage at Hollywood Park, which was used in the film's opening credits sequence. The sequence that Toomayan built from this footage—elegant and dispassionate—was weirdly offset by the producers' decision to support it with a rap song performed by Ice-T and Conway—one of the least likely pairings in hip hop history.

When a rough cut of the picture was ready, the filmmakers were confident they had a winner. Korman said, "You never know whether a movie works until you show it to an audience, but it sure feels good." Nichols felt similarly: "I'm crazy about what I've seen so far." And Conway confirmed that he was pleased with the way Bartel had corralled him, Korman and the other members of the cast: "If Harvey or I had directed [*The Longshot*], it would be closer to television. It would be a raucous kind of comedy, a Disney movie even. Nichols made it a legitimate piece, and Bartel has kept it legitimate."[66]

Upon the movie's release in January 1986, the critics, if anything, argued against its claims to legitimacy, blasting it for being an exercise in television-grade silliness—the very quality Bartel, Conway and Nichols had sought to avoid. The *Chicago Tribune*'s Rick Kogan snarled: "Written by Conway, [*The Longshot*] is strongly influenced by the comic's many years as Carol Burnett's television sidekick. It is little more than a series of related sketches, meant obviously to be funny but consistently buffoonish, frequently crude. Conway's meat-and-potatoes is slapstick, and there is plenty of that. All that's missing are the commercials."[67] And Roger Hurlburt of south Florida's *Sun Sentinel* carped: "Continually punctuated by crude toilet jokes ... and references to the groin, *The Longshot* is tough going. Cleaned up, it might have made a mildly funny TV movie. But running a mere eighty-nine minutes, the flick is hardly satisfying theater fare. Essentially a series of skits linked together, *The Longshot* wastes time and talent in perpetuating the obvious."[68]

For Bartel the real disappointment that came from *The Longshot* was the imposition on his creativity the production had entailed. "It's good to stretch and do different things, but I'm not interested in becoming a director for hire. I'd rather work on my own ideas."[69] He felt, in particular, that Conway had prevented him from making the movie better—more sophisticated—than it could have been: "My sensibility was on some level antipathetic to what Tim Conway wanted. I was trying to find interesting things under the surface, and he just wanted more surface."[70] He also claimed that "the most personal touches were surgically removed by the line producer."[71]

A new opportunity to work on material that interested him materialized, fortunately, in the fall of 1985, after he'd finished his commitment to *The Longshot*. Steven Spielberg, who'd been pleased with Bartel's work on "Secret Cinema," invited him to work up an original script for *Amazing Stories*'s second season. The series' first season had by and large aroused the disdain of critics, who dismissed the bulk of the episodes for being heavy on style and light on substance. Tom Shales of the *Washington Post*, for example, decried its want for originality: "This is one of the worst ten shows of all time, in any category. It's a disappointment every week. You tune in and expect something, and get nothing.... It's incredibly over-cute and over-produced ... with primitive premises about ... things that children could make up."[72] The show was a ratings loser, too, and was sarcastically referred to "in some circles as *Not So Amazing Stories*."[73]

Bartel's "Secret Cinema," which had its first broadcast April 5, 1985, was perhaps the best of the episodes that ran during the first season. The show possesses a high degree of stylistic and thematic cohesiveness that Bartel's longer efforts too often lack. From the moment it opens, with Bartel's character speaking grandiloquently to Penny Peyser's Jane, the episode surges forward, by turns dousing the screen with the gaudy colors of fifties musicals and the thick, sinister shadows of *film noir*. The players—Woronov, Peyser, Dunne, Arden, Bartel—all seem to be pepped up, driven by an excess of caffeine or amphetamine.

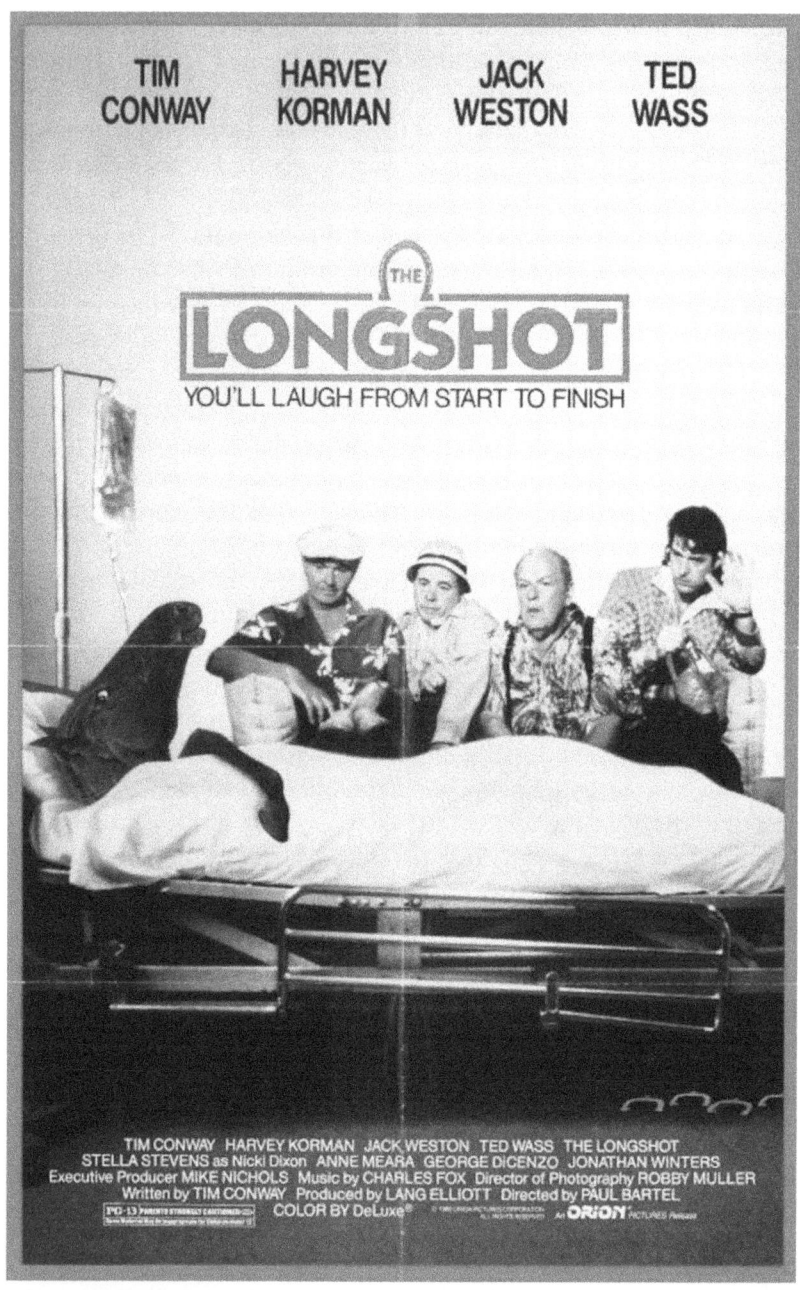

Poster for *The Longshot* (Longshot Productions, Orion, 1986), Bartel's least personal feature.

They shove their arms into the air, from their sides, they scowl, laugh, pout, fall down, jump about, howl—each bringing to mind the befuddled heroes of Clair's *À nous la liberte* or the anthropomorphic creatures in Sally Cruikshank cartoons. Like the first version of Jane's nightmarish experience, the remake is an exercise in postmodern camp that delights in "its love of the unnatural: of artifice and exaggeration."[74]

For his second *Amazing Stories* assignment, Bartel, always more comfortable working with another writer, reached out to John Meyer, with whom he'd written *Not for Publication*. The pair, indulging their fondness for musicals came up with something they called "Gershwin's Trunk." Meyer hammered out a first draft of the teleplay on his "Smith-Corona electric portable, at Paul's glass dining table."[75] The script detailed the moral collapse of a Broadway composer named Jo-Jo Gillespie (Bob Balaban), who is afflicted with writer's block. Upon the advice of his housekeeper, Jo-Jo solicits assistance from Sister Teresa (*Lust in the Dust*'s Lainie Kazan), a medium. In astonishment, he witnesses the transmigration of George Gershwin's spirit into Sister Teresa's body, imbuing her not only with his talent but his physical features. Jo-Jo proceeds to commission this phantasmal thing to write musical numbers for him, out of which he will put together a show.

The show's success, he hopes, will enable him to outshine his rival, an oily composer named Jerry Lane (John McCook). Michael Feinstein, a Gershwin scholar (and celebrated pianist), explains that "both Jo-Jo's and Jerry's shows are opening on the same night, so Jo-Jo decides to postpone his opening by one day because he knows that his score is going to be superior—after all, it's by George Gershwin.... [W]hen Jo-Jo goes to see Jerry's show, the performers burst into the same song that Jo-Jo's show is meant to open with. It turns out that Jerry was seeing the same psychic as Jo-Jo because they shared the same housekeeper."[76] What Feinstein doesn't mention is a subplot woven through the story. A crooked detective, Watts, played by Bartel, has reason to believe that Jo-Jo is a murderer, and he agrees to leave him alone if—and only if—he can get a cut of the profits from the upcoming show. On Jerry's opening night, when Jo-Jo learns what has happened and that his show won't be going on, the detective, sitting beside him, wraps a pair of handcuffs around his wrists—an image that recalls the closing shot of Alexander Mackendrick's *The Lavender Hill Gang*.

The script's exploration of a paranormal theme—so apt for the *Amazing Stories* series—marked the second time Bartel touched on metempsychosis in his work with Meyer; in *Not for Publication*, the mother of David Naughton's character has the ability to communicate with the dead, seeking advice from Charles Lindbergh at one point to help her son land a plane in which he and his love interest, Lois, have been left stranded in the air by the mayor of New York. (The supernatural as a trope would materialize two more times in Bartel's work: a ghost and a talking dog show up in *Scenes from the Class Struggle in Beverly Hills*; and in a short film he made for British TV, "Demonella," the Devil—a woman—occupies the bodies of human beings and animals when she leaves Hell to visit the mortal plane.)

Bartel and Meyer incorporated original music into their story that evokes the appealing melodies of George Gershwin and the clever lyrics of his frequent collaborator, his brother Ira. Among the songs they wrote were "I Discovered You," "They All Laughed" and "Ticklish Toes." Meyer explained, "I wrote a Gershwinesque theme, inflected with *noir*-ish overtones –which orchestrator Larry Hochman scored brilliantly." Meyer's creation so impressed the producers at Spielberg's production company, Amblin Entertainment, they asked "me to repeat my function as composer for a totally unrelated episode ["Miss Stardust"] of the *Amazing Stories* directed by Tobe Hooper."[77]

As much a murder mystery as a "mini-musical," "Gershwin's Trunk" is, like the remake of "The Secret Cinema," a highpoint in Bartel's later career.[78] The episode starts with a tilting nighttime shot of a stark skyscraper and cuts to the interior of Jo-Jo's apartment, where the nebbishy composer struggles to clean a bloodstained floor. A white baby grand bulges into the shot oppressively. Then a bell rings. Jo-Jo scatters sheets of music over the stain, heads up some steps and opens the door. An imposing detective—wearing a trench coat and a fedora—fills the door frame, augmenting the scene's claustrophobic quality. Played with restraint by Bartel, the detective pushes himself into the crowded room and tells Jo-Jo: "I have something that belongs to you." He shows Jo-Jo a pen that he found on the Manhattan Bridge, from which Jo-Jo earlier in the night tossed a corpse into the East River.

In less than a minute of screen time, Bartel establishes the heavy shadows and beckoning sense of doom that characterize *film noir*. As the narrative progresses, he employs a chiaroscuro lighting scheme, setting patches of light and darkness against one another. Neon signs flash above darkened city streets. Singing dancers perform in flashy nightclubs. Corrupted by greed and egocentrism, the principals speak to one another in a hard-boiled, tough fashion, trading sarcastic insults. A jazz-inflected score floats through the story like the tangled scent of cheap perfume and cigarette smoke. Other nods to *film noir* appear. Jo-Jo relates the events that have led up to his crimes in a series of flashbacks, recalling the narrative structures of Billy Wilder's *Double Indemnity* and Delmar Daves's *Dark Passage*. Jo-Jo, moreover, is an example par excellence of a weak anti-hero, a schemer like *Double Indemnity*'s Walter Neff, who overestimates his intelligence. Though he fancies himself a major talent, temporarily struck down by writer's block, in truth he is a mediocre artist, unable to work without the help of a collaborator. (An ironic reference, perhaps, to Bartel's dependence on co-writers for his own creative projects?) Jo-Jo seeks the help of the medium—and proceeds to pass off the new Gershwin songs as his own—because he can't (and never will be able to) turn out memorable material on his own.

But "Gershwin's Trunk" is more than a pastiche of *film noir*. As a story about counterfeits and knock-offs, it critiques the moral deficits and me-first tendencies of Reagan's America just as *Eating Raoul* had, cynically demonstrating that dishonesty is self-justifying when it leads to financial success. While this approach may not work in the end for Jo-Jo, it does for his rival, Jerry. And the blackmailer detective who apprehends Jo-Jo only does so when he's realized the hapless composer can't deliver on his promise to pay him off: Det. Watts enforces the law, that is, only when other options don't appear. The corruption of the police, the story intimates, is so total that the detective in all likelihood won't be punished for his hesitation over arresting the murderer—or why else would he be willing to handcuff Jo-Jo and lead him off to jail when he does?

Fakes and imitative objects appear throughout the story, each its own Maltese Falcon, reminding us that what we are watching itself is a fabrication. The skyscraper that makes up the program's opening shot is a matte drawing, more a symbol of the cityscape than any attempt to render it realistically. Meyer's gorgeous and lush score, as he admitted himself, sounds like Gershwin but of course isn't Gershwin, another fake. Knock-offs of Al Hirschfield caricatures (provided by Bob Schulenberg) hang from the walls of a set meant to evoke Sardi's Restaurant in New York's theatre district. There is also the manifestation of Gershwin himself—an effect produced by makeup, rubber, and a wig. Nothing is at it seems, "Gershwin's Trunk" suggests. Broadway composers draw acclaim for music they don't write. Cops commit crimes when they want to. George Gershwin is a woman, or maybe a man, or perhaps both? An exercise in deconstruction, "Gershwin's Trunk" eschews what general viewers no doubt believe are (or should be) the lines that exist between performance and reality, crime and law, death and life, male and female gender.

Bartel continued to play small roles in film and television projects directed by acquaintances and friends over the course of the eighties. Many of these productions were mainstream studio offerings, such as Amy Heckerling's *European Vacation* (1985) and John Landis's *Into the Night* (1985). He also appeared in *Amazon Women on the Moon* (1987), an anthology movie that delivered viewers an "irreverent attack upon the major and minor annoyances of contemporary life."[79] The film featured directorial contributions from Carl Gottlieb, Peter Horton, Robert K. Weiss, Joe Dante and Landis. With Carrie Fisher, Bartel co-starred in a sketch helmed by Dante titled "Reckless Youth" that at once sent up vintage health awareness films and James Whale's *Frankenstein*. Jim Emerson, who otherwise rejected the film, warmed slightly to this vignette: "One of the best-directed sequences—by Joe Dante—is the final piece, a thirties social disease film parody.... But although it's well done as far as these things go (Woody Allen's sexual hygiene skit in *Love and Death* was a much more outrageous concept), the target is so stale as to be pointless."[80]

Amazon Women on the Moon also recognized Landis, Dante and Bartel's shared background at Corman's New World, closing with the logo for Miracle Pictures, the film company ridiculed in *Hollywood Boulevard*. Bartel in fact went back on the payroll for Roger Corman twice during the second half of the eighties. First, he reprised his role as Paul Bland, alongside Mary Woronov as Mary Bland, in a comedy-horror film titled *Chopping Mall* (1986), directed by Jim Wynorski for Corman's (then) new production-distribution company, Concorde-New Horizons. In the film, the Blands attend an informational seminar for a line of machines called Killbots that provide security at a mall and engage in brief sarcastic exchanges about the gizmos. Years later, Woronov said that she had no recollection of shooting the scene, but she did recall that Bartel had asked her to participate as a favor to Corman. "I remember Paul saying, 'We have to do this for Roger, we have to do this for Roger.'"[81] Was he perhaps angling for financial support from Corman for the *Bland Ambition* project, which he still hoped to

Bartel and Carrie Fisher in the "Reckless Youth" episode from *Amazon Women on the Moon* (Paramount, 1987), which Joe Dante directed.

bring to the screen? The second movie Bartel appeared in for Concorde-New Horizons was *Munchies* (1987), a comedy directed by his old friend Tina Hirsch about almost-cute monsters (like those in Joe Dante's *Gremlins*) that attack people.

Bartel continued to help young filmmakers—"godfathering," he called it—as they embarked on independent productions.[82] "A lot of people have helped me, and I feel incumbent to help others," he told John Stanley. "[M]y name on genre projects gets them easily financed in many cases."[83] When he was approached to appear in a low-budget comedy called *Mortuary Academy*—which his former personal assistant, Zane W. Levitt, was producing and which Michael Schroeder, first assistant director on *Lust in the Dust* and *The Longshot*, would direct—he agreed to play the president of a college for morticians "who falls in love with the corpse of a young cheerleader."[84]

The screenplay's original writer, William F. Kellman, had become "fascinated with the comic film potential of the funeral business after completing an article on California's only school for morticians." He built the story around a pair of brothers named Grimm who will inherit a college for morticians if they can graduate from it. In their way stands the school's necrophilic chief, Paul Truscott, who will take over as proprietor of the school should the brothers fail. Schroeder was aptly suited for directing the picture: his parents owned "a trio of mortuaries and a cemetery in Oregon and Idaho. 'During the summer, I'd help out, digging graves and working around the mortuary. Sometimes my father would get a call in the middle of the night to pick up a body, and I'd go along for the ride.'"

Bartel also worked on rewrites of Kellman's script, for which he received an onscreen credit. And several themes and tropes that work through his movies show up in this picture, too, especially the preoccupation with sex and death and the tendency to swing between broad satire and subversive wit. Schroeder himself recognized the similarities between Bartel's movies and *Mortuary Academy*, telling Patrick Goldstein, "It's like *Eating Raoul* meets *Police Academy*. We do flirt with areas of bad taste, but we hope it'll be funny for people who have good taste too. My family's taking it pretty well."[85] The film ends with a cinematic allusion of the sort Bartel inserted into his films. In this instance, Bartel's character makes off with his decomposing lover on a ship at sea. When it's brought to his attention by the ship's captain that his companion is dead, Truscott contentedly replies that "no one is perfect"—evoking the famous final scene from Billy Wilder's *Some Like it Hot* when a bedazzled millionaire learns that the woman he loves is a man.

Mortuary Academy also brings to mind, perhaps, Arkush's *Rock 'n' Roll High School* with its depiction of an anarchic school where the students are fans of a threatening punk rock band. This time the kids love a band named Radio Werewolf, whose members, bizarrely, put on a concert toward the end of the movie despite being dead! Schroeder and Levitt stocked the cast, too, with several actors who'd appeared in Bartel movies, including the earlier cited Cesar Romero and Nedra Volz, both from *Lust in the Dust*, and Mary Woronov. Screenwriter Bruce Wagner, who at the time was working on the script for the next film Bartel wanted to direct, *Scenes from the Class Struggle in Beverly Hills*, has a small part, too, playing an insanely sleazy character named Schuyler who oversees a used car dealership. One of the models on Schuyler's lot, a "Turbo Stud," is loaded with strange accessories, including automated sex toys.

Schroeder, Levitt and Bartel followed up on *Mortuary Academy* with a blood-soaked thriller, *Out of the Dark* (1988), that exploited narrative scenarios and character types well-known to fans of the slasher genre, which was then experiencing a vogue. Starring Cameron Dye and Tracey Walter, the picture narrows on a serial killer who systematically murders female employees employed at a phone sex chatline service called Suite Nothings. The heavy, played by Bud Cort, bears a close resemblance to the antagonists in pictures like *Halloween* and *Friday the 13th* whose psychopathic hatred of women compels them to torture and kill female victims. Cort's character, Bobo, similarly conceals his face like the bogeymen in these films, in this instance with a freakish clown mask.

Bartel received a producer's credit for *Out of the Dark* and had a small onscreen role as a low-end motel clerk. Filmed in late 1987, the picture again featured cast members from *Lust in Dust*—Tab Hunter, Geoffrey Lewis, Lainie Kazan and Divine. Karen Black had a cameo in the movie, chewing the scenery as the boss at Suite Nothings, who reacts with increasing horror as her employees disappear and die. Bartel was enthusiastic about the picture, and he made statements to the press that highlighted the movie's perhaps not always evident satirical intentions, asserting that it "glows with sex, violence, telephones and all the other things that are dear to the hearts of the American people."[86]

When *Out of the Dark* went into release in May 1989, critics generally panned it. The *New York Times*'s Stephen Holden decried the picture's violence: "Michael Schroeder's misogynistic thriller *Out of the Dark* is a movie so desperate for attention that it will stop at nothing to titillate. Opening with extreme closeups of a psychopathic killer tearing at his own flesh with a knife while growling sadistic warnings to a telephone sex partner, it sinks to a nadir of repellent kinkiness during a motel scene in which turbulent lovemaking is photographed to suggest murder."[87] Dave Kehr, a longtime supporter of Bartel's work, drew a similar conclusion, exclaiming, "[T]his vaguely feminist demystification of pornography is far outweighed by the film's own insistent exploitativeness, in which cheesecake shots segue invariably into brutality and gore."[88] *Out of the Dark* is nonetheless an entertaining movie that at times self-consciously sends up the slasher movie genre's conventions—a strategy Wes Craven would use several years later with his parody of horror pictures, *Scream* (1996), which despite its depictions of women tortured and murdered drew plaudits from critics.

In the decades since its release, *Out of the Dark* has gained an unwanted degree of notoriety for being Divine's final film. His part, at that, is little more than a walk-on. He plays a master detective named Langella, who shows up at a crime scene wearing a moustache, a fedora and an overcoat: a squinting parody of a tough *guy*. After shooting on *Out of the Dark* was completed, Bartel was himself hopeful about directing Divine again. He joked with Michael Musto that he and the actor had "been discussing starring him in the life of Eleanor Roosevelt."[89] Bartel had actually begun to write a musical comedy for the actor, which he wanted to title either *Divine Date* or *Hollywood Dream Date*. He imagined the lithe, diminutive—and fluidly-gendered—singer-actor Prince as his co-star. But after Divine died in March 1988, this endeavor, understandably, was dropped.[90]

7

About Men and Women

The project that possessed Bartel's attention the most in the second half of the eighties was *Scenes from the Class Struggle in Beverly Hills*. "I've had the idea in the works for about fifteen years, even before *Eating Raoul* was written," Bartel explained to John Hartl in 1989. "The title came first. I was thinking of *Scenes from a Marriage* and *Hunting Scenes from Bavaria*—it's a very nineteenth century literary idea. I wanted to do a French comedy in modern dress, very much like *The Marriage of Figaro*, with a lot of Buñuel's *Discreet Charm of the Bourgeoisie* and a lot of Jean Renoir's *Rules of the Game*." Bartel may have also had in mind the documentary *Scenes from the Class Struggle in Portugal* (1977), a scree against that country's right-wing government and its dispossessed poor, which was produced by David C. Stone. Stone was also producer on *The Double-Barrelled Detective Story*, for which Bartel had designed the titles in the mid-sixties.

Bartel wanted with *Scenes* to poke fun at the sex habits and phony politics of the upper crust. "In the early seventies I had the idea ... to do a film about rich and spoiled people in their teens and twenties, living in their parents' mansions, guest houses and pools [sic], and going out to rob banks and give the money to the Black Panthers and other radical organizations. Eventually I decided to meld it with a story of two wealthy women, one divorced, one widowed.... It would be about incest by proxy. One woman would initiate the other's son sexually, and vice versa."[1]

Bartel had initially approached Dick Blackburn about collaborating on the script for *Scenes*, but the writer felt that he was not right for working on what he felt would be an effervescent sex comedy.[2] Blackburn recalls that he encouraged Bartel to reach out to Bruce Wagner, a short story writer and novelist with substantive experience working on movies, who'd earning a writing credit on Wes Craven's *A Nightmare on Elm Street 3: The Dream Warriors* (1987). Bartel, incidentally, claimed that film director Hector Babenco introduced him to Wagner. "Hector is an old friend. I was on the selection committee for the Filmex film festival [in 1981] and selected Babenco's *Pixote*. He knew Bruce and thought we might be on the same wavelength."[3] Wagner, a Hollywood native, was well-qualified for an acerbic picture that ridiculed industry people and the fatuous rich. As Liam Lacey wrote: "[Wagner's] father was marginally in the [entertainment] business and [Wagner] went to school with celebrities' kids [and] walked home past Romanoff's, where Groucho Marx and Warren Beatty dined in the coffee shop. A high school dropout, he was inspired by the prose of writers such as Henry Miller and Jean Genet."[4]

Bartel sensed that his co-writer's attitudes and appetites aligned with his own. "Bruce is very eccentric. That's what attracted him to me. Both Bruce and I are attracted to the marginal and dangerous and perverse and dark. For a long time, I had been looking for a writer to collaborate with. When I met Bruce, I knew that my prayers had been answered.... Indeed, Satan had sent him to me."[5] The pair was also in agreement about the themes and satirical targets they wanted to introduce into the film. Wagner told Jim Emerson that he intended with *Scenes* to create "a kind of radicalized version of *Rules of the Game* or *Smiles of a Summer Night*.... I wanted people to laugh hysterically and be shocked every minute or so by something someone does or says. A constant series of low to high voltage shocks."[6]

In February 1986, Bartel and Wagner had a first draft of their screenplay ready, which documented the interactions of "two wealthy women in Beverly Hills, one a widow and one a divorcee, who live next door and the various sexual relationships between them and their servants."[7] The story's mix of bedroom peccadilloes, social satire and bon mots helped them secure a financing agreement with RKO Pictures, but only after the "production was turned down by every studio."[8] The arrangement with RKO was enough to secure a non-binding commitment in the summer of 1986 from Faye Dunaway to star in the picture.[9] The arrangement with the production company fell through a short time later, however, and Bartel, now working with producer Jim Katz (from *Lust in the Dust*), scrambled for a new source of money. Eventually, he and Katz connected with independent production company Cinecom, having sold the production as "a Faye Dunaway vehicle."[10]

Assured of a $4.5 million budget, Bartel expected shooting to start in early 1988 and proceeded to fill out the cast and crew. While Dunaway would play Clare, a widowed TV actress, *Eating Raoul*'s Mary Woronov in a supporting role would play her next door neighbor, a divorcee named Lisabeth, who needs to stay in Clare's house for a weekend. Lisabeth and her dying son, Willie (Barrett Oliver, Bartel's co-star in *Frankenweenie*), take to Clare's because their home is being fumigated—to destroy the germs of Lisabeth's philandering ex-husband, Howard.

Bartel gave the part of Howard to his friend playwright-actor Wallace Shawn, a frequent collaborator in the eighties with one of Bartel's favorite directors, Louis Malle, on pictures like *My Dinner with Andre* and *Vanya on 42nd Street*. Shawn actually sought the role, enthusiastic as he was over the film's leftist positions. He told Patrick Goldstein:

> I'm not saying I actually got this part without a certain degree of friendship. Paul and I—well, we met at Schwab's if you want to know the truth.... When I heard there was a possibility that I could actually be in this movie.... OK, I begged to be in it, which is very uncharacteristic for me. Usually, I'm extremely ambivalent about being in a film. I find myself hoping that it might be fun, and I would get paid for it, but dreading it because I'd be embarrassed to have my friends see me in it.... I begged. I groveled. I gave up money to be in this film. I could've done something else—if I could think of the title, I'd tell you—that would've paid more money.... It's astonishing to me that this movie could've been made in the eighties. Everyone I know leaps at any sign that the social pendulum might be swinging in a less, well, fascistic direction—though I'm not sure that it is. For me, this is a period where most Americans believe that social satire—satire that I would consider empty or silly or incredibly superficial—is really bitingly savage. I don't know, I guess most Americans simply don't have that degree of anger in their repertoire.[11]

For Clare's dead husband, Sydney, who returns as a ghost to annoy his widow, Bartel cast actor-director Paul Mazursky, a friend with whom he'd appeared in John Landis's *Into the Night*. Bartel gave himself a prominent part, too, as a diet doctor, Mo Van De Kamp, whom Clare hires to help her stay thin. Bartel quipped to Terry Gross: "The doctor is a quack, and God knows Beverly Hills has plenty of them. Actually my role was originally supposed to be the dog's psychiatrist, but Paul Mazursky used that joke in *Down and Out in Beverly Hills*, so we had to revise our script. And Bruce, taking cruel advantage of my problems of keeping my weight down, decided to write me as a thinologist, and

I went along with the joke."[12] Both the doctor's counsel and his morals are dubious. He prescribes treatments like consuming "junk food until you're ready to vomit, then a bracing salt-water enema"; he also runs off at the end of the picture with Clare's young daughter, Zandra (Rebecca Schaeffer).

In addition to Woronov, Bartel and casting director Elizabeth Leustig brought on three more actors attached to *Eating Raoul*. Robert Beltran was to play Juan, a servant who sleeps with Lisabeth, Susan Saiger as an entertainment journalist and Ed Begley, Jr., as a playwright with ridiculous ideas about not only the theatre but life and people in general. Begley, Jr., who'd played a psychotic hippy in *Raoul*, agreed to take the playwright role without hesitation, explaining to Patrick Goldstein: "Paul is a very funny man, on and off the set. He's become a friend, [and] you always enjoy working with him so much that you're happy to hear him call about a part."[13]

The production's start was delayed multiple times, however, as Cinecom dithered over the budget and demanded last minute changes to the shooting script. Bartel worried that delaying the starting date could cost the production its biggest name, and, indeed, during one of these waits, Faye Dunaway's stock as an actor went up thanks to her appearance in *Barfly* (1987), a movie about alcoholics in love that soared with critics. With new offers before her, she begged off the picture, and without a binding contract, she was able to depart with impunity. While her exit disappointed Bartel, he also empathized. "Faye had been waiting on-and-off for a year for the production to start.... I can't really say I'd have done differently in her place," he said. "She obviously can command much more money now."[14]

International Creative Management, the talent agency that represented Bartel, "suggested Jacqueline Bisset as a replacement," an idea he endorsed. With her ability to sound like British gentry when she spoke, her imperial beauty and her reputation, deserved or not, as a film actress who typically took on serious roles in serious dramas, Bisset as Clare would allow Bartel to juxtapose—and contrast—her aristocratic persona with the venal habits of the film's supporting characters. "I don't get offered many comedy parts," she said. "And this humor is ... so raunchy and has such a dangerous quality. It's very on the edge." Her presence enabled Bartel to weave another allusion to French cinema into the story: Bisset had played an actress in Truffaut's *Day for Night* (1973), a film that depicts affairs and trysts crossing class lines. "I'd always thought of Jaqueline as the exquisite heroine of *Day for Night*. But when we met and we talked, I fell in love. She's very funny—as soon as she read her lines, I knew she could handle anything."[15]

Bartel and Wagner made a point with their script to collapse as many customary social barriers as they could. Over the weekend at Clare's mansion, nearly all of the wealthy characters succeed in sleeping with, even forming romantic relationships, with working class characters. As the narrative closes, for example, Shawn's gynecologist character leaves Beverly Hills, taking with him a former porno actress named To-Bel (Arnetia Walker). Likewise Lisabeth and Clare's houseman, Juan, head off to start a new life as a couple. With these two pairings, Bartel and Wagner also flouted the prohibition on mixed relationships, the racist fear of miscegenation. To-Bel is black; her doctor lover, Howard, is white. Juan is Hispanic; Lisabeth is white.

Bartel had first depicted interracial sex twenty years earlier in "Naughty Nurse," incorporating a ménage a trois comprised of a black

The portly thinologist Dr. Mo Van De Kamp (Bartel) chats with To-Bel (Arnetia Walker), a recently retired porno star in *Scenes from the Class Struggle in Beverly Hills* (North Street Films, Cinecom Entertainment Group, 1989).

man, a white man and a white woman. With "Naughty Nurse," he had also tested another social prohibition with the film's implication that its male protagonists are bisexual or, at least, comfortable about participating in sexual experiences together. In *Scenes*, however, Bartel and Wagner treated sex between men more explicitly. Juan and Lisabeth's chauffer, Frank (Ray Sharkey), make a bet that if Juan beds Lisabeth, he'll win $5,000, which he needs to pay off a loan shark. If Juan fails, he will not only *not* get the money, he'll have to have sex with Frank. Although Juan and Lisabeth do become lovers, out of a sense of honor Juan decides to conceal this development and allows Frank to sleep with him. Following the incident, Frank gives Juan $5,000 anyway, and the men part as friends. The gesture is generous, but it also re-casts Juan's submission into an act of prostitution.

Bartel claimed that the inclusion of the subplot about the housemen allowed him to speak to his own ambivalence about being gay and the not-always-pleasant consequences his sexuality had generated for himself as he came of age in mid-century America. "I think I got involved making films about society and especially about problems in society because I used to be a pretty angry guy.... I am gay. And I think that being gay has been the biggest source of conflict in my life. And growing up in the fifties it was taboo to be gay. I don't think it was easy for my parents. But I also had a sense at the time that my parents had misrepresented society to me, and also other passions, which they didn't approve of or didn't allude to and didn't condone. As I grew up I came to terms with that, and with my parents, and more importantly with myself."[16] And to Tommy O'Haver he said: "My one regret about that movie is that the gay relationship was predicated on a bet and the straight guy was obliged to go through with it without particularly wanting to. On the other hand, what I'm proud of is the scene the next morning where it's clear he doesn't think it was any big deal and possibly even enjoyed it."[17]

Principal photography finally commenced on *Scenes* the second week of August 1988 and wrapped five weeks later. "We filmed it in three different locations, in Brentwood, Fremont Place and Hancock Park—everywhere but Beverly Hills, which is too expensive to shoot in," Bartel told John Hartl. "We brought in new furniture, rented paintings and a lot of my art collection wound up on the walls."[18]

Bartel's interactions with the actors often had a festive quality as he invited them to play their characters in broad fashion. As he had on previous films, he invited suggestions about how their performances could be improved, a tendency that impressed Bisset: "What I like is that Paul has a very relaxed attitude—he's not at all autocratic. In fact, he's quite gentle." Woronov was grateful, too: "He's very relaxed. The only things that pressure him are money and time." Wagner was also asked to come to the set to offer his advice whenever Bartel felt the script needed adjustment, for which Wagner was grateful. "[T]o work on something this uncompromising has done wonders for my spirit. It's been like vomiting, but having fun doing it."[19]

Even difficulties that arose during shooting tended toward mirth rather than frustration. Walker and Shawn, for instance, shot a love scene together that put Bartel in the ironic position of asking for more restraint and modesty from his actors. Walker explained:

> I'd tease little Wally. I'd say, "Wallace, our big love scene is coming up. What are you wearing?"
> He said, "I'll wear what you're wearing."
> I said, "I'm not wearing anything."
> So Wallace said, "I'll be there for you. I won't wear anything either."
> Came time for the scene, I ended up wearing underwear, and he did the scene nude. They spent the rest of the time trying to cover him up.[20]

Bartel confirmed Walker's story, telling John Stanley that Shawn "got into bed thinking he had to be completely naked, and ruined four or five takes because his schlong kept showing from under the covers. But we finally got him covered up."[21]

To maintain his mood and energy on the set, Bartel followed a bit of advice Roger Corman often passed on to his protégés: "'I sit down a lot. I even lie down when I can. Whenever there's a long pause like this, I really do relax.' He smiled. 'Take a little nap.'"[22] He also allowed himself to have fun with cast and crew at his home on Fareholm Drive, where he—the lifelong gourmand—often prepared meals. Zane W. Levitt remembered vividly how he would "spare no expense on food. He loved good food. I mean, he liked to eat, he was really into it."[23] At these get-togethers, Bartel would invite his guests to perform musical numbers. "I've found the best way to psychologically energize myself for the week's work is to have a bunch of friends over on Sunday night and sing old show tunes. We do everything—Rodgers and Hart, Gershwin, Cole Porter. Last night Arnetia [Walker] and I sang a duet of 'Baby, It's Cold Outside.' We went till 1:00 a.m. last night, which is a ridiculous hour, since I had to get up at dawn to prepare for shooting. But I feel completely energized—it restores me in some way I don't fully understand."[24] Bartel's fondness for show tunes and sing-a-longs crept into the film, too. Pianist Michael Feinstein has a cameo in the picture, for example, during which he plays "These Foolish Things." And as the film's end credits roll, Cole Porter's "Let's Misbehave," sung by Arnetia Walker, snaps along on the soundtrack.[25]

Once shooting wrapped in September, Bartel bid farewell to actors and crew, and he and Alan Toomayan retreated to the editing room, where they put together a rough cut of the picture. Bartel was insistent on weaving through the soundtrack a series of songs, cues and passages of classical music that he selected himself. One of the finer sequences in the film may be the one during which shots of the principals relaxing *post coitum* in one another's arms proceed across the screen as a passage from Debussy's *The Children's Corner* gently plays—contrasting the cynicism and dramatics that dominate the picture's other sections. Cinecom was not happy, however, with the early cut's running time and told Bartel and Toomayan to return to the editing room. Bartel complied, agreeing to remove footage given to the love affair between Beltran's and Woronov's characters, which he and the actors later realized damaged the romance's plausibility. Woronov felt that Lisabeth and Juan "needed scenes that were not hysterical, so you'd have a feeling for the people. But they [Cinecom] didn't have room for them. They left a little bit of the heart out."[26]

Cinecom's CEO, Amir Malin, pushed for even more changes, but Bartel told them he was done, and "promise[d] to take his name off the film."[27] Bartel also clashed with Cinecom briefly over the film's title. As Scenes had gone into production, a string of films with "Beverly Hills" in their titles were shooting or in the can ready for release, including *Troop Beverly Hills, Terror in Beverly Hills, Beverly Hills Vamp* and *Beverly Hills Brats*. The trend, it seems, had started with the blockbuster *Beverly Hills Cop* in 1984, followed two years later by Mazursky's *Down and Out in Beverly Hills*. Bartel told the *Los Angeles Times*'s Nikki Finke: "I was so sick of hearing Beverly Hills in titles that I suggested ... that we call it *Scenes from the Class Struggle in Southern California* or *North America* or whatever. And [Cinecom] said, 'Are you crazy? Absolutely not! It's got be Beverly Hills.'"[28] Bartel prudently dropped this request.

Once the film was ready for previews, Cinecom got behind it, screening it throughout Los Angeles and vicinity for critics. Bartel tried to crash one of these screenings at the Burbank Studios but was turned away at the door. A staffer at the facility explained: "It was nothing personal. But the screening was strictly for long lead press." As Bartel walked off in the direction of the studio lot's commissary, he spotted Joe Dante, who was at work on *Gremlins 2: The New Batch*. As the friends chatted, Dante asked Bartel to play a movie theater manager who tries to assuage an irate mom with the aid of Hulk Hogan when some gremlins misbehave in front of her and her son. The mother was to be played by Belinda Balaski, a supporting player in *Cannonball!* Bartel agreed to take the part right there.[29]

Bartel's lightened schedule prior to *Scenes*'s release enabled him to turn his attention to other projects. In the last few months of 1988, he and Dick Blackburn reunited with producer Anne Kimmel to resume their efforts on *Bland Ambition*, having been assured financing from Vestron Pictures. With a start date announced for April 1989, Bartel had punched up the script with Blackburn, secured locations and readied his cast. But right before the scheduled start, Vestron told the filmmakers that money for production was no longer available.[30] "We were a week-and-a-half from starting to shoot it when Vestron ran out of money," Bartel told *Newsday*.[31] The company had recently released several costly duds, including Ken Russell's *The Lair of the White Worm* and Michael Almereyda's *Twister*, which had destroyed its viability. Kimmel recalled: "Money was rolling. We'd hired a crew. We were hiring our actors. But when it came to negotiating the pay or play clause with the actors, Vestron started getting cold feet. You can't imagine the disappointment of being in production for two or three weeks and then having the funding disappear. Then Vestron went belly up and that was the end of it."[32]

On June 2, 1989, *Scenes* opened at the Castro Theatre in San Francisco, where, as John Hartl noted, "Bartel hopes to break the box office record he established there with *Lust in the Dust*." The film was subsequently booked in independent cinema houses "in New York, Los Angeles and in Seattle."[33] *Scenes* had its official premiere a few days later on June 5 in West Hollywood at the DGA's Theater Complex. Among those in attendance were Bartel, Katz, Wagner, Beltran and Walker. An admixture of celebrities made appearances, too, including actress Sally Kirkland, rapper Adam "King Ad-Rock" Horovitz and Esther Williams, who'd starred in the MGM musicals *Million Dollar Mermaid* and *Take Me Out to the Ball Game*. At the reception that followed the screening, guests enjoyed a meal fit for Beverly Hills denizens, with caviar and champagne as a pianist played numbers from the Gershwin songbook.[34]

The notices that came in for *Scenes* that summer were generally good, with critics welcoming the picture as a return to form for Bartel, his brightest offering since *Eating Raoul*. Instead of seeing the film as a satire of class pride and prejudices, though, several reviewers responded to it as a send-up of other people's movies, TV shows and plays. Dave Kehr, for example, wrote: "Paul Bartel's bad taste comedy *Scenes from the Class Struggle in Beverly Hills* opens by playing its gilt-lettered titles against an artfully rumpled red velvet background—a moment of perfectly captured kitsch that could have been clipped from one of producer Ross Hunter's lush movie melodramas of the fifties."[35] Frank DeCaro in *Newsday* wrote: "In this delightfully offensive comedy, Bartel skewers the sexual mores and social values of the Robin Leach set. Gentler than John Waters's early work and more wholesome than anything by Pedro Almodovar, *Class Struggle* is sort of an *Upstairs, Downstairs* for the trash-cinema set. It's *Down and Out in Beverly Hills* with subversive undertones."[36] And the *Boston Globe*'s Jay Carr, addressing the film's tendency to swing between arthouse affectation and slapstick, argued that at "its best, *Scenes from the Class Struggle* plays like a cross between Buñuel and the Marx Brothers."[37] (Bartel dedicated the picture to Buñuel.)

Jim Emerson, in contrast, recognized that the film was more than a *Mad*-style spoof of earlier movies and TV shows: "*Scenes from the Class Struggle* succeeds—although … it's often tough (or even impossible) to tell when the movie is laughing at racism and sexism and when it's just indulging in it. But although its sensibility is rooted in camp, this picture at least doesn't play it safe. It gives you moral as well as physical qualms, makes you squirm and question your attitudes and responses to it."[38] The *New York Times*'s Caryn James agreed: "In Mr. Bartel's startling little film—combining farce, black humor and social satire—serious comments lurk beneath a surface as bright and frothy as the billowing orange evening dress Jacqueline Bisset wears in the film's opening sequence. With it narrow focus on characters who are rich or who live within spitting distance of the rich, *Scenes from the Class Struggle* is lightweight social criticism, but social criticism nonetheless."[39]

The favorable attention that came to the film briefly restored Bartel's status as a "hot" director in the industry. "I'm not someone whose doors the studios have broken down in the years since *Eating Raoul*.... In the week after *Scenes* opened, I found that calls were returned very quickly by top people. A number of people have expressed admiration of the film and are interested in working with me.... [S]o I'm reading books and scripts and also talking to Wall Street people about financing for packages of movies. Nobody's interested in one little $4.5 million picture. They say: 'Can't you bring us five $5 million pictures or one $15 million picture and two $5 million pictures,' because, of course, the people in the money-raising business are interested in taking a commission on a huge—instead of a piddling little—thing."[40] All of these exchanges never led to anything, however: Bartel would direct only one more feature, *Shelf Life*, which he primarily financed himself.

The ideas floated around during this period were nevertheless intriguing. One project that went fairly far in terms of development was an updated treatment of the 1958 science fiction movie *The Attack of the 50 ft. Woman*, in which professional wrestler Big John Stud was to play the film's male lead. "This movie will not result in more natural acting, but it may appeal to more kids," Bartel explained to Howie Movshovitz, adding that he agreed to make the picture, a genre parody, because "I'm trying to jump around and do different things, something a little less related to the arcane inspiration of eighteenth century comedy (which led to *Scenes*) and closer to *The Girl Can't Help It*."[41]

With Bruce Wagner, he worked up an original script titled *Getting Away with Murder*. Joan Collins was to star in the picture and Menahem Golan would produce it for 21st Century Entertainment, an independent production company. The story, Bartel said, borrowed plot elements from Malle's *The Bride Wore Black* and Mackendrick's *Kind Hearts and Coronets*, having Collins's character "sanely and methodically [go] around getting revenge" on men who raped her.[42] Bartel referred to the story, rather callously, as a "murder comedy."[43] "Joan is a very interesting person to write for," he said. "We're having a great time. We're laughing a lot."[44] Despite a promised start date in October 1989, the project met the same fate as that befell so many of his creative ventures and evaporated.

Bartel was also hopeful about making a quieter, more personal story with the working title *Modern Marriage*, which re-visited the gay-straight friendship theme he'd integrated into *Scenes*: "It's about two guys who are roommates, one's gay and one's straight, and both are about to enter a long-term relationship with another person though each has a problem with commitment. It's more straight, if you'll pardon the pun, in that I'm not looking to criticize here, but rather to show how people can be brought together. I will do this by minimizing differences instead of exacerbating them."[45] Bartel also attached himself to a planned biopic about Andy Warhol, agreeing to co-write the script with Gus Van Sant, the director of *Drugstore Cowboy* (1989), but spatting with Van Sant ultimately broke the partnership, and the film was never made.[46]

In the summer of 1989, as *Scenes* courted the favor of movie critics, Bartel was invited to give an interview to *Fresh Air*, a popular topical interest program carried by National Public Radio. During his conversation with host Terry Gross, Bartel for the first time discussed his sexual orientation before a general audience. During their conversation, Gross asked Bartel to speak about his relationship with Mary Woronov, whom she mistakenly thought was his spouse.

> GROSS: You and your wife [Woronov] star in your movies—
> BARTEL: Well, she's not my wife.
> GROSS: Oh. She's not your wife? Oh, I'm sorry.
> BARTEL: No. She's my friend. She's only my wife in the movies.
> GROSS: Gosh. I really thought you were married.
> BARTEL: No.
> GROSS: That means you're not lovers, either?
> BARTEL: No. I'm gay. She's a painter.[47]

With friends, it needs to be said, Bartel had never been reticent about being gay. He may have been uncomfortable talking about sex with family, but he was not closeted. Jon Davison remembers: "I was provincial as a youth, and all the gay people I knew seemed to be secretive and unhappy. Paul was the joyous opposite. He delighted in his sexuality and was often hilarious about it."[48]

A little more than a week after the *Fresh Air* interview, a tragedy occurred that spoiled what should have otherwise been a joyful summer for Bartel and *Scenes*'s cast and crew. The actress Rebecca Schaeffer, who'd played the role of Jacqueline Bisset's daughter, Zandra, was murdered in her residence by Robert John Bardo—a deranged admirer whose obsessive personality eerily paralleled George's in *Private Parts*. A high school dropout from Arizona, Bardo had fixated on Schaeffer for several years, having watched her on the TV series *My Sister Sam*, which ran on CBS from 1986 to 1988. "Bardo taped every episode and replayed them endlessly," notes Ellis Cashmore.[49] He had watched *Scenes* in a movie theater and was unpleasantly surprised to see Schaeffer "in bed with an actor [Ray Sharkey]. When Bardo saw Schaeffer in the sexually suggestive scene he became furious and convinced [himself] that she didn't deserve his love any longer and should be punished, believing she had become just 'another Hollywood whore.'" He proceeded to track her to her apartment in Los Angeles, where he "pulled a .357 Magnum from a plastic bag and shot Schaeffer once in the chest with a hollow-point cartridge. A half-hour later, she was dead on arrival at Cedars-Sinai Medical Center."[50]

Bardo was apprehended in Tucson one day later. During the interval between the murder and his capture, *People* approached Bartel for a statement. The director was deeply saddened. "I can only assume that it was somebody who didn't know [Rebecca] but was obsessed with her. I can't imagine that anybody who really knew her would do this. She was so mature and intuitive that she would have made sure this couldn't happen."[51]

For his next project, Bartel took a break from moviemaking to oversee the musical adaptation of *Eating Raoul*, which he hoped would make its way to Broadway. How much Schaeffer's murder influenced this decision isn't clear. He'd loved show tunes since boyhood and had done his best to incorporate musical elements into much of his output as a filmmaker, and now he wanted to create a full-blown theatrical production. The idea of turning *Eating Raoul* into a musical reached back more than a decade, having come to him after the motion picture's release in 1982. "My real idols in life are Gershwin, Rodgers and Hart, Cole Porter, Noël Coward, Jerome Kern," he told the *Chicago Tribune*'s Michael Kilian. "When the film was a success, it occurred to me that I could possibly ride it into the musical theater. That it could be my entrée."[52] Working from the original film script (sans Dick Blackburn), Bartel wrote the libretto and secured Jed Feuer to compose original music, with lyrics by Boyd Graham.

As he went to potential investors, he stressed that a musical adaptation of *Eating Raoul* had a good chance of replicating "the screen-to-stage success of *The Little Shop of Horrors*." *The Little Shop of Horrors*—a horror-comedy about a monstrous plant that eats people in a flower shop—had had its start in 1960 as a quickie low-budget movie directed by Roger Corman, with a Charles B. Griffith script. Corman hadn't retained the copyright on the picture, and after it lapsed into the public domain, the creative team of Howard Ashman and Alan Mencken adapted the original story into a musical comedy, which subsequently won the New York Drama Critics Circle Award for Best Musical in 1982. In 1986, Warner Bros. Pictures and the Geffen Company released a film adaptation of the musical directed by Frank Oz that turned a profit.

Several Broadway stalwarts agreed to hear Bartel out when he approached them but in the end decided against financing. "We auditioned it for Mike Nichols," Bartel explained. "We had a brief romance with Martin Charnin."[53] Eventually, Bartel convinced a group of financiers—Max Weitzenhoffer, Stewart F. Lane, Joan Cullman and Richard Norton—to give $1 million to the production.[54]

Bartel felt that he was not qualified to helm *Eating Raoul: The Musical*, that it "needed a whole new imagination. I wanted to put my talents, such as they are, at the disposal of someone else's vision."[55] In due course Toni Kotite was selected, a young director whose credits included several college productions and an avant-garde play titled *Scooncat* that had run on Manhattan's Theatre Row in 1987. For the parts of Mary and Paul Bland, Bartel and the producers cast, respectively, Courtenay Collins, a Juilliard graduate and Eddie Korbich, who'd recently played the Tobias Ragg role in a revival production of Sondheim's *Sweeney Todd* at the Circle in the Square Theatre on Broadway. The part of Raoul was given to television actor Adrian Zmed.

Over the nine-month stretch leading up to the production's premier in May 1992, the cast and crew workshopped material in storefront theatres, experimenting with set design, actors' costumes and choreography. Bartel had decided that this new version of the Blands' story should be set in the sixties, "to avoid the AIDS-era and to underscore the swinger craze," a change that intrigued Kotite as it allowed her to dress the players in "wigs and psychedelic clothing and all that."[56] Looking back on the production years later, Bartel regretted decisions he made about the staging and set design. "In retrospect I wish I had thrown my weight around more. We made a terrible mistake committing to lots of physical scenery in New York. That production lumbered.... We tied the show down."[57]

On its opening night, May 13, 1992, at Union Square Theater, Bartel was nervous but also confident about the production's chances for success. A telegram sent to him by composer Stephen Sondheim jokingly declared: "Relax. You have nothing at stake but your entire career."

"It's fruition," Bartel said, moved by this gesture. "To be admired even a little bit by someone you admire so much."[58] *Eating Raoul: The Musical* nonetheless failed to impress reviewers. The reviews that came in primarily attacked the production's extravagant attempts at humor and satire; critics felt that it was *too* campy, *too* tongue in cheek, even *too* gay, with swingers dancing in drag and sequences calculated to evoke the sexy goofiness of Busby Berkeley's routines in movies like *42nd Street* and *Golddiggers of 1934*. "In spite of the seeming outrageousness of the material, this adaptation of Paul Bartel's 1982 cult movie is over its head in a vat of whimsy," Mel Gussow of the *New York Times* complained. "The show tries so hard to be with it that it ends up being without it, that is, without anything except a shadow of what made the film funny in the first place."[59] Most damning of all may have been *New York* magazine's theater critic John Simon's assessment: "The music has a couple of moments, but the book and lyrics have none. Although Adrian Zmed brings enough libidinous bluster to Raoul, Courtenay Collins would seem unlikely to lure on the most desperate pervert, except perhaps one enamored of bad nose jobs, and Eddie Korbich is too squishy to swing a garlic press, never mind a frying pan."[60]

The experience disappointed Bartel deeply. How could he not be? "With its edgy black humor and pleasant score, it's surprising *Eating Raoul* didn't enjoy a long run. But audiences didn't come, and so the musical was gone in six weeks," he lamented. "[We had] permitted ourselves the sin of openly expecting a hit. The gods punished us. They sent John Simon in a shower of fire."[61] As the production struggled through the early summer of 1992, though, Bartel managed to have some fun, appearing with his friend Wallace Shawn in the soap opera *One Life to Live*, which was then filmed in Manhattan.[62]

After *Eating Raoul: The Musical* closed, Bartel returned to Los Angeles, melancholy over the production's failure but still interested in theatre. That July, he accepted an invitation from his actor friend Jim Turner to visit the Lex Theatre in Hollywood to watch the final performance of an experimental production titled *Shelf Life*, which featured Turner, O-Lan Jones and Andrea "Andy" Stein as siblings who've spent nearly thirty years living in a bomb shelter.

The play, which the actors also wrote, bombarded its audience with absurdist dialogue and nonsense songs as it mocked the social values and sexual hang-ups of the American middle-class—themes dear to Bartel. "It was so funny, full of meaning and poetry. It said something about our culture, about the relationship between siblings, about men and women, about the child within and the adult. I fell for it." That night, he sensed the play could be adapted into a modestly-budgeted movie, which excited him. "I'd come back from New York, where I'd spent a frustrating nine months doing the musical version of *Eating Raoul* Off-Broadway.... The experience was so costly and complicated, that I wanted to get involved with work that could be done without hundreds of thousands of dollars. I saw *Shelf Life* as a chance to do something small and wonderful."[63]

The cost of *Shelf Life* would eventually reach half-a-million dollars, of which Bartel, "[i]mpatient with the Hollywood shuffle of raising money and schmoozing with studio heads," would contribute $350,000.[64] The play's actor-creators had agreed to re-write the story for the screen, allowing Bartel to pour himself into his duties as a producer, re-teaming with Anne Kimmel to secure the remaining budget from "private sources," including a Canadian investor named Bruce Critchly and, once again, his father, Bill Bartel.[65] He also put together a crew that included director of photography Philip Holahan, editor Judd Maslansky and production designer Dean Tavoularis, who, with his brother, visual consultant Alex Tavoularis, created "a single, 15-by-25-foot set ... [that] looks like a claustrophobic, post-apocalyptic version of Pee-wee's playhouse."[66] Shooting commenced "on a soundstage at CFI [Consolidated Film Industries] in Hollywood" in the first week of August that summer and wrapped just two weeks later.[67]

Shelf Life opens with two adults and their three young children sitting in the living room of their Anaheim home on November 22, 1963, the day Oswald murdered Kennedy. As the terrible news comes in through the TV, the family's patriarch, played by Jim Turner, announces that the killing is just the first of several events that will cause the United States to break down. He ushers the others into the bomb cellar he's built, having them descend into a space that will exclude them from sunlight, fresh air and other people. A title card announces the passage of thirty years, and we soon have the chance to watch the now adult children, Tina, Pam and Scotty, interacting in their squalid home. To amuse themselves and, perhaps, to give their lives a sense of purpose, they perform skits that are shot through with half-remembered ideas passed on to them by their long dead parents or the television in the shelter that sporadically transmits bits of programs and news reports. The siblings attempt to tamp down their anxieties as they realize that their pantry after so many years is just about empty. Before any new suffering occurs for them, though, they are discovered by a construction worker whose crew has drilled down into the earth through the shelter's ceiling.

Though Jones, Stein and Turner with their script nearly doubled the length of their play, the completed film managed to summon the frenetic, breathless qualities that attracted the director to the production in the first place. The principals, manically engaged in pantomimes and dances, shamble about the cramped set through much of the movie, shouting and laughing at one another, weeping at times, too, wearing little more than rags. To reinforce the sense of madness that seeps through their underground lives, Holohan's cameras often jump and pivot violently before settling into soft arcing motions. The set itself is dream-like, with the characters' props and costumes—and treasured artifacts—strewn about like garbage.

As he had with *Eating Raoul*, Bartel submitted copies of *Shelf Life* to prestigious film festivals, expecting to arouse interest from investors and score a distribution deal. Helping him with this campaign were publicists Mickey Cottrell and Doug Lindeman, who believed that recent history, e.g., the Soviet Union's dissolution, had made this surreal comedy set in a bomb shelter particularly timely. The "Cold War mentality can finally be laughed at," Lindeman told *Variety*.[68]

The realization dawned fast, however, that the filmmakers' optimism was misplaced, as rejections came in from two of the most important outlets for independent productions, the Sundance Film Festival and the Toronto International Film Festival. Bartel recalled: "I must say I was the victim of my own hubris. I thought that offbeat and strange and theatrical as it is, I thought it would be a shoo-in at Sundance. Its emphatic rejection at Sundance was my first indication that it would not be universally accepted. I thought that because of my place among American independent filmmakers, it was automatic that they would accept it. This always goes before a fall."

Though his career as a filmmaker had begun with experimental film productions, Bartel surmised that prospective buyers felt that *Shelf Life* marked too much of a departure from the more conventionally-structured features he'd made in the seventies and eighties. "The greatest problem about getting this film released has been because of my earlier work. People expect *Eating Raoul* or *Not for Publication*. They are surprised when they see it, even confused. Even though it has something in common with my other films in that it's also about unconventional subjects. But the style is so completely different, and that's what throws people."[69]

Bartel continued to screen the movie at independent theaters throughout North America, and despite its lack of a distributor, critics came to watch the picture. The reviews varied considerably. The *Village Voice*'s Julie Lang was a vigorous supporter of the movie: "Bartel successfully reenacts the what-if-some-hyper-paranoid-pop-hauls-his-family-into-a-bomb-shelter routine, and if the parents kick the botulism-infected can, what happens if the kids survive without knowledge of an escape? ... I'll tell you one thing, this is no *Blue Lagoon*; these actors are ugly with a capital U, chipped teeth, gnarled hair, farting noises spewing through their teeth. This is nonsense. This is a game, a political commentary, a prediction, nothing to worry about. Enjoy."[70]

Longtime Bartel advocate Todd McCarthy in *Variety* declared that *Shelf Life* "is a distinctive small film, a microcosmic commentary on vaunted family values and the media generation. Based on an original stage piece created by the performers, who repeat their roles onscreen, pic represents something of a departure for Paul Bartel from his usual outrageous comedies, but features some of the best direction in any of his films. Work's intimate scope and conceptual nature position it for specialized audiences, and Bartel's name and hoped-for good reviews would be the selling points for an enterprising distrib.... To be sure, this is an unusual work that will click with some people and pass right by others. Artificial nature of it will put some off, while others will warm to it as its intentions become clear. But pic has been done with talent in a very particular key that could strike a chord with a loyal, if limited, following."[71]

Toronto-based critic Liam Lacey, however, thought the picture was an overheated example of style over substance:

> *Shelf Life* is consistent with Bartel's penchant for broad satire against American family values, which he characteristically views as a smokescreen for paranoia and violent competition. Visually, he manages to do the near-impossible: capture the experience of small theatre on film, moving the camera fluidly around the confined space, and conveying, both through lighting and movement, the shifting nuances of intimacy, menace and innocence.
>
> If only the play were worth the trouble. The script sounds like the sort of pretentious jumble that can come out of improvisation exercises: sudden power

shifts, role changes, playground chants, parodies (of *The Ed Sullivan Show*, teen rebel movies and kitsch pop songs). There is little sense of the disparity between tone and subject that actually makes satire sting. What we have instead is a parade of pop-cult references, garishly reflected through an absurdist's lens, that doesn't so much entertain as congratulate the audience on being in on the jokes. You might think of *Shelf Life* as the intellectual version of *The Brady Bunch Movie*.[72]

Though reviewers' expectations for the film were frustrated by what they perceived as its unusual structure and pacing, Bartel's final feature exploits motifs and themes that preoccupied him over much of his career—death, proscribed sexuality, musical numbers, costumes, even voyeurism (the film ends as Bartel's onscreen persona peers through a crack in the ceiling at the three siblings). And his interest in experimenting with and violating the rules of cinematic form reached back to his earliest efforts behind the camera: *Progetti* (the student production he shot in Italy), "The Secret Cinema," "Naughty Nurse."

Shelf Life, in other words, marks a return to Bartel's avant-garde origins, the one feature-length release in which he explored the ideas that interested him most with the greatest freedom, a result of the control over the project that was his for having underwritten so much of the budget himself. "I hope the money comes back quickly [on this movie], because I want to do this again. There's nothing like the feeling of being able to do things with your own money—even though people say you never should. In my experience, nothing else conveys such freedom. If it's a disaster, it's your *own* disaster."[73]

But the film never did see a return, and the remainder of Bartel's output as a director would be limited to television work. He was, however, attached for a short time to *Four Rooms*, an independent feature comprised of comic vignettes helmed by different directors that was set in the Chateau Marmont on Sunset Boulevard. Bartel was, it seems, let go because the film's principal investors felt he was not young or hip or novel enough for the work. Producer Alexandre Rockwell told *Filmmaker*, "We talked about Paul Bartel doing one [sequence], maybe Alan Rudolph. After that, I went to Quentin [Tarantino]. Quentin got up on it; Lawrence [Bender] got into it. And [they] went to Miramax. And then (I'm probably to blame as much as anyone), it got a little out of control. Miramax wanted to do it, but under the condition that the group of directors represent a New Movement. The casting of the directors' group was key—it was Miramax's hook. So we had to go back and tell Bartel and Rudolph that it wasn't going to be them. It was very tough; they were bummed out."[74]

Throughout the nineties, Bartel spent increasing time with old friend Barry Dennen, hashing together scripts the two pitched to film and television production companies. One of these collaborations served as the basis for a short film Bartel would direct for the British television show *The Comic Strip Presents....* The job came about in part as a result of Bartel's acting work. In 1990, he'd appeared in a comedy feature, *The Pope Must Diet*, which featured Scot actor Robbie Coltrane as a chubby, befuddled priest who, after mistakenly being elected pope by the College of Cardinals, becomes the target of a mafia assassination scheme. Bartel played a character in the movie, Monsignor Fitchie, whom Michael Musto described as "the ecclesiastical equivalent of Mrs. Danvers in *Rebecca*."[75]

The Pope Must Diet was directed by Peter Richardson, a founder of The Comic Strip, a group of actors—Rik Mayall, Nigel Planer, Jennifer Saunders and Richardson himself—that spoofed British culture and politics in stage revues. In 1981, Richardson had successfully negotiated a deal with the U.K.'s newly created Channel 4 to produce several short films for a series to be called *The Comic Strip Presents....* that would feature his troupe.[76]

The primary directors, as well as players, on *The Comic Strip Presents....* during its first decade on the TV were British. But Richardson, who recognized in Bartel a kindred comic spirit, arranged for him to direct an episode for the series after shooting on *The Pope Must Diet* was complete. Happy to work on a new project, Bartel dusted off a script that he and Barry Dennen had written called "The Secret Ingredient" a decade earlier for an unrealized American film production based on the old *One Step Beyond* TV show.[77]

Re-christened as "Demonella," the script borrowed from the legend of Faust, having the Devil offer Arnold Silverstein, a hack songwriter, a tune that will make him rich in return for his mother's chicken soup recipe. The Devil, played by Jennifer Saunders, needs to impress some fastidious epicures at a dinner she is planning: the guest list includes Oscar Wilde, Marie Antoinette, Sid Vicious and Adolf Hitler. Arnold's mother (Miriam Margolyes) refuses to participate, and the Devil in response takes on various personae and genders as she tries to con the recipe from the stubborn woman and her son.

With "Demonella," Bartel created, arguably, his final great work.

7. About Men and Women

The program is an exemplary comedy, a fast-paced examination of the crooked morals permeating the music business—functioning as a synecdoche, perhaps, for the entertainment industry that Bartel had been engaging with for decades. Several markers characteristic of Bartel's style appear in the program: the unscrupulous pursuit of money; a gender-bending protagonist; an overweight protagonist; family conflict; music performed on a piano; dance numbers. Bartel manages as well to put himself, literally, into the composition, playing a foppish Oscar Wilde with a Buster Brown wig, who inexplicably has wound up in Hell and carries on often with Hitler. Playing the Führer is Dennen, who transforms the dictator into a ninny who swats at his companions with a riding crop. As the Wilde and Hitler characters bicker at the Devil's table awaiting the promised soup—the Silversteins, ironically, are Jewish—between them sits Genghis Khan (Peter Richardson).

The last decade of Bartel's life was spent primarily playing walk-on parts in other people's movies and TV shows. *Shelf Life*'s failure, Anne Kimmel suggests, may have discouraged him from working as hard as he had previously to secure directing assignments. "He continued to try, but he was happy getting the roles.... He was disappointed. It was an uphill struggle. He stopped trying as hard as he did when he was younger, but he still loved being involved in film. He started doing more to help other people, like other young directors. And artists. In his house there was no space on his walls at all that wasn't filled with art. Downstairs he had a wonderful basement that had drawers that were filled with unframed art. He would have artists stay with him sometimes, just to help their careers. He wasn't as involved with movies, but he was still creative. He loved the idea of art, of books. He had a huge collection of first edition books that were signed. He was into the arts, not just film."[78]

Bartel was often given parts on TV shows, among them episodes of *Snoops* and *Ally McBeal* that Allan Arkush directed, as well as the Showtime miniseries *More Tales from the City*, which featured adaptations of short stories by gay author Armistead Maupin. He had roles in a pair of low-budget horror movies directed by one-time New World production assistant David DeCoteau—*Jaguar Prey* and *Skeletons*—and appeared in a 1995 re-make of Roger Corman's *A Bucket of Blood*, on which Corman served as executive producer. He showed up in John Carpenter's *Escape from L.A.*, Bryan Singer's *The Usual Suspects* and Julian Schnabel's *Basquiat*—a biopic about Andy Warhol's tragic protégé

Jean-Michel Basquiat. He also played an insufferable photographer, Rex Webster, who creeps through the art world in Tommy O'Haver's *Billy's Hollywood Screen Kiss*, a comic drama dealing "with the frustrations of same-sex attraction."[79] Bartel told O'Haver, "I was attracted to the project [because] ... the role was extravagant and promised to be fun."[80] In his introductory scene, the Webster character pontificates on craft and aesthetics, delivering a drunken statement that arguably summarizes Bartel's treatment of sex in his own films: "But seriously, what does it mean to be a gay artist in today's society? Well, it means responsibility, responsibility to re-create popular culture in a pan-sexual mode." He proceeds to define "pan-sexual" to the sycophants standing around him: "Oh, it means, I fuck him, he fucks her, she fucks me, I fuck—"

Bartel also made appearances in two films that explored both homophobia and the manner in which AIDS had transformed the gay community, Gregg Araki's *The Living End* (1992) and Richard Glatzer's *Grief* (1994). Gary Morris recognized in these film appearances Bartel's continuing desire to assist other directors. "Bartel's ultimate importance may lie less in his directorial efforts, which are variable in quality, than in his unwavering presence as an inspiring figure in the independent film world, particularly to queer filmmakers, an image reinforced by his genial, bearlike demeanor and eagerness to help struggling young auteurs."[81]

What is evident from Bartel's onscreen roles in the nineties is that despite his obvious pleasure in playing campy characters, his love for rich food had caught up with him. Though he'd been portly, if not fat, since the seventies, his large frame had broadened, and he looked older than a middle-aged man should, his distinctive beard now white. His indifference to exercise and his half-hearted attempts at dieting during these last years of life troubled friends. As John Meyer recalls, "Paul ate steak at almost every dinner—which he would salt inordinately."[82] Bartel was not without his own concern or, at least, ambivalence about his epicurean tendencies: "Sex, food, even book collecting," he admitted, "all these pleasures gleam with a fine patina of guilt."[83]

The last work he did as a director came about through a personal connection, his association with director-producer Amy Heckerling, in whose *European Vacation* he'd appeared. In 1995, Heckerling had scored a box office hit with *Clueless*, a comic update of Jane Austen's *Emma* set in Beverly Hills, which follows the exploits of high school-

7. About Men and Women   121

aged debs who scheme and angst over boys and fashion. Heckerling had landed a deal with the ABC television network to develop *Clueless* into a weekly sitcom.[84] Bartel wound up directing two episodes for the program during its first season (1996–1997), "We Shall Overpack" and "Cher, Inc." While the shows are outwardly commercial and safe for general audiences, he managed to invest them nonetheless with subversive flourishes. In the "We Shall Overpack" episode, for example, a student's Thigh Master exercise device slips from between her knees and springs across a classroom. Bartel cast himself in this episode as a stuffy substitute teacher who takes orders from the school's principal—*Scenes from the Class Struggle in Beverly Hills*'s Wallace Shawn.

In 1998, new interest in Bartel's "Secret Cinema" films abruptly materialized thanks to the release and popularity of Peter Weir's comedy, *The Truman Show*. The life of Weir's eponymous protagonist, much like the Jane characters in Bartel's works, serves as a source of entertainment for audiences: he lives in an enormous TV studio surrounded by cameras that record his existence. Several critics had noted these resemblances. Todd McCarthy argued, "The similarities are obvious to anyone who has seen them. '[The] Secret Cinema' played the New York Film Festival ... and it was remade by Bartel as an episode of the *Amazing Stories* TV show." The fuss in the press prompted Weir's screenwriter, Andrew Niccol, to issue a statement, saying that "he hadn't heard of 'The Secret Cinema' when he devised the script, and still has not seen it." Bartel was asked for his thoughts, too, and responded graciously to the likenesses between Weir and Niccols's movie and his. "In a sense, their interest in the idea (the idea of exploitative storytelling) validates my own interest."[85]

This renewed attention failed to lead to a new feature directing assignment or funding for any of Bartel's personal projects. He continued to enjoy recognition among industry colleagues as a knowledgeable cinephile, though, and was presented with numerous opportunities to attend international festivals as a panelist or jury member. In September 1999, for instance, he went to Switzerland to chair the jury for the Locarno Film Festival. The festival functioned as an informal New World reunion as Mike Finnell, Joe Dante, Jon Davison, Allan Arkush, Dick Miller, Mary Woronov, Bartel and Roger Corman came to the city for a panel presentation that addressed Corman's incredible impact on American motion picture history.[86]

During the last six months of his life, Bartel sensed that he might be ill—Wendy said that he consulted with a doctor about the health of his liver—but he continued working as he had more-or-less since the sixties, making up new ideas for movies, working on scripts and keeping himself available for acting jobs. Just before Bartel died, in fact, he had been negotiating with financiers. "He had possible money from England here, potential money from Israel there, potential money from Germany. He was trying to get it off the ground. It could have reinvented him. It could have given him another chance to be one of the top directors."[87]

Given Bartel's age when the heart attack killed him—he was only 61—news of his passing startled friends, family and admirers. "He was just amazingly generous and hilariously funny," Bruce Wagner said. "He really had a deadpan hilarity that was soothing. He was really epically funny in just daily conversation.... I was talking to Buck Henry about [Bartel's death].The consensus was that everyone said, 'What a bummer.'"[88] Film critic Jon Bowman, who'd reported on *Lust in the Dust* during its filming, was similarly saddened by the news, though he approached the death with humor: "In an ironic twist he might appreciate were he still among us, Paul Bartel has died ... the same year as the hit-and-run carnage he laid out in his wickedly funny B-movie *Death Race 2000*.... Wherever you are, Paul, rest assured Miss Togar is watching over you."[89]

Services to commemorate Bartel's life and his films were scheduled on both coasts. The first event, hosted by the American Cinematheque, took place in early June at the Egyptian Movie Theater on Hollywood Boulevard. A blurb that ran in *Variety* announced: "Friends and colleagues of the late-director-actor-writer are invited to attend, and an open microphone will be available to anyone who would like to share reminiscences."[90] For those who showed up, Jon Davison and Joe Dante "ran 35mm prints" from Bartel's films and the two episodes he made for *Amazing Stories*, which Davison considered some of "his strongest work."[91] A second event was held at the end of June Lincoln Center in Manhattan, the same place where Bartel had savored watching new movies from Europe decades earlier.[92]

At the time of his death, Bartel was perhaps recognized by general audiences and critics more as an actor than a director. The stuffy persona that Paul projected—hearkening at once to Alfred Hitchcock, Charles Laughton and William F. Buckley—was not so much an extension of his own, but rather another invention, like his films, that he used to send-up the temperaments and beliefs of tyrants, prigs and other conservatives. Paul Sherman in a commemorative essay claimed, "With his trademark bow tie, distinguished air and deep voice, Paul Bartel—the writer, director and character actor—had the outward appearance of a snob who looked down on the less cultured. But in his movies and his movie roles, that was just the sort of person he repeatedly ridiculed."[93] His acting was another instance of his subversiveness, another strike at the figures of power who disdain and too often exert control over people like Bartel himself—writers, musicians, liberals, filmmakers, gay men—who challenge social prejudices.

His readiness to defy social conventions, to "combine black comedy with a keen cultural critique," is another of his signature traits as a director.[94] The best movies—*Private Parts, Death Race 2000, Eating Raoul, Scenes from the Class Struggle in Beverly Hills, Shelf Life*—are those in which he turns his bemused but still angry attention toward the American superstructure, its ideals and its ability at times to mutilate people's personalities: an artist like George in *Private Parts* becomes a murderer under the weight of homophobia; a vicious American government dismembers public servants like Frankenstein in *Death Race 2000*, using them up like the soldiers McNamara and Kissinger sent to Vietnam or the students shot by National Guardsmen at Kent State; the pursuit of happiness is a pursuit of prosperity, turning the ambitious poor into killers (*Eating Raoul*) and the established rich into a venal aristocracy (*Scenes*). Even in his weaker efforts—*Cannonball!, The Longshot*—the effort to improve one's standard of living leads to humiliation and death.

Though he treated such serious material obliquely and with a degree of levity, his movies all the same betray an undeniable dislike for bourgeois American values and its adherents, a tendency that aligns his work thematically, if not stylistically, with the output of more obvious radicals like Kenneth Anger, the Kuchar brothers and John Waters. Bartel would have challenged an allegation of this sort, no doubt, yet with patience and perhaps a joke.

PART TWO:
INTERVIEWS

Joe Dante[1]

Stephen B. Armstrong: You and Paul were friends pretty much from the beginning at New World.
Joe Dante: Even before that.
SA: Tell me—
JD: The first time that I met Paul was at a screening of *Private Parts* in New York. I can't remember why I was there because I didn't know Paul before that. I remember seeing him, though, in the lobby beside the actor in the picture who plays the villain, John Ventantonio. He was seeing the movie for the first time, and he was very concerned about what his mother was going to think, which Paul handled with some aplomb, I thought.

Paul and I got along well enough to start co-writing a script that was called *Love Kill*. This was at his New Jersey beach house. My friend Mike Wakely and I were working on it with him. Actually, it was more a treatment—about a disturbed young woman in a beach house with a bunch of young guys.

Paul was called out to California for whatever reason—I don't know what happened between the New Jersey-period and New World-period. I was living in Philadelphia and working on a trade magazine called *Film Bulletin*, where I was the reviewer. I would only see Paul when I went to New Jersey or New York. Then I think he got called to do *Death Race 2000*.
SA: He had worked on *Big Bad Mama*, right?
JD: He did second unit on *Big Bad Mama*. What was the first thing he did for Corman? I'm trying to think if there was anything before *Big Bad Mama*. I know he was doing the second unit for that and that led to him getting the *Death Race* job. Paul was a good filmmaker.

He did a lot of good second unit work. At that time, second unit work was the key to first unit work. At New World Pictures, Roger would try you out in various capacities, in the editing room, in second units, sometimes re-shoots for some picture that needed another scene. You really got a dose of filmmaking. It was all non-union, so he could hire anybody he wanted. There were no strictures. There was very little money, of course, but we were working on actual feature films. It wasn't film school, although in a certain sense it was, but these were real movies.

When Paul got the *Death Race* job it was a big breakthrough for him. I'm of the opinion that *Private Parts* is the best movie he ever made. I don't know that he agreed with that. I'd seen his shorts. He did "The Secret Cinema" and then he did "Naughty Nurse," which was pretty much an underground classic to see when you could find it. We all had 16mm projectors, and we would get together and run a lot of movies. It was very useful to have a 16mm print of something you had done to be able to show people.

When he got the *Death Race* job he tried to make a satire for a producer who didn't really want a satire. He wanted an action movie, and so there was a certain amount of tension between Roger and Paul. The first time Paul showed it to Roger, Roger thought it didn't have enough violence.

SA: So many of Paul's movies and so many of yours have satirical qualities. What's the appeal of satire, from your point of view?

JD: Some people have said that I make my movies and *Mad*-magazine-parodies of them at the same time. I think probably *Mad* was a pretty major influence on me, and I tended to like the more absurd comedians like Ernie Kovacs and Steve Allen, people like that who would do the material and also comment on it. I never had a style, or I never intended anything when I got a job; I just took it and did stuff out of my head. Paul and I both agreed that the only way that you could distinguish yourself in this particular field was for your movies to have some sort of personality. Naturally the producers would often want to knock all the personality out because it was too weird or esoteric or eccentric, and that would cut into the box office receipts.

So with *Death Race*, for which Paul had a very mordant satirical view of what he was doing, he was eventually let off the picture.

Chuck Griffith, who'd written part of the script, came in and reshot. Lewis Teague directed a bunch of re-shoots, too, which were all sandwiched into the picture. Paul was still around, though, hovering in the editing room. I was doing trailers in a room that was right next to where [Bartel and editor Tina Hirsch] were cutting. I would look at the dailies. I'm in the movie, as a matter of fact.

It was quite apparent that a lot of the jokes that Paul put in were jokes that Roger didn't think were funny. To Roger there was a difference between people laughing at a movie and laughing with a movie. I think he felt that Paul's approach was too arch for the audience that he was aiming at. So there are a number of sections in the movie where scenes are build-ups to punchlines that don't exist because they were removed. This gives the movie a kind a disjointed quality.

However, there's no overcoming the incredible cartoony nature of the movie, particularly if you compare it to the re-make. It is literally a cartoon. When Don Steele comes out with his take on his character [Junior Bruce], it's beyond over-the-top, which I think is how Paul felt that the material needed to be treated in order to be taken seriously. Obviously Roger went along with that to a degree because Don Steele is the most outrageous thing in the movie; he gets all the good lines; he encapsulates the movie at the end. Although compromised, it was still quite an unusual movie—and it was a big hit.

It led to Paul, of course, getting an offer for his next picture, which was another car movie! I don't think Paul felt that he had any particular affinity for cars; it's just that once you make your mark in a particular genre then [industry people] want you to do it again. "Give us another one like that." But that one [*Cannonball!*] was not really done for Roger but for Run Run Shaw and an independent producer named Sam Gelfman. Roger ended up distributing it. It's a much straighter movie than *Death Race 2000*. It preceded all of the star-studded "cannonball road race" movies that followed. Definitely the forerunner of those pictures.

Paul's take on *Cannonball!* as I said was a little more conventional, though there are some outrageous characters in the movie: the character that James Keach plays, the German who looks at all the world as if this is all going to be Germany; the Mary Woronov girls. I met a lot of people in that movie I ended up using in subsequent pictures. Belinda Balaski. Archie Hahn. And Dick Miller, of course, is in it—he actually gives one of his best performances.

But again the movie is a little disjointed. It's probably because there were lots of other car crashes added, and there was a terrible [theme] song. You're serving many masters when you're making this kind of movie, which dilutes your personality. I would not call *Cannonball!* as personal a Paul Bartel movie as the previous two.

It may have been the first picture, because I was in it, in which I was closely associated with the entire making of the picture. I was there on the set. I knew all the people. I went to the dailies. And I persisted in the feeling that there was a better movie in those dailies than actually got on screen

SA: Was the picture cut at all by New World people? I can't remember.

JD: No. The editor was Mort Tubor, who was an old guy, an older editor. I'm not a pro; I'm not a particularly inspired editor. But there were performance choices and the way the picture was cut that failed to get the best out of the material. There were just better things. I don't know if they were settling or if it was that somebody insisted on using this version [of a take] or that or whatever. I don't know. But it's an interesting movie. It's got a lot of interesting characters in it. Judy Canova came out of retirement to be in it. And it did well. It was a pretty successful picture.

SA: What I understand is that Paul was at Schwab's having coffee and Don Simpson came and said he'd been reading about the race in *Time* magazine. Together they worked on the script

JD: I'm sure that's true. Don's in the movie, too.

SA: But Carradine said that Paul hated the project, that he was miserable making another car picture. How could he develop the property and turn around and hate it?

JD: You have to remember that one of the things in Hollywood is that people want to work. They need projects. If Paul has been successful with a car movie and Don Simpson comes to him and says, "Here's an idea for a car race movie that we could probably get made." Paul's not going to say, "I'm the wrong guy for it." Paul's going to say, "Fine." He may in the course of making the movie decide that this isn't really that good a script or it isn't the kind of movie he wants to do or whatever, but once you're in for a penny you're in for a pound. You've got to make the movie. You've got to make the best movie you can out of it. I wouldn't be surprised if he told David at some point that he really didn't like the movie or he hated it while they were making it, but that probably didn't diminish the amount of work he put into it.

SA: How about your memories of *Hollywood Boulevard*?

JD: *Hollywood Boulevard* happened after *Death Race*. Roger wanted us [Dante and Allan Arkush] to do trailers because we were the trailer department that he had never had before. He'd just had to bring in piecemeal editors and try to explain to them how to make the trailers, and it was time-consuming. This way he had these two guys who knew what he wanted and knew how to make the trailers and had already made successful trailers for pictures that made money. To let them just go willy-nilly off and make a movie wasn't going to help his bottom line, so what he basically told us on *Hollywood Boulevard* was: "You can make the movie. Make this the cheapest movie we've ever made. You've got ten days to do it, but you've got to keep the trailers going. You can't stop making trailers." So while we were shooting we were literally also making trailers for whatever pictures were current.

But we had two directors. Our motto was "Two directors, no waiting." I would set up something and start shooting it on one side of the hill, and while I was shooting, Allan would set up his stuff with the different actors. Then I would say, "Cut." He'd call, "Action!" And while he was shooting I would do my thing.

It was shot in late '75 and then released in '76. Believe me, that didn't take a lot of time out of [Paul's] schedule. It was a ten-day movie, and he was probably in five days of it. Allan and I were getting our first shot at directing a movie, and we figured that we knew so little about directing a feature that it would be useful to have other directors on the set. We hired Jonathan Kaplan and Paul to be in the movie so that in case we made mistakes because we were in a hurry, they would be there to say, "No, no, no. Get a close-up, you need a close-up here. Because you can't cut these two things together if you don't get it." Little simple things like that. But they are very useful.

SA: So you and Arkush did *Hollywood Boulevard*, and then there was *Rock 'n' Roll High School*.

JD: There were two projects. One was *Piranha* and one was *Rock 'n'*

Roll High School. I thought *Piranha* was a bad idea because it was several years after *Jaws*, and it just seemed like a *Jaws* rip-off, which it was. *Rock 'n' Roll High School* was much more interesting because it was something that had begun as *Girls' Gym*. We had dictated some stuff into a tape recorder, and later the Writers Guild found out and sued Roger Corman on our behalf. Of course we were still working for him, and so we had to go to him and say, "Don't fire us! We didn't do it!" But he took it pretty well because apparently it happened before. Allan had the chops and the background to do *Rock 'n' Roll High School* because he used to work at Filmore East, and his student film was this rock 'n' roll film. So I inherited the fish.

Rock 'n' Roll High School was made in 1979 right after we shot *Piranha*, which I'm also in. You had to be in these things because it was cheaper. Allan got sick on the last couple of days. I had been doing second unit. I did a scene with Ron Howard that got cut out of the movie with boys looking into the girls' gym. It's the only nudity in the picture, and they cut it out, which was tragic especially if you could see what P. J. Soles looked like in those days. I did my stuff and went home. Then I got a call from Mike Finnell, the producer, the next morning at 5:00 a.m., saying, "Can you come in and direct? Allan is in the hospital." I finished the last two days, two or three, I can't remember. Even though I have a script credit, I never actually read the entire script. I just showed up and started directing. Unfortunately it was the big "Rock 'n' Roll High School"-gym-song-scene with P. J. that Allan had apparently in his head and knew how he wanted to shoot it. Dean Cundey was the DP. I said, "Did Allan give you any notes?" And he said, "Yeah, he gave me these." He had this yellow-lined paper with little X's and O's and arrows that didn't make sense to anybody, so we just figured, "We don't have time to shoot this and choreograph it. Let's just shoot it in pieces." And so we did a *Hard-Day's-Night* sort of thing, where it's just shots that don't have to come together. The girls were very upset that Allan wasn't there. I did a bunch of other stuff, but I can't remember what the scenes were. It worked out fine.

So Paul was Mr. McGree in the movie. He doesn't have a lot of screen time, but he plays the sort of would-be square music teacher who learns to love rock 'n' roll, an AIP-type cliché they wanted to stick in there. The picture came out and proceeded to not do much. The Ramones were not at the time as well-known as they later became. The secret of the charm of the movie is the Ramones. It's not a bad movie in other ways, but without the Ramones, with Cheap Trick or the Clash or whatever they were thinking of getting, it just wouldn't have worked. There's something about the Ramones. They are the people your parents warned you against. That's why the transgression of the movie works so well. And the obsession of the girls about these guys about how gorgeous they are and of course they're not gorgeous and that's why they're gorgeous. And they're hilarious because their lack of personality becomes a personality.

And the music is good. The shooting of that picture was pretty wild, I mean bringing crowds in with the idea of a Ramones concert and then having to shoot the same thing over and over and having them get really raucous, threatening to kill people. It got pretty hairy.

While Allan was sick, I put the first rough cut into shape, and then he came back and finished the movie. It worked out fine for him.

SA: And *Piranha*?

JD: *Piranha* worked out fine for me. It was made in Texas, and I was away from everybody. I was convinced it was the worst movie ever made. I didn't leave the editing room for months because I was so terrified that this was going to be my last movie. People later came to me and said things like "I came to visit you, and you didn't act like you recognized me." And it was because I was literally living in the editing room and trying to figure out "Is it better when the piranhas are eight-frames-long or is it better when they are three-frames-long?" It was a very low-budget movie. It turned out fine. It was a UA co-production, so there was a little bit more money. They distributed it in South America, where it proceeded to make a fortune. And it became one of New World Pictures's most successful movies.

SA: Did you have any points on that, or was that just a job of work?

JD: You don't get points with Roger on those kinds of pictures. You get a salary and a salary is what you got. And you're lucky to get that. All the money goes to Roger. I didn't make any money on a movie until after I'd done *The Howling*. I wasn't in the Directors Guild while I made *The Howling* even though there's *The Howling*

9 and *The Howling 10* and re-issues galore I never see a dime. You have to be in the DGA for that. Nobody ever made any money from those except the studios.

SA: *The Howling* was AVCO?

JD: Yes. But they were still making non-union movies; that's the only way you could make it for a million dollars.

SA: Wow.

JD: Yeah. All those movies from that period that were so popular were all made by people who weren't officially in the Directors Guild, and that included Paul. I'm not sure when he got in. I'm sure he got in because he did an *Amazing Stories*, and you had to be in for that.

SA: I've looked through his papers and haven't found anything yet regarding membership in the Directors Guild.

JD: *Lust in the Dust*. Was that a union picture or not?

SA: I don't know. It was independently financed. *The Longshot* was an Orion production.

JD: Now *Longshot*, probably he would have been in the DGA by then.

SA: *Not for Publication* was independent with Thorn EMI backing.

JD: That could have *not* been [a union picture]. But here's the trick: once you're in, you're in. You can't say, "On this one I'm going to work as if I'm not in the DGA." You can't do that. You have to take a minimum, and there are residuals in them that have to be paid to directors. It adds up. That's why Roger made all those movies [with New World]. When he was working for AIP, AIP had a union deal. The reason he started New World was because he could compete with AIP for the same screens for much less money because his movies were not made union. AIP had gone union in the fifties, so they were stuck with union pictures and DGA directors and all those payments and things. And that's ultimately what killed them because they tried to go beyond their usual kind of movie, and they made pictures that were meatier, which they just didn't know how to make. As a result, the pictures weren't as good as the competition, and they cost way more than they were used to spending. So they went out of business. If [James H.] Nicholson had stayed I think the company would have survived, but when he left it to Sam [Arkoff] it all fell apart.

SA: How do you square that with Roger Corman—he's counting money with left-wing posters on the walls of his office?

JD: That's part of the myth. That's part of Roger's mythos. That's why we love him. He'd have these posters on the wall, and he'd be handing you a little piece of paper that said you were going to be paid $1000 to direct this movie. He never said it out loud. He would just write it down on a little piece of paper. You'd have to unfold it and look at him, and then you'd have to pass it back to him.

SA: Tell me about the shared film collection that you had with Paul.

JD: Jon Davison and I came from New Jersey, where Jon had introduced me to the art of film collecting 16mm films. We actually hired a truck to drive from Philadelphia all the way out here and found a vault on Seward and started putting our films in this vault because you have got to keep [a collection] temperature-controlled. We had quite a few pictures as we came out here. We started accruing more and more, and other collector friends of ours, like Tim Hunter and Miller Drake, people who had films, we all sort of chipped in. And whenever Paul bought a movie or if he had some materials, some outtakes or whatever, we put that stuff in that vault. Paul didn't have that many movies. I don't think he had more than ten or fifteen.

SA: Do you know what they would have been?

JD: I know there're Arrabal movies. *Viva la Muerte.* He had a Kodachrome print of that, which is a movie that I never quite warmed to. I can't remember what his movies were now. Jon might know. There weren't a lot. And he didn't need to because he knew us and we had lots of movies.

SA: What movies did you have?

JD: We had everything, everything we ever wanted to collect. We had the Hollywood movies. We had foreign movies. We had the movies from the thirties, forties and fifties. We had Technicolor, CinemaScope, black & white. We had the best pictures we could find. These were all thrown out by TV stations. You weren't supposed to collect them. In the seventies there was a big scandal back when the newspapers still had really big headlines. "FILM PIRATES JAILED!" They were going to people's houses like Rock Hudson and Roddy McDowall, people who were film collectors and who'd been given the films legitimately by Daryl Zanuck and by Universal and whatever, because that was a part of their deals. Abbott and Costello used to have all their films. But now there was a push against—it wasn't even piracy because there was no internet—the illegal showing and owning of these pictures. So they decided, the MPAA or somebody, decided to get tough on film collectors. This ended up biting them in the ass. Warner Bros. discovered that they needed materials that had been thrown out from *A Star is Born*, the "Born in a Trunk" number, which was missing. Where did it exist? Some collector had it because he took it out of a Dumpster. When Warner Bros. contacted him to try to get to use that footage, they said, "You shouldn't even have that footage because you stole it." He said, "I didn't steal it. I got it out of a Dumpster." And they said, "That's impossible. We never throw anything away." Which is complete bullshit: they were throwing things away by the mile. There were junked prints in every garbage can in town in every studio. Some of them became pictures you couldn't find anywhere else. They ended up having to go back to these same film collectors to get this stuff that they should have been keeping themselves because they were too cheap or stupid.

SA: Arkush has said Corman threw out the extra footage from the Ramones concert in *Rock 'n' Roll High School*.

JD: He would have thrown out anything that was in a warehouse that wasn't being used.

SA: What do you remember about *Eating Raoul*?

JD: *Eating Raoul* was a project that Paul was putting together literally in bits and pieces. I don't know where he got the money. We gave him short ends from *The Howling* to shoot on. I would not say he was making it like *The Other Side of the Wind*, but he was making it in sections and pieces. He would shoot on a weekend. He would get some money together and shoot for a couple of days. Then he'd shut down again. So it was made over a longer period than most movies. I cut a few scenes. I remember Paul had me cut a scene between him and Mary, the scene at the dinner table when they are opening their mail. I thought Mary was really good in the scene, so I cut it around her. When Paul saw the scene, he said, "Thank you," and he didn't ask me to cut any more scenes. He re-cut it so there was more of him.

SA: Like *Limelight* with Keaton and Chaplin.

JD: Paul was a better director than actor. When called upon to play somebody fatuous, he was great. But when he was called upon to play somebody sympathetic, he wasn't quite as sympathetic as he thought he was. That's why I think there are some scenes in *Eating*

Raoul that would be improved if they played more on Mary. But that's just my opinion.

SA: There's a scene with Denny Tedesco and Anne Kimmel when Paul is waiting for the crooked wine buyer (Hamilton Camp). And the waiter—

JD: I'm the waiter, but I'm only seen from the back.

SA: Any recollections of that experience?

JD: Just "Why didn't he shoot me from the front?" is the only thing I can think of. He shot all my stuff with faraway long shots. I remember where we shot it: it was a little restaurant right across from USC that had been closed-down for the afternoon, and we had to get out quick. I haven't seen the movies in years.

SA: How about *Gremlins 2*?

JD: He did a fatuous theater manager for me in a scene where the audience has been led to think the gremlins have broken the film, and it turns out that we're in a movie theater and a woman comes out and is upset that it's such a terrible movie. Paul comes out. He gets Hulk Hogan to yell at the gremlins and make them stop interrupting the film. It took a couple of hours to shoot at the Vogue Theatre out on Hollywood Boulevard. He did it as a favor.

SA: Why do you think he made some really bad movies?

JD: He made the movies that they let him make. We all make the movies they let us make. We don't get to just pick and choose unless we're Spielberg. When you're a working director and you're trying to put projects together, you take what you can get, and you try to make them better. You try to make *Not for Publication* a better, funnier script than it is. If you succeed, great. If you don't succeed, there are a million reasons why. Maybe you don't want this actor, but they want the actor in the movie or else you're not going to make the picture. There is any number of reasons why a movie doesn't work. But anybody going into a project has to say to themselves, "I'm going to make the best"—which we did with Corman's—"the best movie that I can make out of this junk." And that's the only way you can approach it. The people who approach it the other way and say, "This is beneath me. This is crap. I'm just going to walk through it," they never went anywhere. Because that's not how you get anywhere. You have to be as good as your material is, and you have to try to be better than your material and lift it up a little if you can.

Allan Arkush[2]

Stephen B. Armstrong: Let's start with your early experiences at New World Pictures. How did you land a job in the company's trailer department?

Allan Arkush: I went to NYU film school, and I graduated in 1970. The people that I graduated with were Jon Davison, who later on produced *Airplane!* and a bunch of other movies, and Jonathan Kaplan, the director. Those two were instrumental in me getting to New World. Jonathan had gotten a chance to direct a movie called *Night Call Nurses*—that was, I'm going to say, '73-ish. He probably got it through our teacher from NYU, Marty Scorsese, because Marty was doing *Boxcar Bertha* [a Roger Corman production for American International Pictures filmed from late 1971 through early 1972]. Roger was starting New World at the time, and he had come up with the concept of hiring film students to direct movies after working with Coppola and Bogdanovich in the sixties.

Jonathan did *Night Call Nurses*, which was a success, and then he did *The Student Teachers*, which was also a success. While he was doing *Student Teachers*, Jon Davison, who was a huge Roger Corman buff and loved all his movies, came out to work with Jonathan and eventually got a job as Roger's assistant. Then Jon invited out his friend from high school, Joe Dante, who was also a film student. I had met Joe once. When they started working out here [in Los Angeles] I'm going to guess that it was about '74.

Joe was cutting trailers, and they needed somebody else in the editing room—the business at New World was getting so big. I came out because Jonathan said, "If you're out here, a job might show up." Jonathan as a matter of fact had moved on when I got there. He was now doing *Truck Turner* or *The Slams*. But Jon was still working at New World. I lived in Jon's house for a while. And then out at Jonathan's house in the garage on the floor on a foam mattress. We had no money back then. No one had any money.

New World needed someone to help out with Joe and Jon in the trailer department who had a car so that we could drive out to show Roger the trailers [at New World's offices on Sunset Boulevard] and go to the labs and pick up all the lab work—everything that had to be done for making trailers. I would say at some point in spring 1974 that's when I started working in the editing room. The editing room was located in Jack Rabin & Associates [in Hollywood]. You know who Jack Rabin was?

SA: Sort of.

AA: If you look him up, Jack did special effects. He started out as an animator, I believe, for Max Fleischer and then went on to do special effects in movies like *Rocketship X-M*, *The Monolith Monsters*, *Viking Women and the Sea Serpent*. Lots and lots of special effects with varying degrees of quality. Anyway, we were in his editing room, where I was assisting Joe and working with Jon. Basically by default, we were New World's post-production department.

Not long after I came, Roger started distributing Ingmar Bergman [*Cries & Whispers*] *and* making movies like *Caged Heat and* releasing the women in prison movies, the Filipino ones, *and* was about to go into production on *Death Race 2000*. I guess he was in production already on *Big Bad Mama*. There was all this work that had to be done. We realized that a trailer, two TV spots, a one-sheet and a press booklet had to be completed just about every three weeks. This was not a professional, trained staff. All we knew about advertising was that we'd watched it, not much else. We had some knowledge of these movies—Jon and Joe certainly had a lot more than I did—and we were all of a sudden cutting trailers for them. These trailers, you know, were all very broad and irreverent, as suited New World, which was this growing independent film company.

Here was the process for us. The director's cut of whatever movie Roger was making, whether it was *Death Race 2000* or *Cockfighter* or *Big Bad Mama* or any of the Filipino movies, would come in and Roger would screen it. We would go to the screening, too. We would watch the cut, and he'd comment on something he thought maybe should be in the trailer. Then we would take the movie and run it on our Moviola. These were black-and-white workprints with single-track sound. We didn't do any dailies in color. There was no mix, no layering of dialogue, no sound effects. You really had to know what you were looking at. You can't imagine what a New World picture looked like in a black-and-white dupe with one track! We would then run the movies on the Moviola, and we'd take a section that we would choose to duplicate—getting a black-and-white dupe of a black-and-white workprint. Then we would synch those up and have them coded and then start to cut the trailer.

Right around that period, in the fall of '74, New World started production on *Death Race 2000*. When I first got there, Joe was cutting the majority of the trailers. I would assist him. As more pictures had to get made into trailers, I would start doing trailers separately. But we were all in the same room. Joe and I were working side-by-side. Jon would come by almost every day. That was how we came up with ad campaigns. Jon sort of was the one who was in charge, writing catch-lines and so forth. You'd cut a trailer and stand next to it and run it and read off the copy that you had written. If Jon liked it, we would have Roger come by, and we'd read copy while Roger watched the trailer. You had to imagine what it would actually sound like in the end. The posters were pretty much Jon, who would design them with the artists. He would talk to Roger about what Roger wanted, and Roger was very often very specific. "I want all the girls with low-cut tops, with machine guns in their hands, and a 1930s roadster." That was the poster for *Big Bad Mama*.

While all this was happening, we saw the director's cut of *Death Race 2000*. I thought it was really, really funny. It was quite a different movie from what happened to it later. There was much more odd stuff with the Frankenstein character. Sylvester Stallone had a bigger part; he was quipping a lot. Everyone had more comic bits. And it had much less action. During the course of Roger previewing and editing *Death Race* he kept cutting out the humor. He just didn't think that that was important to that picture. He wanted more of a straight-ahead action thing. He had a preview of it that got a lot of laughs, and that bothered him. That's when he really jumped on it and cut a lot of stuff out. It was one of the times that we were all very upset. Especially Paul, but Jon Davison also. We all felt there was a much better movie than the one that came out, funnier, more outlandish. Roger had Paul go back—and Lewis Teague, as well—and shoot more action scenes and more gore, which were added in to the picture. Joe cut the trailer.

It was then we met Paul, in the editing room. Thank God, I should tell you, for Paul's editor, Tina Hirsch. Tina was the professional, and Joe and I were just figuring it all out. She showed us the things that you had to do just to function. We had talent, but we didn't know that the track had to be labeled with red and the picture in black so the projectionist would know in a glance which to do. We didn't know about coding the film so that you could match it up later and keep it in synch. We didn't know much about breaking it down into tracks to mix it. We learned all of that by going from editing room to editing room and getting the film and learning from each editor what they were doing.

SA: Did you know Tina Hirsch when you were in New York, or was that something that came about in Hollywood?

AA: I didn't know Tina in New York. I must have met her at the *Death Race* screening briefly. That's probably how we met. She was great. Sometime around then, she moved into our editing room. You see, Jack Rabin had four rooms. You can't underestimate in the history of New World Pictures the importance of the editing rooms that Jack Rabin rented out. That's where everybody met and where everybody was everyday. Almost all the pictures made by Roger Corman from '73 through '79 were edited in Jack Rabin & Associates's post-production space. Jack did optical work for New World, and he rented out the back [of his facilities] to Roger. If you go down the list of every New World picture from that time, everyone was in those spaces; I mean the vast majority of them. Jonathan Demme was regularly there. Lewis Teague was there all the time. Paul certainly was there. Jon Davison was there because he was in charge of post; he was involved with all the movies and was mostly Roger's right-hand person. David Cronenberg came in there when he had pictures to release [*Rabid*, *The Brood*] and needed something to be done. John Sayles came through there. Teri Schwartz, who became the dean of UCLA film school, and was an AD and a production manager and a producer on the Corman movies, was in and out of there. Tina Hirsch. All the editors. It was a very communal space. We'd all go out to lunch together. That was part of our day. We would have lunch near the CFI lab [on Seward Street in Hollywood] in this little dinette. It's now a pretty fancy Italian restaurant, and the CFI lab we used to go to is gone. But I used to be able to recite the daily specials by heart.

We were together all the time. That's how I got to be friends with Paul. He was a great guy and, as I said, we loved his movie. During that period, I guess I saw the movie Paul did before *Death Race* in a screening room—*Private Parts*—the one where they inject the dolls with the blood. I certainly didn't expect that when I saw it. I knew Paul socially and I knew *Death Race* and thought he was a really funny guy. I hadn't seen that weird, horror aspect of him in anything. Somewhere in there as well I must have met Mary Woronov because she was in *Death Race*.

At the start of *Death Race*, by the way, those are Jack Rabin matte paintings, the futuristic stuff, the one of the stadium. Jack did all the matte work for New World. He built the Hollywood sign and the letter Y that falls over on Mary's character in *Hollywood Boulevard*. He was like a second father to us. He had been in the business all these years. I guess he was in his fifties at the time. We were all in our twenties. The editing rooms were near Santa Monica Boulevard off at Cole. When Jack moved the place from Cole to the Las Palmas-and-Sunset area, we moved with him. He was our guy. He would talk to Roger. Julie Corman would come in and out, too. That's how we functioned. That was the atmosphere. That's how we all got to be friends.

It was like being in a religious order and what you worship is film. I would get up in the morning and pick up Joe and come to the editing room, or we drove directly to the MGM lab. Roger had an account with MGM to do the color work on all his movies. Because he had such a good deal for himself, and such a shitty deal for MGM, we never got the prime time—which would be for people who were paying real money—when we had to go look at answer prints. Roger was doing black-and-white dailies, for Christ's sake, and these small orders of prints or trailers so that he could move them around the country and not spend all his money up front. Roger didn't make 1,500 prints of a movie and release it on a weekend. He would make maybe a hundred and do it territory-by-territory. Anyway, we used to drive back and forth to MGM, and during that time we would write down ideas for movies. Joe and I would just riff on them, and we'd talk to Jon about it. Then we'd go into the editing room, where we'd work all day on Corman movies.

Roger would be offered movies that had gone into bankruptcy or were about to by labs and financiers. As he got to trust us more and more, he would send us to watch these movies. If a name person hadn't created one of these films, we'd watch it, and then we'd tell Roger what we thought, if it was worth his time to watch it or buy it. If it was a known person, even a semi-known person, who created the movie, Roger would watch it himself, and we would go and watch it also. If he liked it he bought it on the spot, and we would borrow the print and start the trailer immediately. That's how the *Amarcord* trailer got to be made over a Labor Day weekend in '74.

SA: All of this sounds crazy.

AA: Un-huh.

SA: So you were buddies then with Joe and Jon and Tina and Paul, and all these people would come together for *Hollywood Boulevard*. Tell me about that film's history.

AA: In 1974, Roger had given us what he claimed was a vacation, but without pay. This happened when there was a little lull in movies coming to the trailer department. Then he re-hired us, so he didn't have to pay us for two or three weeks. In August '75, we saw that he might try the same thing again. Jon figured out that the equipment that Roger owned would be idle during the lull and that we should make a movie with it. He went to Roger and said, "You're not using it. You know there's always a lull in the department. Rather than laying us off, why don't you let us make a movie? We'll make a movie cheaper than any movie you have made." Roger was intrigued.

The idea was that we would use footage from all the other pictures New World had. We knew every inch of it because we'd done the trailers. We'd seen everything, including outtakes, as well as what was left in the pictures, the action scenes. Joe would direct dialogue, and I would do the car crashes and things like that. We would make it as cheaply as possible. We figured out it would take about ten days, with two units going full-time.

The murder-on-the-movie-set plot came in because we had to integrate all the footage. We were talking about it one night, and Danny Opatoshu, who was going to write the film, and Joe thought of some movie called *Murder by Television*, which was a Bela Lugosi picture. We thought a behind-the-scenes story about moviemaking [echoing aspects of the plot used in *Murder by Television*] would give us a way to integrate all the footage. We were basically doing a roman à clef: making a film about making a film, about what we were doing with our friends, and using all our friends as we did it. In a way it paralleled the way the novels and poems of the Beat Generation came into being. Stay with me here. We're not as good as the Beats by any stretch of the imagination, but Kerouac's *On the Road* is a story of him and his friends going on the road, fictionalized, with names changed, but essentially an account of things that really happened. He did the same thing with *Dharma Bums* and *Desolation Angels*: Ginsberg's poetry reading of "Howl" makes it into *Dharma Bums*. We were doing something along the same lines for our first movie!

We worked practically around the clock. Being on the set all the time with Paul and Mary—this bonded everyone even further. Jonathan Kaplan was in it, too. We were all friends and helping each other out. That's the spirit with which *Hollywood Boulevard* was made. There are times when you watch the movie and you get that from it. The places where the picture doesn't succeed are when it's trying too hard to be a real exploitation movie. Like the Candice [Rialson] rape scene. That was a bad idea from the beginning. There are some scenes in that movie that were bad ideas, but there's a lot of it that is fabulous, like the drive-in sequence. And so much of the Philippines stuff is hilarious.

SA: Before you went into shooting, did you know Paul would be the director character [Eric von Leppe] and Mary would be his star?

AA: Yeah. We knew Mary would be Mary McQueen, the villain. That was absolutely set. We also figured out what shots and sequences we needed, and from which movies we were going to use footage. We'd gone through all the movies and had duplicated the action scenes that we were going to use. We then figured out how many shots we would need to shoot to make everything fit—where we would get in to the action footage, where we would get out and which new shots were needed. Joe would do a scene about Paul and his cast arriving at the Philippines. Paul's character would say, "Okay, go out there, and don't get killed." And they'd go out. Joe would do everything up to there. I had looked at the action scenes and saw the guys falling out of trees and explosions, and so I had to shoot shots of the actors in the correct screen direction and eyeline to make sure everything would work together. I knew—I had a list—that I needed four machine guns firing left-to-right. So, whoever was available who wasn't in the scene that Joe was doing would run over to me. I was about 100 yards away, set up in this swamp setting. I'd give them the gun and say, "You fire close left-to-right," and then I'd check it off the list.

 A lot of stuff was created in the editing room. You remember how Mary came running down the hill firing that gun right into the lens? It's sort of an homage to *The Great Train Robbery*. When we started cutting the scene together, we used "Ride of the Valkyries." We went to a library of stock music and bought music for a $100 dollars apiece. We couldn't afford a composer, though Andy Stein did some of the score. We cut sequences to the pieces of music or else laid the music in and edited it to fit better. For instance the music that plays when Mary cuts the wires on the *Death Race*-car. That came from a library of old horror movie music you could buy by the minute. That corny Theremin made everything seem very funny.

SA: Mary and Paul had worked together in *Death Race 2000*, and they had been friends even before they came to Los Angeles, but it was you and Joe and Jon who must have said, "Hey, these two work together on-screen." How did you know they connected like they do? They've always struck me as a sort of low-budget Hepburn and Tracey.

AA: I guess because we would have lunch together, and they were friends. You know I'm involved with *Trailers from Hell* [a website that has film professionals discuss trailers and the films they promote]? I did a commentary for it on *Adam's Rib*, which meant doing some research. Obviously I knew that Garson Kanin and Ruth Gordon had written the movie, and they had written other Cukor movies, but I was really struck by the depth of the friendship of Cukor and them and the fact that they had brunch as a ritual every Sunday at Cukor's house. People talk at these sorts of lunch things, of course, and creative people come up with ideas.

As *Hollywood Boulevard* was gestating, I think, over one of those lunches we had, ideas for our movie were fleshed out and talked about and the thought came up that Mary should play Mary McQueen. "Who's going to play the villain?" "Mary could do it. She's funny." And Mary's sitting there. "Hey, Mary, you want to play the villain?" She just seemed so arch and funny and Cruella Deville–like, and like Natasha in *Rocky and Bullwinkle*. If you're George Cukor and you're having lunch with Garson Kanin and Ruth Gordon and talking about writing a movie about lawyers—and across the table there's Spencer Tracey and Katherine Hepburn—you go, "Hey, you guys would be really great as lawyers and a married couple." Same impulse with us. Except we didn't eat as well. But we did have the ham special every Wednesday.

SA: So you're directing your friends in *Hollywood Boulevard* and would do it again with *Rock 'n' Roll High School, Heartbeeps, Get Crazy*. Why did you go back to them so often?

AA: It only seemed natural. Who else would work for that kind of money? That's the way it was.

SA: So Paul was kind of a go-to actor for you? You maybe would need an effete, fey character at some point, say in *Rock 'n' Roll High School*, and Paul was good for it?

AA: Well, I just I thought of him more as the music teacher [Mr. McGree]. "Hey, Paul! You should be the music teacher. The one who teaches classical music and then gets into rock. The 'Roll over Beethoven' idea." We always thought Mary should be the principal, that was a foregone conclusion. There was never any doubt of that. I've got to say, and Mary will agree with me, her hairdo does about half the acting in that picture. Gigi Williams, who did her hair and makeup, certainly deserves some credit for helping create that character because Mary's not like that. She's funny, but she's Mary. She's not that kind of cruel person. That's not her. Everything that her character believes in, Miss Togar, is the opposite of what Mary believes. By the way, Paul snuck into the *Hollywood Boulevard* preview with a hat on and sunglasses.

SA: The two great Nazi characters of the mid-seventies are the one Shirley Stoler played in *Seven Beauties* and Miss Togar in *Rock 'n' Roll High School*.

AA: I had certainly seen *Seven Beauties* by that point.

SA: Tell me about the scene you and Joe Dante did in *Cannonball!*

AA: So Paul's directing *Cannonball!*, and he says, "Hey, you guys want to be in it?" Just like that. He needed somebody to give David Carradine a replacement car. My dialogue was about the carburetor. We showed up one night out in what I now know to be San Fernando Road, where all the car and junk shops are, to do our scene. We probably hadn't seen Paul all week because he was shooting. We saw him all the time otherwise because at night we would all watch movies at each others' houses. That was part of being in the religious order. Since there were no VHS tapes or DVDs, Jon and Joe kept a vault full of 16mm movies that they shared. We would go and take a movie out of the vault and watch it, sometimes several. We had a whole stack of movies we were working our way through.

I'm sure Paul had got the job to create *Cannonball!* because of *Death Race*. I knew about the actual event that the film story was based on because when I was a young teen I used to read car magazines. There was a race across the country sponsored by *Car and Driver*, an illegal race. The participants had to break the speed limit in places. So that night—it was a Friday, don't ask me how I remember—we headed out and Paul's there. He's shooting stuff, and he says: "Here's David." We meet David Carradine. Paul says, "You guys should go rehearse." "Sure, let's run our lines." We go into David's trailer, and David immediately pulls out this big bag of pot. "You guys want to smoke a joint?" It was—I believe the term is 'Acapulco Gold.' It was a really, really light-colored Acapulco Gold. I had seen some heavy-duty pot working the rock 'n' roll stuff before New World, and so I knew that this was really potent. If I took one puff off this thing I would not remember a line. So David's smoking this, and meanwhile his son, whose name was Free at the time, was running around the room with no clothes on. David was more than a vegetarian. He was on some kind of fruit diet, and he offered us fruit while the son ran around the room naked. He smoked joints, and we ran lines with him, and then we went out there and shot the scene. I have not seen that footage in years.

SA: The big movie in Paul's career was *Eating Raoul*. Jon Davison is in it, in one of the orgy scenes. And Joe Dante plays a waiter. You weren't in *Eating Raoul*, too, were you?

AA: No. I think I was working on *Heartbeeps* at the time.

SA: John Landis and Joe Dante gave him spare footage to use. Did you do anything like that?

AA: No. But I remember going to see Paul's cut of the picture. He screened *Eating Raoul* for all his friends. It was hilarious. I think I probably saw three different versions of it.

SA: Mary in an interview I found said that after the success of *Eating Raoul,* Paul sort of dusted the New World people. He made three films that were okay, with *Not for Publication, Lust in the Dust* and *The Longshot.* For the most part they don't have his New World friends in them. Any thoughts about that? She seemed a little hurt.

AA: I think he was just trying different things. Remember that we didn't have any money. I got paid $85 for directing *Hollywood Boulevard.* I think I got paid total about $3,000 for directing *Rock 'n' Roll High School.* That's like six months of your life for that kind of money, plus whatever salary I would get in the editing room—while I was directing the movie I had to be editing trailers, too. That was subsistence-level, you know? If someone offers you a job, and you've got a chance to do it, to shoot a movie *and* to get a little money, you just do it. The most I ever got paid on a weekly salary for Corman was $400, maybe $450, and that was to write, re-write, re-direct and edit *Deathsport.* I don't know what Paul's decisions were before directing those movies, but it probably seemed like a good thing to do professionally.

SA: You stayed friends with him all the way to 2000 when he died.

AA: I was really hit hard when Jon Davison called and told me Paul had passed away. I happened to be in Washington Square Park at the time. I got the call on my cellphone.

SA: There was a memorial service in Lincoln Center, and there was another one in one of the theaters on Hollywood Boulevard. Did you get to either of those?

AA: Yeah, the *Hollywood Boulevard* one.

SA: Tell me about that.

AA: He was the first of our friends to pass away. The first of our group of people. There was tremendous sadness to it. This was a long time ago. I can't remember many specifics except looking around and seeing everyone I knew in one place. I loved Paul very much. He was very instrumental in helping me, as well as just being a friend and making me laugh out loud. We went to the movies all the time together. We spent a lot of time together. I guess I used him on everything, didn't I? *Heartbeeps. Caddyshack II.* He was in *Fame* [TV series] and also *Snoops* [TV series], which must have been 1999, right before he died. I think I used Mary on *St. Elsewhere* [TV series]. I always hired them because it was fun to show up on the set and have a friend of yours there.

Roger Corman[3]

Stephen B. Armstrong: In the early seventies Paul made *Private Parts* for your brother, Gene, for MGM. The film floundered, and he was out of work. Reputedly he came to you in person to ask for a directing job at New World. Is that true?

Roger Corman: That is true. He directed *Private Parts* for my brother, and then he came to us and talked. My brother recommended him highly, and we went from there.

SA: When he came to your attention, Steve Carver was already working on *Big Bad Mama*?

RC: Yes. Steve was the director of *Big Bad Mama*. We hired Paul to be the production's second unit director.

SA: And you were impressed by his work?

RC: Yes. I thought he did a very good job, and just talking with him and knowing that he had a flair for comedy, I decided to have him direct *Death Race 2000*, which was an important picture for us. The film is about a futuristic science fiction action race from New York to New Los Angeles. It had some black humor in it, and I felt Paul would do very well.

SA: As I understand it, you had a script already written for *Death Race* and gave it to Paul, but Paul wasn't happy with it.

RC: That I don't remember. I believe I had the script completed before Paul came on. We got along well. The only difference between us, and it was a slight difference, was that I felt that the film was to be a satirical comedy, and he wanted to play it a little broader. I don't think he did anything on the script.

SA: I want to say that it was Robert Thom who initially wrote the script, and then Charles Griffith came in and worked on it.

RC: Yes. Bob Thom did the first version. Chuck Griffith did the second version. The script was essentially written by Bob Thom and Chuck Griffith.

SA: So, as production on *Death Race* got underway, Paul understood that it was going to be an action movie with comic elements. But then the story is that tension arose between you two because he was going in a more farcical direction, and you felt the movie should go more into an action-adventure direction.

RC: No. I envisioned it as black comedy. He thought it should be a little bit more of a farce, while I thought of it as a black comedy. There were only a couple discussions. There was no real problem. We got along well, and the picture, of course, was quite successful.

SA: That was the one movie he directed for New World, but he did go on to appear in a number of features for the company. He also directed *Cannonball!*, which was not a New World production, right? But the movie had financial support directed to it from New World and the Shaw Brothers. Can you tell me about that?

RC: I just remember *Cannonball!* vaguely. I know Paul directed it. I think we put money into it and distributed it and had something to do with the production, but it wasn't a fully New World production.

SA: You made a cameo appearance with Don Simpson in that film.

RC: Oh, that's right. I had forgotten.

SA: There is quite a bit of writing out there suggesting that there was conflict between you and Paul over the final cut of *Death Race*, and that Paul was sort of sour on it, although the film did so well. Yet it seems that there probably couldn't have been all them much conflict given how he cast you in the next movie he made.

RC: There was never any real tension. There were different interpretations. But we both agreed on the final cut. I wouldn't say that there was any real tension at all. I was pleased with what he did, and the picture, of course, was quite successful. As you may or may not know, *Death Race 2000* won *Maxim* magazine's poll as the greatest B-picture of all time.

SA: I remember that! Paul acted in some movies that New World made, too. For example, *Eat My Dust!* and *Grand Theft Auto*. He was also in *Hollywood Boulevard*.

RC: He was very good in that picture. He played the director. He didn't direct the film. Joe Dante and Allan Arkush co-directed. The director's name was Eric von Leppe, which was a tribute to my old picture *The Terror*, in which Boris Karloff played a character named Baron von Leppe. Paul was very funny. He was a very good comic actor. The idea was that he was making this outrageous, cheap exploitation picture, but talking about it as if it were a great art film, explaining away the outrageous exploitation scenes in terms of their artistic concepts. He was very, very funny. I thought that was one of his best performances.

SA: He also gave a strong performance in *Rock 'n' Roll High School*.

RC: Yes. He was excellent as the teacher who…. It was so long ago…. I believe he was doing some experiment with animals.

SA: A mouse.

RC: Yes. He was attempting to prove that rock 'n' roll caused animals to become degenerates. Again, he was *very* funny in *Rock 'n' Roll High School*.

SA: And of course his character becomes one of those degenerates himself at the end.

RC: Yes.

SA: Often directors who passed through New World, well, they weren't paid very much, but at the same time they were given this incredible opportunity to make a movie. The expectation, as I understand it, was that sooner or later they'd leave and make movies on their own, which is what happened with Joe Dante, Jonathan Demme, and others you mentored. Paul was ultimately one of these directors. He made his movie and moved on. But it seems that when he got started on *Eating Raoul* he came *back* to you about possibly financing it. Do you remember anything about that?

RC: Yes. I thought it was an interesting idea. I didn't think it was commercial, though, so I didn't finance *Eating Raoul*. He asked me to look at a cut of the film and tell him what I thought, and I gave him a couple of ideas, though I wouldn't overrate what I did. It was a very good picture, very funny. It should have had more success than it did, although it did do reasonably well, as I recall.

SA: After *Eating Raoul*, Paul had an opportunity to move on into more feature projects. He did a movie, *Not for Publication*, which failed commercially and critically. It may have hurt his chances for future work. There is a story that in 1985, when Paul was asked to appear in the *Chopping Mall* movie, he said to Mary Woronov, "Look, we've got to do this for Roger, we've got to do this for Roger." I can't help but wonder if he said this to Mary because he was angling for or at least hoping to secure potential financing from you for a project he had in mind. Would you say that the two of you still had a relationship at that point?

RC: Yes. We worked with Paul on a number of films. He wasn't only in *Chopping Mall*. A year or so later he appeared in *Munchies*. We continued to be on friendly terms.

SA: Did he possibly hope to return to the fold, to maybe direct for Concorde-New Horizons? In the mid-eighties, he was often scrambling for projects. I wonder why he didn't come to work for you later in his career.

RC: He was acting quite a bit. Paul was known as both an actor and as a director. I don't know how many films he acted in. A great many. He was a very successful character actor.

SA: About eighty films or so, and of course numerous television appearances. So, final question, what is your assessment of Paul Bartel as a professional and as a person in general?

RC: He was thoroughly professional. And a very good person. I don't think anybody ever had anything bad to say about Paul. He was well-liked, everywhere, and as a director he got along not only with the actors but the crew. He had a successful career—perhaps a little more as an actor—but he was a very good director, too.

Richard Blackburn[4]

Stephen B. Armstrong: When did you start working in motion pictures?

Richard Blackburn: I went to the UCLA film school same as Paul, and graduated with a BFA. Actually my first semester was Francis Ford Coppola's last semester. From there I moved to New York, where I worked for a film production company before being hired on a magazine in San Francisco as an editor-writer to interview people in film and the entertainment business. In 1972, I directed what eventually became a cult movie called *Lemora: A Child's Tale of the Supernatural*, which Synapse put out a couple of years back on DVD—easily the best version of it in any format. Bob Fern, whom I had met at UCLA—when we were about the only ones doing comedies for our thesis films—and I co-wrote it. It was a horrific shoot. The AD tried to take over as director, my storyboards went out the window the first day, and we doubled our budget. The list of woes just goes on and on. At about the same time, Paul made a movie called *Private Parts*. Although we didn't know each other then, both films have a little girl in jeopardy going through a strange journey. Paul's is much more perverse. Mine is more romantic-gothic.

SA: How did the two of you meet?

RB: We became acquainted after he'd finished *Private Parts*. My girlfriend at the time [actress Mary-Robin Redd] knew him and invited him to a party she gave. He mentioned he was doing a movie called *Death Race 2000* and left the script with us. There was a scene in it with a close-up of, quote, "a bomb disguised as a baby," and I just thought that was so funny. I told Mary-Robin,

"I think I could work with this guy," and she related it to Paul. When he had finished *Death Race*, he wanted to do a movie to be called *Frankencar*. That was his idea—the lead character built into a car after an accident in which his head and torso survived. The rest of his body was to be a car. A modern centaur myth. It was to be this wild film, and he asked me did I want to work on it? I said, "Well, are there any sensitive relationships in it?" "None that I can think of." "Well, fine, let's do it. Just for fun."

That was our first collaboration. That script is still out there. Maybe once or twice a year I will get some inquiry from somebody who wants to do it. It probably never will happen. It's just one of those scripts. People love the concept. Of course by now it would have to be very much re-written. At the same time it seems to fire people's imagination. After we had written it, Paul got word that the Sex Pistols wanted to do a movie called *Who Killed Bambi?*, and we were supposed to do that. But that fell through, as well.

At one point he called me up and said, "You know, Roger Corman is interested in doing a script with Mary and me"—meaning Mary Woronov, whom he had first worked with on film in *Death Race 2000*. And he said, "He wants us to do something. He'd be in interested in financing something." Which I found out later was a total lie. He just wanted to get me to work on something. Because all my scripts were in the weird pile at the studios. I said, "Sure, did you have anything in mind?" He said, "I thought we could be detectives in Florida. What do you think of that?" I said, "Not a great deal." "Why not?" "I don't think anybody cares about *Tony Rome* stuff." "Well, what would you suggest?" I was literally lying in my pullout bed looking up at the ceiling in my garage apartment, and I said, "I think you should be a sexless married couple that murders people for money." There was a big pause, and then he goes, "Let's discuss this further at Schwab's."

The famous coffee shop was still extant on Sunset where Lana Turner was discovered. Paul lived minutes away from me, and about ten minutes later, we got to Schwab's and sat down in a booth and had something—Coca-Cola, a sandwich. And we started talking. He said, "You know, if we do this, and we're going to be a sexless married couple, I think we need somebody for Mary, maybe a Latin lover." I said, "Well, that's okay as long as the guy is a street guy, not some José Villalonga type." "No, that's fine."

"Good, then I know his name, and I know what he does." It was that fast, really. There was a lock-and-key maker in a kiosk on Fairfax near Santa Monica Boulevard called Raul's Key Service, which is still there. I said, "He's a phony locksmith." He said, "That's good."

The initial idea came together incredibly fast, which shows you how well we worked together when we were working well. We got our characters figured out and hammered out ideas. I remember he wanted a dominatrix. He loved the idea. I said, "Okay, then we should have somebody really, really suburban and very, very normal. You know, what you wouldn't expect." "Fine," he said.

I wrote the script in Berlin, at the Berlin Film Festival. Paul would go to many, many film festivals. He made it his business to know lots of people. Anyway, they wanted him on the judges' panel, and he told the festival people, "I need to bring my collaborator. We're working on this script." "Oh, fine, that's fine," they said. "We'll send you both tickets to Berlin." In those days, film festivals had more money. Winter in Berlin was pretty bleak. I was holed up in a hotel room with an electric typewriter, hammering out the script while Paul was swanning around, going to all the screenings, meeting Julie Christie, and so forth.

With the first draft written in Berlin, we came back and tried to interest people in it. *Eating Raoul* was Paul's title. From the start, I know Anne Kimmel, the producer, thought it sounded too much like a porno movie. But Paul and I felt this was the only thing we had to make people want to read it because they'd wonder, "What the hell is this?" We couldn't call it—I don't know—*The World of Swingers*. So we kept that title.

At that time Art Fein, a friend of mine, had a very mid-century 1950s apartment. He'd had it all done up that way. In those days you could do that pretty cheaply, the furnishings, clothes and everything. Not like today where it's a big deal—you can go down to Palm Springs and spend a fortune on that stuff. So when Paul's friend, who was the art director, Bob Schulenberg, came in to take a look at it, he said, "I don't even have to do that much here." The problem, though, was that they were going to raze the apartment building. So we shot twenty minutes' worth—a lot of it was short ends and all kinds of stuff that Paul had cadged from various friends and acquaintances. We got that together with the hope of getting backing, but we didn't get any at all. We did get Buck Henry, though, who said, "I'll be in it."

In the meantime, I had gone over to London and was working on scripts there. One day I got a call from Paul. He said, "What are you doing?" I said, "Well, I just finished this thing. I'm basically free. I'm not working on anything at the moment." He said, "Good. You should come back because I've got the financing. My parents sold their house in New Jersey. They've moved to Florida and given me the money." They said they'd back the film. This was good and bad because when the film became sort of a success, and we talked to people at screenings, a lot of eager film students wanted to know how this low-budget production got on. We had to say it was a parental production. I don't know what would have happened if the parents hadn't sold the home. That was just the reality of it. Anyway, I went back, and we resumed shooting. As I said, they were going to raze the apartment building, so we had to finish there first.

SA: What were you contributions once the production resumed?

RB: I basically was directing Paul. He needed someone to watch his performance, so that he didn't get too big, so that he blended with the rest of the cast. That was one thing—another was rehearsing some of the other actors. We hadn't enough money for the luxury of a long shoot, so we were doing our best to get everything in the can as quickly as possible. We would discuss how scenes would be played and what we should leave in, or maybe there was a prop we discovered—a lot of back and forth. I remember that little squeezable doll. The goo goo doll. I loved that thing. Art Fein had it there in his apartment. I said, "Let's use this." So we had Raoul hit it with a gun at the end and say, "None of this cheap crap."

I also made a contribution to the soundtrack. I had been to a Hollywood rock 'n' roll club called Cathay de Grande and saw a group called Los Lobos. They were just beginning. I told Paul, "Look, we've got to get these guys on the soundtrack." He said, "I don't know anything about rock 'n' roll. I'll leave it to you." So that's how Los Lobos got into the film. And for years after they would introduce "Devil in a Blue Dress" saying "Here's something we sang in the movie *Eating Raoul*."

SA: What about casting?

RB: We tried to get Pee Wee Herman—Paul Reubens—as the guy who works in the sex shop. He was just sort of getting underway, and I think even at that time they might have been talking about *Pee Wee's Big Adventure*, because I got offered that project later. But he felt a little squeamish about being in a low-budget weirdo movie like ours. He passed us on to a fellow Groundling, John Paragon, who was terrific. I remember Paul and I going up to Reubens's place to speak to him. He had all these little toys, and I remember him saying, "I don't want to be a jerk about this, but would you guys like a joint?" Well, Paul hardly ever drank, and as for pot or anything like that, he never did it. The only reason he *would* ever do it was to be part of the process or be friends with somebody—he didn't do it was because he wanted to. So, of course, he goes: "Oh, yes. I'd love one." I'm looking at him like he's out of his mind and said, "I'll pass." So I saw him with this joint, smoking it with Pee Wee Herman. And later on—this may be, to coin a phrase, "not for publication"—I remember him once telling me he took heroin with Mike Nichols. I didn't even ask him if he got a kick out of it. I don't even know if he did get a kick out it. If so, it was probably only because he was taking it with Mike Nichols.

Another casting that was interesting involved Robert Beltran. Now Robert told us he had graduated from the Royal Academy of Dramatic Art. Completely false! Paul had initially promised the part to an actor friend, but when we saw Beltran he looked so much better, so much "righter" for the part. So we decided to go with him even though he was basically an untried actor. When he did his first scene, which is when he comes into the hospital, the both of us were behind the camera, nervous as cats, because we just didn't know. Then he said his first line, and we looked at each other and let out our breaths and knew it was going to be fine. Susan Saiger, I don't remember how we got her. Oh, yes—one of my contributions was to pick up Mary Woronov and get her to the set on time.

SA: What about shooting locations?

RB: We shot all around Hollywood. Knocked off things. A lot of times we didn't have a permit. We just shot it on the sly.

SA: Any script problems?

RB: At one point when we were writing the script we didn't have an ending. At that time, I was going around with a gal who worked for a sort of self-help line for people who were depressed or suicidal.

They could call the line, and she would try to make them happier or not contemplate suicide or whatever. Anyway, she got invited to some party, and she asked me did I want to go to it, and I said, "Sure." It was in an A-frame house in the Hollywood Hills. With a hot tub. Somebody said, "Okay, everybody, strip down, and we'll jump into the hot tub!" I'm like "What?" Everybody strips down and jumps in. So I'm inside the place looking through the sliding glass doors. Nobody left in the house. They're all cavorting in this hot tub. And there are these big heaters on stands, surrounding it. I look at the hot tub, and I'm looking at the heaters, and I go over to the phone and call Paul. I woke him up. I said, "I got the ending."

SA: How did you all support yourselves during the shoot?

RB: I was pretty well-fixed after I came back from working in London, so I could coast a while. I think Paul had some money from his other projects. We could devote ourselves full-time to the film.

SA: After you had the film shot, what happened?

RB: Once we had it shot, Paul was very, very good about seeing if things were working. No matter how funny, if a scene held up the story, he was much better than I at saying "Take this out." I would be falling in love with stuff because I wrote so much of it. I had more of an attachment. He was more objective. In most writing teams you've got the more objective person and the more subjective person. It just sort of falls that way when you have a good partnership.

Anyhow, we'd screen the movie for audiences, cut it, screen it, tighten it again. Then there was the process of trying to sell it and get distribution. So we went to Cannes Film Festival. The strategy was—this was Paul's thing—which was very, very smart—he rented the smallest theater at Cannes to show the film for the first time and did as much publicity as he could. Then because the venue was so small, people had to be turned away. So the news went out the next day that people couldn't get into this crazy American black humor comedy. The next day it went to the second largest theater, and then it went to the third largest theater. Each time, people were turned away. And at that point Richard Roud of the New York Film Festival saw it and nodded at Paul at the end of the screening and said, "You're in." That's how we got into the New York Film Festival.

SA: How were you affected by the movie's critical and commercial success?

RB: It made me hold out, probably unwisely, to do my own projects. I wanted to direct them. As a matter of fact, I was to direct the sequel to *Eating Raoul*, *Bland Ambition*. I also wrote a little piece for *American Film*, something about our fifteen minutes' worth of fame after the movie came out and was making a splash. Anyhow, all kinds of projects popped up. I got an agent. Or rather, I moved up from one agent to another.

SA: Were you involved at all in the script for *Scenes from the Class Struggle in Beverly Hills*? In interviews given around the time *Eating Raoul* was released, Bartel said that *Scenes* would be his next movie.

RB: Paul came to me with the idea first. In many ways he was a producer-director. He thought like a producer. He would get a concept. He would imagine what an audience would like. He would decide on what he thought he could sell and would balance that with his own interests. He came up with *Scenes from the Class Struggle in Beverly Hills*, which is a pretty funny title. But when he told me the story, I said, "I don't think much of this." And he said, "Well, it's the basis for *The Marriage of Figaro*." I said, "It may be the basis for *The Marriage of Figaro*, but I'm not that crazy about it. But I know somebody who would probably like to work with you on it," and I introduced him to Bruce Wagner. Bruce had written some short stories that basically updated Fitzgerald's Pat Hobby stories. They came out in a small limited run paperback, and they were great. He was very involved in the entire power structure of Beverly Hills, the money, that type of thing. I think he was from the wrong side of Beverly Hills, and he knew the social stratas cold. So I put them together, and they did in fact write the movie. But that is as far as my involvement with the film went.

Paul would come up with these insane things as far as I was concerned. Once I remember him saying to me, "Dick, what do you think of this? Divine in *Luxury Liner*." And I was like "Are you kidding?"

SA: How did you get attached as an actor to *Not for Publication*?

RB: First of all, I begged him not to do it. He had written it some years back with his friend Johnny Meyer. It was to be a romp, a throwback screwball comedy thing. Too me it was just too light. It was going backwards from *Eating Raoul*.

This goes to something I'd like to say about the way we worked together, which shows the differences in our approaches. We both liked Alexander Mackendrick's *The Ladykillers*. His thing after that, his touchstone, was the musical *Sweeney Todd*, and mine was *The Honeymoon Killers*. You can see that my viewpoint was much darker than his. Although he had that black humor, that sort of outrageousness, it was more—how can I explain it?—more frothy. If it had been left to me, if I was making *Eating Raoul*, it would probably have been much darker, even despairing. I think the contributions of both of us were good and made the film successful, a good balance.

At one time I said to him, "I think we should go down and check out this whole swinger scene and go to the parties in some of those big apartment complexes." He responded with "I have absolutely no interest in them at all." He just wanted them in the background. That was one of the things about Paul—he would love an idea of something rather than the reality of it. "I think the audience at this time would like elephants to charge through the restaurant," he might say, as an example. And then it would fall to me to try to find the reason for elephants to do that.

So we would have these arguments. I'll tell you an example of that in *Raoul*. That is the scene, the sequence actually, where Paul's on top of Raoul's car. I said, "Paul, it's very obvious where you are. The guy's going out selling clothing and coming back to the car. How's he not going to see you?" "I won't put myself in the same shot, and the audience will accept it." I said, "They might accept it, but unconsciously they'll know it's impossible. Can't we put a camper up there?" "Oh, no, we don't have to go to that trouble."

He came from, in large part, the Roger Corman school, which is very high concept. Get the concept, write the script and get it out there. So it's not detail-oriented. I am hardly the Phil Spector of screenwriters, but a lot of our arguments would result over what's real and what isn't and how can we make it to feel real as opposed to just, oh, the audience will accept it because they would want this to happen. The old "suspension of disbelief."

SA: Can you speak more about *Not for Publication*? It has great moments, but it doesn't have the cohesion or interest that *Eating Raoul* has.

RB: You want me to address why this is so?

SA: Yes.

RB: In *Eating Raoul*, what you had is two people who cared for each other, and then somebody appears who splits them apart. Basically that's the story. Actually, in the follow-up, *Bland Ambition*, that is the very problem with the script. Mary and Paul are *united* against the disruptive character, a little girl who causes them trouble, but she doesn't split them up. I think a great deal of the strength of *Eating Raoul* is having one character who threatens the unity of the hero and the heroine and their perverse affection for one another. *Not for Publication*—it seems written by people who want to return to the style of comic movies of the thirties. Also, it isn't grounded in any real feelings. It's just too airborne.

After *Eating Raoul*, Paul really had a shot, and that's why I was begging him, "Don't, don't do this." But he was in love with it. He thought it was great. He asked if I would be in it. I said, "Sure. I just wish you'd do something else." He had a big ego, which you need to succeed in this business. But it's double-edged because sometimes it gets out of hand, and he got over-in-love with some projects—didn't or couldn't see their flaws. I think also he was wanting to do things that were more gay-themed, you know? Not everything, but the *Luxury Liner*-Divine idea, *Lust in the Dust* and *Scenes from the Class Struggle* were basically gay. In fact, for the opening of *Class Struggle*, Bruce jokingly asked if he could wear a T-shirt saying "NOT GAY," and Paul said only if *he* could wear one saying "NOT JEWISH." Anyway, we were taking different paths and couldn't get back to collaborating.

But we did get back to together for *Bland Ambition*, and that was because the little girl who was in the *Annie* movie was still under contract to the studio, and they needed a project for her before the time of the contract ended. Paul thought that what he could do, smart producer that he was, would be to use her in a sequel to *Eating Raoul*, which was a fine idea.

SA: This was the *Annie* that John Huston did?

RB: Yes. That little girl [Aileen Quinn] being under contract to Columbia Pictures was the genesis for the *Bland Ambition* idea. We knew the characters, of course. I had met John Waters—I put him in it—and later on after Paul's death when people were wondering, "Could this ever be done?" I said, "I don't know. I guess if you cast other people in it." At the same time, they were thinking maybe

Waters would direct it. I said, "I doubt it. He only does his own stuff." I called him. "I'd be in it if you ever get it on," he said, "but it's true, I only direct my own things." So *Bland Ambition* probably is never going to be made. But even if it were, it has that weakness that would need to be corrected in a re-write.

SA: Can you give us a summary of *Bland Ambition*?

RB: It's a political movie, if you can call it that. Paul and Mary have their restaurant. The Governor of California arrives with his entourage to have lunch. The idea comes from a restaurant I know in Newport called the Crab Cooker, where no matter who you are you have to wait in line. So, of course, the Governor says, "You don't understand. I'm the Governor of California." And they tell him, "Sorry, sir, you have to get in line." The Governor and his people become vindictive to Paul and Mary. They try to shut them down, putting the board of health on them after planting dead rats in the kitchen. So then there's this televised thing, and Paul and Mary, or Paul anyway, is tapped to run against the Governor in the primaries. They get a campaign manager who tells them that to look like the All-American family, they need a child. That's where the little girl comes in. She's a little kid from Hell. John Waters is running an orphanage and glad to get rid of her. She makes life miserable for them, blackmails them, everything. That's basically the plot.

SA: What a movie that would be.

RB: It was really fun to write, knowing that Waters would be in it, and putting in characters like this old Republican-type ex-governor who is just completely out of his mind. But then Paul, as you know, put together a musical of *Eating Raoul*. When it was written— leaving aside how good or bad the musical was—my name wasn't anywhere on it. It just said "Based on a film by Paul Bartel." When my agents found out, they said, "Hey, this is wrong. You're the one who was primary writer of the script. You've got to get your name on this." I had to get a lawyer. Paul and I would talk sometimes, but obviously it put a rift between us. I remember him telling me something like: "Federico Fellini, on some musical that was done from one of his movies, just used 'From a film by Federico Fellini.'" I said, "Well, I don't know how they do it in Italy, Paul, but you're disappearing my credit here." Later, I heard that he actually told Mary-Robin that he was wrong in *not* putting my name on it. In the end it was basically a wash because what I was eventually paid after winning this thing, or settling—it never went to court—was just enough to pay the lawyer. Typical story.

SA: Why do you think he did that?

RB: Paul was a person who loved to bestow gifts, but he did not like to be asked for them, even if it was a person's right to ask. In his estimation, I think, he believed this to be a gift I was seeking. I don't know. He just got very stubborn about it. And I think, also, there might have been a legal thing—that I could actually ask for money were my name on it. I said, "I don't want any money. All I want is a credit." At any rate, it was a fairly unhappy thing, because although the musical was put on, I believe, in Berlin, here in L.A., and Off-Broadway, it didn't do very well. I never actually saw it. I was going to, but then I didn't. And I didn't think from what I'd heard, picking up bits and pieces here and there, that it was going to be a success. But my agents told me, "You don't know that. You have to protect yourself."

SA: In the late nineties, *Bland Ambition* almost got made. What happened?

RB: So after I got paid, and I paid off the lawyer, we got back together to re-write *Bland Ambition*. By now it had been I don't know how many years. We re-wrote the script, things were getting ready, the money was nearly in place. And then…. I guess you know the story. Paul had to have an operation, after which the doctors told him, "Take it easy." And never able to deny himself, he went right off to a film festival. It put a strain on him, and he passed away. And so that was that.

SA: What are your thoughts about Bartel as a professional?

RB: As a professional thing he loved to schmooze. He loved being with people in the industry, talking to them, just the opposite of me. I can remember one time we were going to be hired to write a script based on a book, *Krippendorf's Tribe*. This was in the eighties when it was very fashionable to wear braces, or suspenders, and he and the producer were both wearing them. They talked for about twenty minutes about their suspenders. My eyes were rolling around. He was just that way. He could make small talk effortlessly with anybody in the industry whether he liked them or not. He was very good at that. And as I mentioned before, he was a real mix of self-indulgence and discipline. He always kept a very positive attitude, and his sense of wicked humor, wit and fun went into his best ideas. Also he loved movies—both seeing them and making them.

On a personal level, he was incredibly good company. Very funny. He was extremely generous—if he wasn't asked. That's another funny thing. He gave me an extra percentage point on *Raoul*, telling me, "Well, you did a lot in this movie."

Inside he was a terribly clever and gleefully naughty little boy, and when I think of him that's what I find the most endearing. He supposedly said during his final hours that he had lived a wonderful life and regretted nothing. I believe him.

John Waters[5]

Stephen B. Armstrong: To what extent did you know Paul Bartel? In interviews he called you a friend.

John Waters: Yes, we were friends. We were business friends. You know what I mean? I saw Paul. I knew his films way before I knew him. "Secret Cinema" and *Private Parts*. I had seen them in Baltimore at the Howard Theater and all the exploitation theaters downtown. I'd hook school and go see them. No, that was after school, really. I followed his career. I can't remember how I met him. It might be through—you know, I don't remember how I met him. Was it at a film festival? I knew Mary Woronov a little, too. I was just a fan of his movies. He knew about mine, too. When was Paul born?

SA: 1938.

JW: Oh, he was older than me. He was almost ten years older than me. Eight years older. I guess we both knew each other because we were both film directors, and we had similar tastes in some ways.

SA: Where do you think his movies fit in—independent, gay, comedy, exploitation? Where do you place him?

JW: Certainly the audience that made *Death Race 2000* and *Cannonball!* hits didn't especially think of them as gay movies. I don't think the audience was predominantly gay at all. I think the audience was there for real exploitation movies. They didn't think the films were campy. They didn't like them for ironic reasons. They reacted because they were good action movies. That's how his hits were. His exploitation hits also got good reviews. He was one of the few who made exploitation movies that were well-reviewed.

He was one of the first who did that. He was thought of as an art director and as an exploitation director, but not so much as a gay director, at least he didn't limit himself to that.

SA: But there are gay elements that he dropped into some of the movies. *Scenes from the Class Struggle in Beverly Hills* climaxes with Robert Beltran and Ray Sharkey's characters actually having a sexual experience. In *Private Parts* there's a man who presents himself as a street preacher, and he keeps pictures of beefcake weightlifters on his walls.

JW: You have to remember by that time in 1972, the Warhol films were out. Porno had just become legal. The underground cinema. All that stuff had already happened. And that was a big influence on him, certainly. He took just like I did from every genre and used it *commercially*. I think Paul was a commercial film director. And I don't know mean that in a negative way at all.

SA: But he did make something of a transition in his approach to directing. He had those underground, independent films in the sixties. "The Secret Cinema"—

JW: I don't think the *Corman* movies were underground movies. They were exploitation movies. They were made to make money. And they didn't open in one little art theater: they played widely.

SA: He had a movie named "Naughty Nurse," and actually Grove Press was behind it.

JW: Yes, and I understand that. Grove Press, of course, released *The Queen* and *I Am Curious (Yellow)* later and everything. I think Paul Morrissey, I think myself, I think Paul—we were all influenced by the sexploitation hit movies and everything of the time. And the fight for freedom. And all the censorship barriers that were coming down. The horror stuff. And we satirized that in a way. But Paul went a little further. He made films that worked totally within their genres, especially in the beginning, and he certainly acted in movies like that for his whole career. The Paul Bartel that will be remembered the most, I think, will be the director that made the art hits, like *Scenes from the Class Struggle Beverly Hills* and the movies with Mary Woronov. That's when he got really praised as an art director. I think those are the films he would have been most proud of.

SA: That tendency of his to have the bad taste element but with a certain skill and depth of theme, that to me somewhat resembles your work.

JW: I've always said I made exploitation films for art theaters. He made exploitation films for exploitation theaters. And then he made art films for art theaters. There was some crossover, but I think that the movies that were obvious Paul Bartel movies were the ones that he liked the best. He also made a lot of movies that you maybe wouldn't have instantly recognized were his. Like *Cannonball!* Would you have instantly known that one was his?

SA: No. Parts maybe within it. Little jokey sequences.

JW: Yes. But you know what I mean. And it was a hit, too.

SA: Let's then go to *Lust in the Dust*. He was not interested in having Edith Massey appear in it.

JW: Which broke her heart, but I get why. I mean here's the thing. Tab and Divine and I had just made *Polyester*. Tab loved making the movie with us. He was rediscovered in a whole different hip world. He got along with Divine great. And he had always wanted to make this movie called *Lust in the Dust*. I don't direct movies I didn't write, and nobody will ever believe me when I say that. But I really don't. I never have and I never will. I wouldn't know how to do it, really. So I kept telling Tab, "Well, you should direct it. It's your movie. You thought this movie up. It's your baby. And you want to do it." He was really sort of Heartbroken that I didn't want to do it. But I really didn't want to do it. I had just made a movie with Tab and Divine, so it seemed like the newness of that was not quite as fresh as it was. I had just done that. I wanted to do something different, but I thought that Paul was a good choice to do it. I'm not sure that Tab\ and Paul ever quite decided who really the director was. But as I said, I can see why Paul didn't want to make the movie with all the same cast because then it was like him making a John Waters movie. The same way I didn't use Mary Woronov at the time. We each had our own stock group of people. Tab and Divine had been so publicized. *Polyester* had just come out. We had Odorama, and the movie was a hit. For Paul to do *Lust in the Dust* exactly with the same cast, I think he wanted to make it different. Correctly. I think. And I don't know what the experience was like making the movie. It still seems as though *Lust in the Dust* was Tab's movie.

SA: It does have some themes, though, some motifs that you can trace through the earlier movies: costumes, transvestitism, performance.

JW: Of course, Paul would put his touch on it. He was way too good of a director not to. Did he and Tab get along?

SA: When you read the articles from the set it seems like there was tension. When I talked to Tab a couple months ago, he said, "Oh, you know, there were some arguments about ways to handle a shot, a sequence, but all in all we got along fairly well."

JW: Well, I believe that. What movie doesn't have tension? I never made one that didn't. Especially a low-budget movie and especially a movie where Divine had to do physical stunts and was very, very heavy at the time. Not in good shape. But Divine loved making that movie. He had a great time. I think the movie went well, and it certainly got a lot of attention, too.

SA: It's had a long shelf life. One of these campy movies that people go back to and enjoy. Sometimes it's compared to *Rocky Horror*.

JW: They mistakenly put it on my filmography a lot. People have said to me, "Oh, I like this movie of yours. I like this one. I like *Lust in the Dust*." And I say, "Well, I didn't make *Lust in the Dust*." They just get them confused because of the cast.

SA: Divine saw *Lust in the Dust* as his first mainstream movie. It had a modest budget, but he had his own trailer.

JW: He had a trailer in *Hairspray*, I think. I think he thought *Lust in the Dust* was his first starring movie away from me, which was good for his career. Face it, it was hard for Divine to get roles: he wanted to play men, too, and everything. The day after he died he was supposed to start on *Married with Children* playing a male, gay uncle, which would have been very controversial at the time, but I bet it would have been a hit. And it would have changed his career forever. I was always for him to make the other movies. He didn't want to be only in my movies because he was a working actor. He was thrilled to make *Lust in the Dust*, to go on location and shoot it. I think he's very good in the movie. I think everybody is. And I would think Paul and Divine got along very well. I never heard that they didn't.

SA: Paul's best known movie may be *Eating Raoul*, the one with Mary Woronov. He and his co-writer Dick Blackburn were planning a sequel called *Bland Ambition*. On a couple of occasions Paul mentioned that you were going to be cast in the film as a sinister orphanage director.

JW: I vaguely remember something about that. But I don't think I ever even got a script or anything. I would've.

SA: At that point you weren't acting. You weren't appearing in other people's movies.

JW: Well, I was in *Hairspray*, my own movie. But I would have done it probably. Yes, because I was such a fan of Paul's movies. And I'm a huge fan of Mary Woronov. I think she is a great actress. I loved her in the Warhol movies. I think she is an amazing writer. I'm still a big fan of Mary Woronov. She and Paul had a great run together.

PART THREE: FILM AND TELEVISION WORK

An Excrescence of Style: Paul Bartel and the Grotesque

Throughout his career as a director, Paul Bartel regularly alluded to the films of Alfred Hitchcock, replicating shots first used by the Master of Suspense, as well as lighting schemes, character types, visual and aural tropes and so forth. The inclusion of referential material allowed him at once to display his admiration and to signal through his reworking of the older director's ideas what Noel Carroll describes as "the personal stamp of the new auteur." As Bartel revised Hitchcock, he interpreted Hitchcock, and through this "privileged hermeneutic filter" he invested his work with his own thematic and stylistic markers.[1] A good example of this allusionist tendency occurs in the "Gershwin's Trunk" episode Bartel directed for the *Amazing Stories* TV series. John Meyer—who co-wrote the episode's script and composed the program's score—can be seen leading an orchestra in a Broadway theatre: Bernard Hermann, Hitchcock's frequent composer, conducts an orchestra in the 1956 version of *The Man who Knew Too Much*.

Bartel visited several of Hitchcock's signature themes, too. The duplicity of political loyalties that crops up in *North by Northwest* and *Torn Curtain* seeps through *Death Race 2000*, with the patriotic driver Frankenstein who overthrows the American government. Female characters like those in *Notorious*, *Marnie* and *Frenzy*, who experience tough, even violent, treatment from men because they have strong personalities, similarly materialize in *Private Parts*, *Cannonball!* and *Lust in the Dust*.

Bartel often exploited voyeurism in his films, too, an activity that

Peter Wollen argues "dominates [Hitchcock's] films, both in the narration and in the narrative, in his style as director and in the relations between the dramatis personae."[2] For Hitchcock and Bartel, the act of looking serves as an expression of power and as a source of pleasure. It is also risky. In Hitchcock's *Rear Window*, the professional photographer, Jeff, eases his boredom by peering through an apartment window at neighbors, sometimes using just his eyes, sometimes with the aid of his camera; after he witnesses what he thinks is a man named Torvald's efforts to discard the body of his murdered wife, his fascination quickly gives over to fear as he finds himself on the receiving end of Torvald's malice. In *Private Parts*, the amateur fashion photographer George satisfies his desire for control by murdering models during photo shoots. George enjoys watching women bathe through a hole he's cut into a wall, as well, an interest he shares with *Psycho*'s Norman Bates, who, like George, is transgender.

While voyeurism functions as "a dramatic element" in the fictional worlds the two directors create, it also provides them with the opportunity to inculpate viewers, to emphasize how watching movies is a scopophilic act as it allows us to peer into "a hermetically sealed world which unwinds magically, indifferent to the presence of the audience, producing for them a sense of separation and playing on their voyeuristic fantasy."[3] The photographers Jeff and George frame their gazes and compose their fantasies through lenses not unlike movie directors as they work with actors on sets. In these characters we find, perhaps, onscreen projections of the directors' worries and desires. Jeff in *Rear Window* may have a deeply flawed ethos, yet with his camera he not only discovers Torvald's guilt but thwarts the killer, using a flash to blind him and drive him over a balcony to his death. The actions and compulsions of the voyeur-auteur in this instance ultimately serve the greater good. The men with cameras in Bartel's movies, in contrast, are either doltish—Barry in *Not for Publication*—or dangerous—George in *Private Parts* and the director in "The Secret Cinema," who manipulates the unknowing Jane for the movie serial he is making.

Bartel's allusions to Hitchcock's treatments of voyeurism may be most apparent—and frequent—in *Private Parts*. The film's opening credits begin with the same burst of light that the flashbulb emits from Jeff's camera in *Rear Window* as he defeats Thorwald. As the credits sequence progresses, a series of images appears that include a kitchen knife held aloft by a hand—a not too subtle reference to the first murder scene in *Psycho* when Norman stabs to death Marion Crane in the shower. Bartel proceeds to offer his own distinctive depictions of voyeurism the moment the credits end. In the movie's first shot, the female protagonist, Cheryl, parts a curtain in a beach apartment doorway and leers into a narrow bedroom where her roommate is having sex with a man. An underage teen and, likely, a virgin, Cheryl giggles at the lovers, revealing herself to them. A fight follows, prompting her decision to move out of the apartment and seek lodging at her Aunt Martha's decrepit hotel in downtown Los Angeles. This castle-like setting where Bartel places his soon-to-be-endangered heroine is thick with both shadows and weirdos, not unlike the cloistered, gothic settings in Hitchcock's *Jamaica Inn*, *Rebecca* and, again, *Psycho*.

The hotel's most distressed resident, Aunt Martha's son, George, experiences an immediate attraction to his cousin Cheryl when he first sees her. She in turn quickly learns that George is a lot like her—he enjoys watching intercourse, which she discovers after following him into a city park at night, where he photographs a couple having sex. Intrigued rather than revolted, Cheryl subsequently encourages his advances, and finds it amusing when George lets himself into her room and lays out an outfit he'd like to her to wear, a black negligee with a mask that lacks eyeholes, accompanied by a note that reads: "You would drive me crazy if you'd let me see you with these things on you."

Bartel continues to knead grotesqueries and allusions into *Private Parts* as the film proceeds, further exploring the links between voyeurism and film direction. In Hitchcock's *Vertigo*, the neurotic lead, Scottie, similarly selects clothing for a woman, Judy, to wear in order to fulfill a personal fantasy. But unlike Judy, who experiences anxiety and guilt under her suitor's gaze, Cheryl delights in George's efforts. She puts on the skimpy costume he's given her and moves into a bathroom, where she undresses before a two-way mirror that she rightly senses conceals his hungry eyes. As he stares at her, she places the mask over her eyes and takes a step toward the bath, an unseeing, but hardly unaware, exhibitionist.

The allusion here to the first part of the shower sequence in *Psycho* is unmistakable, the difference being that here the bathing female is a co-participant, a sharer in the transgressive fantasy, not an imminent victim. Cheryl deliberately engages her voyeur, performing an erotic dance in which she drapes her nakedness with soapy bubbles, turning her obscured face repeatedly to the mirror—which glints with light as a camera lens sometimes will. The scene then takes a more overtly theatrical aspect as Cheryl stands up and sweeps a shower curtain horizontally along the tub—a visual echo of the curtain she peered through in the picture's opening shot—bringing an end to the act.

Cheryl's willingness to take direction from George, however, is not limitless. After sneaking into *his* room (which doubles as a studio) fairly late in the movie, again wearing the lacy black outfit he's given her, she adopts at first the role of the ingénue when he finds her, even inviting his guidance as he aims his camera at her. "How should I pose? What's the best way?" She kneels on his bed. He stands over her. "I don't know what the idea of this costume is, but I'm glad you're getting a kick out of it," she says. The pair's proximity is greater than in the bathroom scene, but George, presented here with the opportunity to explicitly direct Cheryl, cannot draw a good performance from her. She is clumsy, awkward, while before she preened in a manner that was both sensual and confident. Her artistry as a performer has been checked, rather than enhanced, by George's attentive direction. When his insanity seconds later envelopes him and he strives to exert control, grabbing a poison-filled syringe that he believes will help Cheryl pose in ways that will meet his standards, she understandably rebels and pulls a heavy light stand onto him, cracking open his skull.

The process of creating art with a camera undoes George. He has tried too hard to elicit a convincing performance from his star. His aesthetics surpass the bounds of the acceptable, and in this sense, he belongs to the same doomed group of artists comprised of Victor Frankenstein, Humbert Humbert and Walter Paisley, the killer in Roger Corman's *A Bucket of Blood*, who turns his victims into hep artworks. George never seeks to share his work with an audience, though, keeping it locked up in his strange room to be seen by no one but the models he brings up to kill. Whereas Cheryl has delighted in the attention exhibitionism yields, the secretive George prefers to stick to himself in the shadows of city streets or in the blinding brightness of his studio lights. He conceals himself as a matter of course in all areas of his life, even obscuring his gender under layers of masculine clothing.

The degree to which George experiences estrangement may be the condition that links him most closely with *Psycho*'s Norman, just as it differentiates him most evidently from *Rear Window*'s Jeff. For Jeff, the camera is a source of power that partly delivers him from the confinement of his wheelchair and saves him from a killer's attack.

George, in contrast, is killed by his photographic equipment. Moreover, George's camera plays a critical part in his ritualistic killings of women, the lure that brings them in to his studio. Voyeurism, photography and film direction may have overlapping qualities, Bartel infers, but not in the ultimately acceptable manner Hitchcock renders. For him, voyeurism is a symptom of a sick personality. Is film direction, perhaps, as well?

A similar ambivalence about the resemblances between the act of looking and the direction of acting marks *Eating Raoul*. In this film, Paul Bland on several occasions watches costumed swingers act out fantasies in scenarios he's concocted with his wife, Mary. Disgusted by these individuals' lasciviousness and the ludicrous qualities of their acting—he waits for that moment during each performance when he can seize upon them with his iron skillet—and thump the player rather than call "Cut!" For him, sex-related behavior delivers no pleasure, and directing is an unbearable annoyance. The situation is all the more ironic, even grotesque, as Bartel plays the role of Paul himself.

John Meyer sensed in Bartel's first treatment of film direction as a theme, "The Secret Cinema," a correspondence between the story's director-antagonist and the darker parts of Bartel's personality: "Notwithstanding Paul's soft-spoken manner, and his impeccable politesse, there roiled beneath his placid surface a swamp of resentment and hostility, directed primarily, I think, at his mother; for what reason I have no idea, but his antipathy toward women is readily apparent, from his very first short feature, 'The Secret Cinema,' in which the innocent heroine is betrayed and traduced by all her friends, lovers and even her mother, as they repeatedly humiliate her by placing her in degrading situations. This is presented to us, the audience, as a huge joke: all her associates are in on this prank—each degradation is being secretly filmed. What does this say about Paul?"[4]

The destruction and re-formation of the personality might be Bartel's quintessential theme, showing up not only in the projects he finished but also the ones that eluded completion. Following the commercial success of *Death Race 2000* in 1975, he and Dick Blackburn drafted a script for a film they hoped to make titled *Frankencar*. Their story focused on a racecar driver named Todd whose body is nearly destroyed in a wreck, which a rival driver has purposefully caused. Todd's neurosurgeon father manages to combine what's left of his son with the body of a performance automobile, allowing the hero to regain his ability to move, to think and to feel. As a result of this "recovery," the young man finds himself in a liminal predicament: neither dead nor alive, not man or machine, but something in-between.

The Todd character is just one of many created (or co-created) by Bartel who experiences confusion, social estrangement and anger because his body is sick, damaged or conspicuously different from others.' Gags built around people's size proliferate in his films. In *Eating Raoul*, one of the Blands' swinger clients, a dwarf, shows up at their apartment with a Great Dane. In *Not for Publication*, Odo, a little person, drives about New York City in a vintage convertible that tows an enormous milk wagon. In *Lust in the Dust*, the prostitute Rosie (played by an obese Divine) breaks a dwarf's neck with her enormous thighs.

Although Bartel was willing to squeeze laughs out of his actors' not always lovely features—including his own—he would target them for deeper thematic ends, too. Through much of *Not for Publication* Odo tries to draw Louise's favor—the irony seemingly lost on him that the beautiful reporter is only interested in men with conventional good looks. "You know dwarf love is the strongest of all," he says. "We never let go. Only death can douse a dwarf." Before the end of the movie, though, Odo discloses that he indeed understands that his chances with the beautiful Louise are nil because he is ugly. Beset as he is by regret and self-hatred—and devotion—he brings to mind Quasimodo, Esmeralda's self-sacrificing servant who can never be her lover.

A similar admixture of loyalty and sweetness between male and female characters materialize amidst the crime and perversion of *Eating Raoul*, where, again, sharp contrasts in physical appearance factor into the presentation. Gorgeous and thin Mary participates in the murder of Raoul because, in the end, she loves Paul; her spouse may be a chubby, plain, fussy, boring guy, but his friendship and their shared ambitions matter more to her finally than Raoul's muscular beauty. Likewise in *Scenes from the Class Struggle in Beverly Hills*—where racial differences often displace disparities in looks—Juan lies to Frank about having had sex with Lisabeth, and consents to sleep with Frank to honor the terms of their bet, because he doesn't want to degrade the closeness he feels has developed between him and his employer. Importantly, the Mary and Juan characters each set for themselves goals that initially appeal to their personal desires—for Mary, sex with Raoul; for Juan, a chance to pay off loan sharks. But as they pursue and achieve these objectives, their personalities undergo profound changes, and by the end of their stories, the fancies that initially meant so much to them

An Excrescence of Style

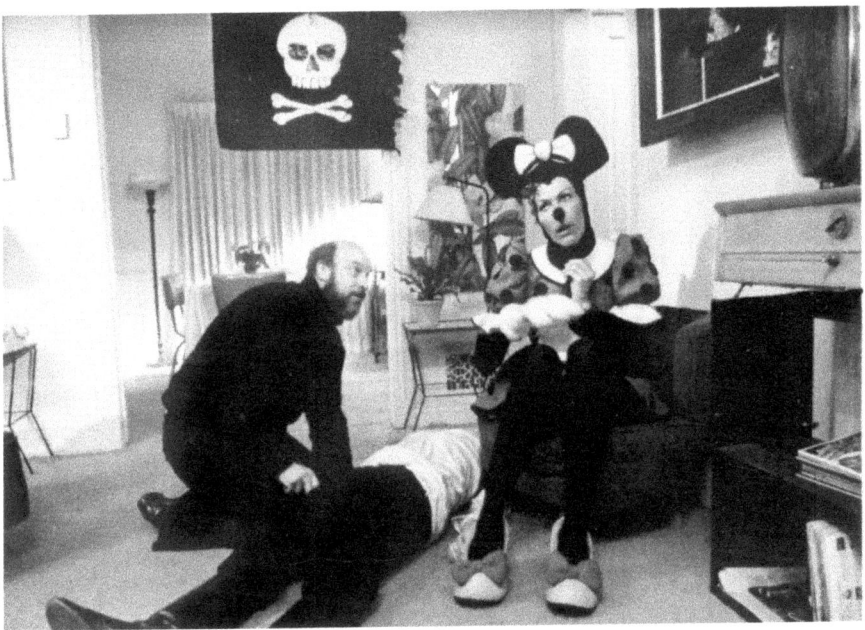

The affable Paul (Bartel) and Mary Bland (Mary Woronov) at work in *Eating Raoul* (Bartel Film, 1982).

appall their moral codes. An analogous scenario presents itself for Cheryl in *Private Parts*. In the film's opening moments, this eccentric character peers into a bedroom and giggles at the sight of her roommate having sex with a boyfriend. When she moves into her prudish (and startlingly plain) Aunt Martha's hotel, Cheryl finds new opportunities to explore sexual behavior. The young and beautiful woman enjoys encouraging and indulging her cousin George's voyeuristic, incestuous impulses, even allowing him to watch her bathe. But George's violent behavior prompts a psychic change in her. Her appetite for sex culture vanishes. And in the film's final shot, having adopted her aunt's prudish convictions, she tells a group of cops gathered in the lobby, whom she misperceives as potential guests: "This is one of the last respectable hotels in the city, you know, and we have to be extremely selective about or clientele."

Such incongruous developments in Bartel's narratives, along with the distorted conditions of his characters' personalities and bodies, exemplify the *grotesque*, used here in the sense of an aesthetic construction that thwarts what Justin Edwards and Rune Graulund call "the conventional oppositions of refined/foul, high/low, or culture/savagery." Bartel, that is, often employs a representational strategy that demonstrates "how the boundaries between the 'normal' and 'abnormal' are fluid, not fixed."[5] The heroes in *Death Race 2000* and *Frankencar* are both men and machines; the adult occupants in the fallout shelter in *Shelf Life* think and behave like children; the vivacious Marguerita performs a dance number with a corpse in *Lust in the Dust*. Bartel was in fact cognizant of this tendency in his work to upset oppositions and sought it actively. To Michael Singer, for example, he explained that for *Eating Raoul*: "There's a synthesis of a genteel approach and raunchy and outrageous material, which was the basic concept of the movie."[6]

The grotesque in Bartel's cinema permeates everything, not unlike the incorporeal nausea Sartre describes in his famous novel. The grotesque is not so much a product of the actions and decisions of his onscreen characters, as it is a defining condition of their existence, a prime mover, always already present. Its expressions can be comically surreal: at the end of *Cannonball!*, the clients who've hired the driver Beutell (Stanley Clay) to transport their car across country calmly climb into the vehicle, despite its nearly destroyed condition, when Beutell picks them up on a New York City street corner. Or perverse: at the end of the same film, Coy comes to the hospital to visit his girlfriend, Linda (Veronica Hamel), and finds her and her extraordinary beauty completely concealed in a body-cast. Or bitter: Jane's mother in both "Secret Cinema" treatments draws more pleasure watching her daughter suffer in the movies that have been made about her than spending actual time with her. Or goofy: the grafter who swindles the four bettors in *The Longshot* walks awkwardly because he wears two left shoes.

Bartel's exploitation of the grotesque imbues the films with a discordant quality that some contemporary critics responded to favorably. It impressed contemporary critics at times. Joe Baltake, for example, detected the grotesque particularly in Bartel's work from the seventies: "Part of what made Bartel's earlier works so charming and palatable, in spite of their raggedness, was the man's innate urbanity. He brought an undeniable sophistication to schlock. He made films that one could watch while eating popcorn and drinking champagne—an unlikely combination that's great."[7] Others, especially Roger Ebert, despised this inclination to forge together raunchy humor and social satire. Ebert was unable to appreciate how the world Bartel presents in his pictures has, like his characters, been disfigured—by technology ("The Secret Cinema," *Death Race 2000*, *Shelf Life*), capitalism (*Eating Raoul*), politicians (*Not for Publication*) and morality (*Private Parts*)—and any attempt to render this world in a manner that isn't abrupt, outlandish or irrational would be unsuitable for his thematic objectives.

Critics faulted Bartel on several occasions as well for lacking a distinctive visual style. Often obliged as he was to shoot fast with minuscule budgets, the time needed to introduce technical flourishes was not available to him. Aside from the occasional allusions to other directors' shooting and lighting choices, his camerawork is indeed generally unremarkable. But when we look at what he shot with the camera rather than how he shot it, we find a fecundity of unsettling events, things and ideas: bizarre performances, expressionist sets and grotesque objets d'art like the goo goo doll in the Blands' apartment or the photographs of freaks that adorn the walls of Troppogrosso's office in *Not for Publication*.

Actually, this tendency to pack the screen with grotesqueries may be the hallmark of Bartel's visual style. Through his persistent insertion of the monstrous and the weird into his mise en scene—from injury and amputation (*Death Race 2000*) and SM (*Private Parts*) to cannibalism (*Eating Raoul*) and madness (*Shelf Life*)—he shapes and comments in expressive fashion upon the damaged psyches of his characters. The content of the film frame for Bartel, in short, matters more than the mobility and manipulation of the camera.

Directing Credits

Film

"The Secret Cinema." 1966. Production: Hacienda-Tropicana-Madness. Distribution: Film-Makers' Cooperative. Producers: Paul Bartel, Robert Schulenberg. Script: Paul Bartel. Photography: Fred Wellington. Editing: Sam Moore. Music: Dick Heller, Sam Pottle. Cast: Amy Vane, Gordon Felio, Connie Ellison, Philip Carlson, Barry Dennen, Mimi Randolph, Estelle Omens.

Summary: A malicious movie director draws upon the techniques and conventions of cinéma vérité and screwball comedy as he films the life of a young woman without her knowledge. Her adventures are screened for a secretive movie club that meets in an old grocery store.

"Naughty Nurse." 1969. Production: Hacienda-Tropicana-Madness. Producers: Paul Bartel, Katherine Dexter. Script: Paul Bartel. Photography: Jan Oonk. Editing: No Credit. Music: No Credit. Cast: Valorie Armstrong, Ron Grathwohl, Chris St. John, Alix Elias, Dennis Helfend, Bob Downey.

Summary: A female nurse and two doctors meet in a shabby New York City hotel room to play sex games.

Private Parts. 1972. Production: Penelope Productions. Distribution: Premier Productions. Producer: Gene Corman. Script: Philip Kearney, Les Rendelstein. Photography: Andrew Davis. Editor: Morton Tubor. Music: Hugo Friedhofer. Cast: Ayn Ruymen, Lucille Benson, John Ventantonio, Stanley Livingston, Charles Woolf, Laurie Main, Ann Gibbes, Len Travis, Dorothy Neumann.

Summary: A teen runaway moves into her aunt's skid row hotel and becomes the obsession of her psychopathic cousin, who may or may not be a man.

Death Race 2000. 1975. Production & Distribution: New World Pictures. Producer: Roger Corman. Script: Robert Thom, Charles Griffith. Story: Ib Melchior. Photography: Tak Fujimoto. Editor: Tina Hirsch. Music: Paul Chihara. Cast: David Carradine, Sylvester Stallone, Simone Griffith, Roberta Collins, Mary Woronov, Wendy Bartel, Harriet Medin, Carle Bensen, Sandy McCallum, Louisa Moritz, Fred Grandy, Martin Kove, John Landis, Don Steele.

Summary: In the year 2000, the national American sport is a transcontinental race in which drivers earn points by killing people. A revolutionary movement tries to thwart the race in an effort to weaken the totalitarian government. The most popular driver, Frankenstein, empathizes with the revolutionaries' objectives.

Cannonball! 1976. Production: Cross-County Productions, Shaw Brothers, Harbor Productions. Distribution: New World Pictures. Producer: Samuel W. Gelfman. Script: Paul Bartel, Donald C. Simpson. Photography: Tak Fujimoto. Editor: Morton Tubor. Music: David A. Axelrod. Cast: David Carradine, Archie Hahn, Victoria Hamel, Mary Woronov, Dick Miller, Bill McKinney, Belinda Balaski, Robert Carradine, James Keach, Gerrit Graham, Stanley Clay, Roger Corman, Paul Bartel, Donald C. Simpson, Jonathan Kaplan, Martin Scorsese, Sylvester Stallone, Allan Arkush, Joe Dante, Carl Gottlieb, Mike Finnell, Shaw Brothers (Hong Kong) Ltd., Harbor Productions, Inc., A Cross-Country Production

Summary: An illegal transcontinental race brings drivers around the world together to compete. Betrayals, murders and crashes gradually eliminate drivers, their navigators and their vehicles. When the driver who crosses the finish line first discovers his success has resulted from an unfair advantage, he repudiates his victory.

Eating Raoul. 1982. Production: Bartel Film. Distribution: 20th Century–Fox International Classics, Quartet/Films, Inc. Producer: Anne Kimmel. Script: Richard Blackburn, Paul Bartel. Photography: Gary Thieltges. Editor: Alan Toomayan. Music: Arlon Ober. Cast: Mary Woronov, Paul Bartel, Robert Beltran, Dan Barrow, Ed Begley, Jr., Richard Blackburn, Hamilton Camp, Billy Curtis, Garry Goodrow, Buck Henry, Darcy Pulliam, Allan Rich, John Shearin, Don Steele,

Anna Mathias, Edie McClurg, John Paragon, Richard Paul, Susan Saiger, Joe Dante, Jon Davison, Wendy Bartel, Anne Kimmel, Chuck Griffith, John Landis, Mark Woods.

Summary: An embittered and financially undone married couple murder and rob swingers in order to put together a down payment for a restaurant they hope to buy. A crooked locksmith threatens to expose their scheme and ruin their marriage.

Not for Publication. 1984. Production: Thorn EMI Films, North Street Films. Distribution: Samuel Goldwyn Company. Producer: Mark Forstater, Anne Kimmel. Script: John Meyer, Paul Bartel. Photography: George Tirl. Editing: Alan Toomayan. Music: John Meyer. Cast: Nancy Allen, David Naughton, Laurence Luckinbill, Richard Blackburn, Richard Paul, J. David Moeller, Alice Ghostley, Jeanne Evans, Don Peoples, Barry Dennen, Cork Hubbert, Anne Kimmel, Paul Bartel.

Summary: A tabloid reporter who doubles as a press flack for the Mayor of New York exposes a secretive criminal ring—organized by her publisher and the Mayor—that trades in the stolen goods.

Lust in the Dust. 1985. Production: Fox Run Productions Ltd. Distribution: New World Pictures. Producer: Allan Glaser, Tab Hunter. Script: Philip John Taylor. Photography: Paul Lohman. Editing: Alan Toomayan. Music: Peter Matz. Cast: Tab Hunter, Divine, Lainie Kazan, Geoffrey Lewis, Cesar Romero, Henry Silva, Gina Gallego, Nedra Volz, Gonzales Gonzales, Woody Strode, Courtney Gains, Daniel Frishman.

Summary: A loner rides into a southwestern town where prostitutes, bandits and killers are searching for a map that will show them where to find hidden treasure.

The Longshot. 1986. Production: Longshot Productions. Distribution: Orion Pictures. Producer: Lang Elliott. Script: Tim Conway. Photography: Robby Müller. Editing: Alan Toomayan. Music: Charles Fox. Cast: Tim Conway, Harvey Korman, Jack Weston, Ted Wass, Anne Meara, Stella Stevens, Gary Goodrow, Jonathan Winters, Frank Bonner, Eddie Deezen, George DiCenzo, Jorge Cevera, Edie McClurg.

Summary: Four working class friends are duped into borrowing money from criminals in order to place a bet on a horse that needs drugs to run fast.

Scenes from the Class Struggle in Beverly Hills. 1989. Production: North Street Films, Cinecom Pictures. Distribution: Cinecom Entertainment Group. Producer: James C. Katz. Script: Bruce Wagner. Story: Paul Bartel, Bruce Wagner. Photography: Steven Fierberg. Editor: Alan Toomayan. Music: Stanley Myers. Cast: Jacqueline Bisset, Mary Woronov, Ray Sharkey, Robert Beltran, Arnetia Walker, Ed Begley, Jr., Wallace Shawn, Paul Bartel, Paul Mazursky, Barret Oliver, Rebecca Schaeffer, Edith Diaz, Susan Saiger, Michael Feinstein, Bruce Wagner, Allan Glaser, Zane W. Levitt.

Summary: Over a weekend in a Beverly Hills mansion, horny people from across the social spectrum take on new lovers, finding that physical attraction transcends class prejudice.

Shelf Life. 1993. Production: Shelf Life, Inc., Northern Arts Entertainment. Producers: Brad Laven, Anne Kimmel. Script and Story: O-Lan Jones, Andrea Stein, Jim Turner. Photography: Philip Holahan. Editor: Judd Maslansky. Music: Andy Paley. Cast: Tina O-Lan Jones, Andrea Stein, Jim Turner, Paul Bartel, Jazz Britany, Shelby Lindley, Justin Houchin.

Summary: Three siblings spend three decades in a bomb shelter, engaging in strange rituals that incorporate song, dance and acting.

Television

Amazing Stories. "Secret Cinema." 1986. NBC. Executive Producer: Steven Spielberg. Script: Paul Bartel, John Meyer.

Summary: A film production crew records the mishaps of a young woman, turning her life into a serial movie for others to enjoy without her knowledge or approval.

Amazing Stories. "Gershwin's Trunk." 1987. NBC. Executive Producer: Steve Spielberg. Script: Paul Bartel, John Meyer.

Summary: A show tune composer seeks help from a clairvoyant who seemingly transforms into George Gershwin.

The Comic Strip Presents… **"Demonella."** 1993. Channel 4. Executive producers: Peter Richardson, Michael White. Script: Paul Bartel, Barry Dennen

Summary: The Devil negotiates with a show tune composer for his mother's chicken soup recipe.

Clueless. "We Shall Overpack." 1996. ABC. Executive Producer: Amy Heckerling. Script: Amy Engelberg, Wendy Engelberg.

Summary: Chinese dissidents serve as a model for students who protest their principal's decision to prohibit them from bringing backpacks to school.

Clueless. "Cher, Inc." 1996. ABC. Executive Producer: Amy Heckerling. Script: Amy Engelberg, Wendy Engelberg.

Summary: A bit of clothing worn during the Russian Revolution inspires Cher to create her own fashion company.

Chapter Notes

Epigraphs

1. David Hinckley, "Mild-Mannered Bob Newhart Also a Standup Rebel," *New York Daily News*, April 15, 2014.
2. Gene Siskel, "Strange Movies Earning Bartel Fame," *Wisconsin State Journal* (Madison), April 17, 1983.

Introduction

1. Matthew Reynolds, "Paul Bartel," Yorah Alom, Del Cullen and Hannah Patterson, eds., *Contemporary North American Film Directors: A Wallflower Critical Guide* (London: Wallflower Press, 2002), 106.
2. Beverly Gray, "Lessons from the Roger Corman School of Moviemaking," *MovieMaker*, Spring 2001, 48.
3. David Everitt, "Paul Bartel," *Fangoria*, July 1982, 33.
4. Peter Stack, "*Eating Raoul*: A Meaty Morsel for Film-Goers," *San Francisco Chronicle*, October 29, 1982. See also John Hartl, "Maker of *Eating Raoul* May Have Another Hit Film on His Hands," *Seattle Times*, May 31, 1989, and John Stanley, "Down and Kinky in Beverly Hills," *San Francisco Chronicle*, May 28, 1989.
5. Lainie Kazan, interview for "More Lust, Less Dust," dir. David Gregory (2001; Beverly Hills: Anchor Bay Entertainment, 2001), DVD.
6. Terry Kelleher, "The Arbiter of Bad Taste," *Newsday* (Long Island), June 4, 1989.
7. Paul Bartel, interview by Terry Gross, *Fresh Air*, 91 WHYY FM, Special Collections, University of Maryland Libraries, NPR Audio Collection, July 5, 1989.
8. Sheila Benson, "*Lust* Gets Caught in Its Own Dust," *Los Angeles Times*, March 8, 1985.
9. Hal Hinson, "Bartel's *Struggle* to Be Clever," *Washington Post*, June 17, 1989.
10. Deirdre Kelly, "Paul Bartel's Bittersweet Taste of Success," *Globe and Mail* (Toronto), February 23, 1995.
11. Alonso Duralde, "End of the Reel," *Advocate*, July 2000, 57.

Chapter 1

1. Todd McCarthy, "Maverick Indie Director Bartel Dies of Heart Attack," *Variety*, May 19, 2000. See also Carrie Rickey, "Paul Bartel, 61; Moviemaker," *Philadelphia Inquirer*, May 18, 2000.
2. Duralde, "Reel," 53.
3. Skip Sheffield, "Film Fest a Cultural, But Not Financial, Success," *Boca Raton News*, December 5, 1986. See also "Deaths," *Palm Beach Post*, April 4, 2000.
4. McCarthy, "Maverick."
5. Wendy Bartel, in discussion with author, February 14, 2014.
6. Michael Dare, "Not Necessarily for Publication," *L.A. Weekly*, November 30–December 6, 1984, 42.
7. Wendy Bartel, e-mail message to author, January 9, 2015.
8. Wendy Bartel, interview for "The

Importance of Being Paul," dir. David Gregory (2003; Beverly Hills: Anchor Bay Entertainment, 2003), DVD.
9. Paul Bartel, "Dialogue on Film," *American Film*, April 1985, 12.
10. Michael Singer, *A Cut Above: 50 Film Directors* (Los Angeles: Lone Eagle, 1998), 16.
11. Michael Goodwin, "Making Raoul: Gourmet," *Village Voice*, February 21, 1983.
12. Wendy Bartel, e-mail message to author, January 9, 2014.
13. Bartel, "Dialogue," 12.
14. Adam Abraham, *When Magoo Flew: The Rise and Fall of Animation Studio UPA* (Middletown, CT: Wesleyan University Press), ix.
15. Lawrence Van Gelder, "Director and Star of *Eating Raoul*, Dies at 61," *New York Times*, May 18, 2000.
16. Paul Bartel, "Two of a Kind," *Advocate*, July 21, 1998, 69.
17. Jim Pickrell, "Cult Stories," *UCLA Summer Bruin*, July 24, 1989.
18. Singer, *Cut Above*, 16.
19. Robert Schulenberg, in discussion with the author, November 13, 2014.
20. Barry Dennen, in discussion with the author, February 18, 2015.
21. Wendy Bartel, e-mail message to author, January 9, 2015.
22. Robert Schulenberg, in discussion with the author, November 13, 2014.
23. Wendy Bartel, e-mail message to author, January 9, 2015.

Chapter 2

1. Van Gelder, "Director and Star."
2. Pickrell, "Cult Stories."
3. Press materials for *Not for Publication*.
4. Press materials for *Cannonball!*.
5. Wheeler W. Dixon, *The Exploding Eye: A Re-Visionary History of 1960s American Experimental Cinema* (Albany: SUNY Press, 1997), 21.
6. "Paul Bartel; Directed Cult Film, *Eating Raoul*," *Los Angeles Times*, May 19, 2000.
7. Duncan Petrie and Rod Stoneman, *Educating Film-Makers: Past, Present and Future* (Chicago: Intellect, 2014), 67.
8. "Online Catalog," *The New American Cinema Group/The Film-Makers' Coop*, accessed July 1, 2016, http://filmmakerscoop.com/.
9. Paul Bartel, "My Amazing Story," *American Film*, October 1985, 56.
10. Mark Olsen, "On 'The Secret Cinema,'" *Scenario*, Winter 1998/1999, 173.
11. Press materials for *Cannonball!*.
12. Alix Elias, in discussion with the author, June 24, 2015.
13. "Helen G. Scott, 72, Writer for Truffaut and Other Directors," *New York Times*, November 24, 1987. See also Tino Balio, *The Foreign Film Renaissance on American Screens, 1946–1973* (Madison: University of Wisconsin Press, 2010), 104.
14. Dennen, in discussion with the author, February 18, 2015.
15. Olsen, "Secret," 173.
16. *Ibid.*
17. Bartel, "Amazing," 57.
18. Olsen, "Secret," 173.
19. Bartel, "Amazing," 56.
20. Olsen, "Secret," 173.
21. Dennen, in discussion with the author, February 18, 2015.
22. Olsen, "Secret," 173
23. Dare, "Not Necessarily," 41.
24. Jonas Mekas, "The First Statement of the New American Cinema Group," Scott MacKenzie, ed., *Film Manifestos and Global Cinema Cultures: A Critical Anthology* (Berkeley: University of California Press, 2014), 58.
25. Bartel, "Amazing," 57–58.
26. Notice of the performance is included in a lobby card prepared for the films' co-premiere.
27. Gary Morris, "Paul Bartel," Claude Summers, ed., *The Queer Encyclopedia of Film and Television* (San Francisco: Cleis Press, 2012), 46.
28. David Mikics, *A New Handbook of Literary Terms* (New Haven: Yale University Press, 2010), 251.
29. Martin Manning, *Historical Dictionary of American Propaganda* (Westport, CT: Greenwood, 2004), 87.
30. Frank Sanello, "Bartel Devours Praise for his *Eating Raoul*," *New York Daily News*, October 13, 1982.
31. Robyn Karney, *The Hollywood Who's Who: The Actors and Directors in*

Today's Hollywood (New York: Continuum, 1993), 36.
32. "Mary Woronov, Paul Bartel, *Eating Raoul*," prod. Ira H. Gallen (1982; New York: Ira H. Gallen Video Resources, 1982).
33. Olsen, "Secret," 173.
34. Sanello, "Bartel Devours."
35. Wayne M. Bryant, *Bisexual Characters in Film: From Anaïs to Zee* (New York: Harrington Park Press, 1997), 109.
36. Pickrell, "Cult Stories."
37. "Cheap Thrills at the Circus," *Hoya* (Washington, D.C.), February 2, 1973.
38. Frederick M. Winship, "Grove Press to Market Erotic TV Film Tapes," *Ludington Daily News* (Michigan), December 30, 1970.
39. Pickrell, "Cult Stories."

Chapter 3

1. Alix Elias, in discussion with the author, June 24, 2015.
2. Roger Greenspun, "*Viva La Muerte*," *New York Times*, October 26, 1971.
3. Dare, "Not Necessarily," 41.
4. Everitt, "Bartel," 31.
5. Bartel, "Dialogue," 12.
6. Everitt, "Bartel," 31.
7. David Ehrenstein, "Murder Most Delicious [essay]," *Eating Raoul* (2012; New York; Criterion, 2012), DVD.
8. Dave Kehr, "Four Auteurs in Search of an Audience: B+," *Film Comment*, September–October 1977, 9.
9. Stanley, "Down and Kinky."
10. Roger Greenspun, "*Private Parts*, Film by Bartel, Arrives," *New York Times*, February 2, 1973.
11. Jay Cocks, "Heartbreak Hotel," *Time*, March 5, 1973, 92.
12. Bartel, "Dialogue," 12.
13. Michael Musto, "La Dolce Musto," *Village Voice*, September 3, 1991.
14. Sam Tweedle, "Chip Happens: A Conversation with Stanley Livingston," *Confessions of a Pop Culture Addict*, July 15, 2011, accessed July 11, 2016, http://popcultureaddict.com/interviews/stanlivingston/.
15. "Mary Woronov, Paul Bartel, *Eating Raoul*."

16. Jon Davison, e-mail message to author, July 28, 2015.
17. Dorothy Manners, "Hollywood: Angie's Latest Is a Shocker," *Register* (Danville, VA), July 26, 1974.
18. Paul Bartel, "Another Evening with David Carradine," *Take One*, July 1978, 15.
19. Chris Petit and Tony Rayns, "Getting the Show on the Road," Jim Hiller and Aaron Lipstadt, eds., *Roger Corman's New World* (London: British Film Institute, 1981), 27.
20. Everitt, "Bartel," 31
21. Singer, *Cut Above*, 15.
22. Mary Woronov, interview for "Cooking up *Raoul*," prod. Issa Clubb (2012; New York: Criterion Collection, 2012), DVD.
23. Cynthia Roe, "Exploding Plastic Inevitable Dancer ... Mary Woronov," *Psychotronic* 7 (1998), 34, 35.
24. "Cult-Film Staple Mary Woronov on Andy Warhol, Roger Corman, and Being Typecast," Will Harris, *A.V. Club*, September 7, 2012, accessed April 17, 2015, http://www.avclub.com/article/cult-film-staple-mary-woronov-on-andy-warhol-roger-84658.
25. Petit and Rayns, *Corman's New World*, 30.
26. David Carradine, *Endless Highway* (Boston: Journey Editions, 1995), 401, 402.
27. Chris Nashawaty, *Crab Monsters, Teenage Cavemen, and Candy Stripe Nurses: Roger Corman: King of the B Movie* (New York: Harry N. Abrams, 2013), 145.
28. *Ibid.* 143–144.
29. Bartel, "Evening," 15.
30. Carradine, *Highway*, 403.
31. Paul Bartel, "Lost in the Garden of the World," dir. Tony Williams (Auckland: Tony Williams Productions, Pacific Films, 1975).
32. Carradine, *Highway*, 403.
33. Tina Hirsch in discussion with author, December 3, 2014.
34. Ed Naha, *The Films of Roger Corman: Brilliance on Budget* (New York: Arco, 1989), 80.
35. Mark Thomas McGee, *Roger Corman: Best of the Cheap Acts* (Jefferson, NC: McFarland, 1997), 81. And Paul Bartel, interview for *Fresh Air*.

36. Charles B. Griffith, interview for "Playing the Game: Looking Back at *Death Race 2000*," dir. Robert Nuñez (2005; West Hollywood: Telekinetic Entertainment, 2010), DVD.
37. Michael Schelle, *The Score: Interviews with Film Composers*, Los Angeles: Silman-James Press, 1999), 129.
38. Bartel in "Garden of the World."
39. Kevin Thomas, "Nine Directors Rising from the Trashes," *Los Angeles Times*, December 21, 1975.
40. Singer, *Cut Above*, 17.
41. David Carradine, "David on *Death Race*." Produced by Aine Leicht (2010; Los Angeles: Red Shirt Pictures, 2010), DVD.
42. Peter Sobczynski, "Miss Togar Speaks! An Interview with Mary Woronov," *eFilmCritic* May 8, 2008, accessed June 23, 2015, http://www.efilmcritic.com/feature.php?feature=2476.
43. "*Death Race 2000* is Short on Satire," *New York Times*, June 6, 1975.
44. Kehr, "Four Auteurs."

Chapter 4

1. Bruce McCabe, "*Eating Raoul*: The Essence of LA Theatricality," *Boston Globe*, October 31, 1982.
2. Bill Davidson, "King of Schlock," *New York Times Magazine*, December 28, 1975, 13.
3. Naha, *Brilliance on a Budget*, 75.
4. Denis Boyles, "Hollywood 'B's' Make the Box Offices Buzz," *New York Times*, August 3, 1980.
5. Joe Baltake, "Joe Dante," *Knight-Ridder Newspapers*, June 13, 1984.
6. Harris, "Cult-Film Staple."
7. Boyles, "Box Offices."
8. Baltake, "Joe Dante."
9. "*Hollywood Boulevard*," *Variety*, April 28, 1976.
10. Richard Blackburn, in discussion with the author, November 11, 2014.
11. James Verniere, "For Publication: Interview with *Eating Raoul* Director Paul Bartel," *Heavy Metal*, April 1985, 54–56.
12. Dare, "Not Necessarily," 41.
13. Mark Williams, *Road Movies* (London: Proteus Books, 1982), 37.
14. Everitt, "Bartel," 33.
15. "The Cannonball Dash," *Time*, May 5, 1975, 69.
16. Peter Biskind, *Gods and Monsters: Thirty Years of Writing on Film and Culture from one of America's Most Incisive Writers* (New York: Nation Books, 2004), 354.
17. Everitt, "Bartel," 33
18. Dare, "Not Necessarily," 42.
19. Carradine, *Highway*, 432.
20. Singer, *Cut Above*, 15.
21. Kirk Honeycutt, "Movies," *Valley News* (Van Nuys, CA), September 17, 1976.
22. Roger Ebert, "Cannonball," *Chicago Sun-Times*, August 13, 1976.
23. Press materials for *Scenes from the Class Struggles in Beverly Hills*.
24. Biskind, *Gods and Monsters*, 354.
25. Paul Bartel, interview for *Fresh Air*.
26. Jordan Fox, *Cinefantastique*, April 1982, 9.
27. Bartel, "Evening," 15.
28. Paul Bartel, "Where I Shop: Paul Bartel," *Buzz*, March/April 1992, 44.
29. Kim Newman, *Nightmare Movies: Horror on Screen since the 1960s* (New York: Bloomsbury, 2001), 93.
30. Kevin Thomas, "Ramones Features in *High School*," *Los Angeles Times*, October 12, 1979.
31. Roe, "Plastic," 38.
32. Alan Spencer, *Starlog*, "Director with a Heart," November 1981, 28.
33. Thomas, "*High School*."
34. Press materials for *Rock 'n' Roll High School*.
35. Paul Bartel, "Guilty Pleasures," *Film Comment*, September–October 1982, 60.

Chapter 5

1. Notes for Filmex Society Screen of *Eating Raoul*, October 13, 1981.
2. Peter Stack, "*Eating Raoul* on a Budget," *San Francisco Sunday Examiner & Chronicle*.
3. Diane Jacobs, "Bartel's Parables," *Washington Post*, January 4, 1983.
4. David Chute, "Paul Bartel Has Lots More in Store for Us," *Los Angeles Herald-Examiner*, October 25, 1982.

5. John Landis, interview for "The Importance of Being Paul."
6. Stack, "Budget."
7. Siskel, "Strange Movies."
8. Jacobs, "Parables."
9. Melody Kimmel, "Paul Bartel," *Films in Review*, December 10, 1982, 626.
10. McCabe, "Theatricality."
11. Paul Bartel, interview for *Fresh Air*.
12. Dale Pollock, "Having Dessert After *Eating Raoul*," *Los Angeles Times*, November 1, 1982.
13. Dare, "Not Necessarily."
14. David Chute, "A Shout in the Dark," *Los Angeles Herald-Examiner*, April 2, 1981.
15. Jacobs, "Parables."
16. Todd McCarthy, "How 'Independent' Can You Be? A Year on *Eating Raoul* Pic," *Variety*, April 21, 1982.
17. John Landis, interview for "Kicks and Crashes," dir. David Gregory (2004; West Hollywood: Blue Underground, 2004), DVD.
18. Alan Toomayan, in discussion with the author, November 5, 2014.
19. Art Fein, e-mail message to author, July 5, 2015.
20. Bartel in "Mary Woronov, Paul Bartel, *Eating Raoul*."
21. McCabe, "Theatricality."
22. Jacobs, "Parables."
23. Pickrell, "Cult Stories."
24. McCarthy, "Can You Be."
25. Productions notes for *Eating Raoul*.
26. McCarthy, "Can You Be."
27. Paul Scanlon, "*Eating Raoul*: Paul Bartel's Tasty Stew," *Rolling Stone*, November 11, 1982, 34.
28. Stack, "Budget."
29. Paul Bartel, interview for *Fresh Air*.
30. Denny Tedesco in discussion with the author, January 29, 2016.
31. Chris Walters, "On Screen: Bartel Runs Amuck in *Raoul*," *Austin American-Statesman*, March 5, 1982.
32. Chute, "In the Dark."
33. "White Dog," *Variety*, December 31, 1981.
34. Jon Davison, e-mail message to author, July 28, 2015.
35. Stack, "Budget."
36. Scanlon, "Tasty Stew," 34.
37. Productions notes for *Eating Raoul*.
38. Robert Beltran, interview for "Cooking up *Raoul*," prod. Issa Clubb (2012; New York: Criterion Collection, 2012), DVD.
39. Production notes for *Eating Raoul*.
40. Susan Saiger in discussion with the author, November 3, 2014.
41. M. Kimmel, "Paul," 626.
42. Sobczynski, "Togar Speaks."
43. David Chute, "More in Store."
44. Roe, "Plastic," 38.
45. Productions notes for *Eating Raoul*.
46. Alan Toomayan, e-mail message to author, November 5, 2014.
47. McCabe, "Theatricality."
48. "Bartel's Scourge of the Swingers," *Screen International*, January 8, 1983.
49. McCabe, "Theatricality."
50. Richard Blackburn in discussion with author, November 11, 2014.
51. Van Gelder, "Obituary."
52. "Aljean Harmetz, "Hollywood Thinks Small in a Big Way," *New York Times*, March 13, 1983.
53. Anne Kimmel in discussion with author, November 8, 2014.
54. See Pollock, "Having Dessert" and "Scourge of the Singers."
55. Harmetz, "Thinks Small."
56. Dare, "Not Necessarily," 42.
57. Carol Lay, e-mail message to author, June 9, 2015.
58. Vincent Canby, "*Eating Raoul*, Comedy with an Offbeat Couple," *New York Times*, September 25, 1982.
59. Richard Corliss, "Soufflé Surrealism," *Time*, October 4, 1982, 122.
60. McCabe, "Theatricality."
61. Desmond Ryan, "*Eating Raoul*: Macabre Humor," *Wisconsin State Journal* (Madison), April 7, 1983.
62. Jack Kroll, "The Joys of Swingercide," *Newsweek*, October 11, 1982, 103.
63. David Denby, "Naughty Nibbles," *New York*, October 11, 1982, 86.
64. Sheila Benson, "*Raoul*: One-Joke Premise for Film," *Los Angeles Times*, October 15, 1982.
65. "Paul Bartel, 61, Actor-Director,"

People, December 25, 2000–January 1, 2001, 16.5.
66. Jacobs, "Parables."
67. John Barron, "Director Thrives on Black Humor," *Milwaukee Sentinel*, March 11, 1983.
68. Production Notes for *Eating Raoul*.
69. Chute, "More in Store."
70. Siskel, "Strange Movies."

Chapter 6

1. Stack, "Budget."
2. Peter Szatmary, "Paul Bartel Eats His Heart Out about Raoul," *Playbill*, April 9, 1998, accessed January 12, 2015, http://www.playbill.com/article/paul-bartel-eats-his-heart-out-about-raoul-in-houston-apr-15-com-74572.
3. Kelly, "Bittersweet."
4. Richard Blackburn, "Digesting Raoul," *American Film*, May 1983, 64.
5. Kelleher, "Bad Taste."
6. Scanlon, "Tasty Stew," 41.
7. John Hartl, "Bartel Makes *Class Struggle* without Compromise," *Austin American-Statesman*, June 8, 1989.
8. "Q&A with Mary Woronov," *Chicago Reader*, November 26, 1982, 8.
9. Lawrence Van Gelder, "At the Movies," *New York Times*, July 14, 1989.
10. Terry Kelleher, "Fine Young Cannibals: They Placed *Raoul* on a Very Bland Diet," *New York Newsday*, May 15, 1992, 82.
11. Desmond Ryan, "Disney's Production of a Sequel to *Oz* Is Now Uncertain," *Philadelphia Inquirer*, December 11, 1983.
12. UPI, "Screwball Comedy Rolls in Dallas," January 7, 1984.
13. Stanley, "Down and Kinky." See also Dare, "Not Necessarily," 42.
14. Chute, "More in Store."
15. Lawrence Van Gelder, "*Stranger Than Paradise*: Its Story Could Be a Movie," *New York Times*, October 21, 1984
16. Peter Belsito, "Interview with Jim Jarmusch/1985," *Jim Jarmusch: Interviews*, ed. Ludvig Hertzberg (Jackson: University Press of Mississippi, 2001), 41.
17. Van Gelder, "Stranger."
18. John Hartl, "Disney's *101 Dalmatians* Likely to Fetch Big Sales, *Seattle Times*, April 5, 1992.
19. Singer, *Cut Above*, 18.
20. Verniere, "For Publication," 55.
21. John Meyer, e-mail message to author, January 27, 2015.
22. Harris, "Cult-Film Staple."
23. Philip Wuntch, "Big D Substitutes for Big Apple," *Dallas Morning News*, November 2, 1983.
24. Anne Kimmel, in discussion with author, November 8, 2014.
25. John Meyer, e-mail message to author, January 27, 2015.
26. Vincent Canby, "Film: Not for Publication, A Comedy," *New York Times*, November 1, 1984.
27. Patrick Goldstein, "A Slapdash *Publication* by Bartel," *Los Angeles Times*, November 16, 1984.
28. Dare, "Not Necessarily," 42.
29. Paul Bartel, interview for "More Lust, Less Dust."
30. Michael Dare, "Not Necessarily," 42.
31. Bartel, "Dialogue," 15.
32. Pat H. Broeske, "With Hot Films, Tab Hunter's No Longer Out in the Cold," *Register* (Orange County), March 10, 1985.
33. Tab Hunter, in discussion with the author, September 11, 2014.
34. Broeske, "Hot Films."
35. Tab Hunter with Eddie Muller, *Tab Hunter Confidential* (Chapel Hill: Algonquin Books, 2005), 312.
36. Bernard Jay, *Not Simply Divine* (New York: Fireside, 1993), 97.
37. Hunter, *Confidential*, 317.
38. Tab Hunter, in discussion with the author, September 11, 2014.
39. Lawrence O'Toole, "Yule Trees become Money Trees," *Globe and Mail* (Toronto), November 8, 1983.
40. Tab Hunter, in discussion with the author, September 11, 2014.
41. Hunter, *Confidential*, 323.
42. Bartel, "Dialogue," 14–15.
43. Siskel, "Strange Movies."
44. P. Gregory Springer, "You Are What you Eat," *American Film*, October 1982, 14.
45. Chute, "More in Store."

46. Cree McCree, "Lust in the Dust," *Santa Fe New Mexican*, May 11, 1984.
47. Jim Katz, interview for "The Importance of Being Paul."
48. Jay, *Divine*, 165.
49. Cree McCree, "Lust Star Ecstatic," *Santa Fe New Mexican*, May 11, 1984.
50. Anne Thompson, "Adults Only," *L.A. Weekly*, June 1989.
51. Tab Hunter, in discussion with author, September 11, 2014.
52. Allan Glaser, in discussion with the author, February 3, 2016.
53. Allan Glaser, interview for "More Lust, Less Dust."
54. Hunter, *Confidential*, 325.
55. Quentin Crisp, *How to Go to the Movies* (New York: St. Martin's Press, 1989), 65.
56. Vincent Canby, "Screen: Bartel's *Lust in the Dust*," *New York Times*, March 1, 1985.
57. Jay Scott, "Spoof Lassoed by Limp Script," *Globe and Mail* (Toronto), April 8, 1985.
58. Roger Ebert, *Great Movies III* (Chicago: University of Chicago Press, 2010), 193.
59. Leslie Bennetts, "NBC-TV Lures Spielberg to Produce Action Series," *Globe and Mail* (Toronto), August 1, 1984.
60. "Keys to Persuading Some of Hollywood's Top Talent," *Syracuse Herald-Journal*, September 12, 1985.
61. Bartel, "Amazing," 58–59, 80.
62. Susan Saiger, in discussion with the author, November 3, 2014.
63. Bartel, "Amazing," 80.
64. Jay Boyar, "There's Reality in His Sad-Sack Role," *Orlando Sentinel*, January 25, 1986.
65. Joseph Dave, "This Movie's No Winner, But It May Show," *Chicago Sun-Times*, January 20, 1986.
66. Jack Matthews, "An Odd Collaboration May Pay on *Longshot*," *Los Angeles Times*, July 17, 1985.
67. Rick Kogan," *Longshot* Is Too Silly and Sketchy," *Chicago Tribune*, January 21, 1986.
68. Roger Hurlburt, "*Longshot* Short on Comedy," *Sun Sentinel* (Fort Lauderdale), February 2, 1986.
69. Matthews, "Odd Collaboration."

70. Kelleher, "Bad Taste."
71. Hartl, "Another Hit."
72. Tom Shales, "TV Review: Amazing It Ain't," *Washington Post*, September 30, 1985.
73. Carolyn McGuire, "Monday Night Amazements," *Chicago Tribune*, June 30 1986.
74. Susan Sontag, "Notes on 'Camp,'" *Partisan Review* 31, Fall 1964, 515.
75. John Meyer, e-mail message to author, January 27, 2015.
76. Michael Feinstein with Ian Jackman, *The Gershwins and Me: A Personal History in Twelve Songs* (New York: Simon & Schuster, 2012), 332.
77. John Meyer, e-mail message to author, January 27, 2015.
78. Press materials for *Billy's Hollywood Screen Kiss*.
79. Laurie Deans, "LA Clips: From Director of *The Decline of Western Civilization*," *Globe and Mail* (Toronto), September 11, 1987.
80. Jim Emerson, "*Amazon Women*: A Spoof That'll Go Poof," September 18, 1987.
81. Harris, "Cult-Movie Staple."
82. Sheffield, "Film Fest."
83. Stanley, "Down and Kinky."
84. "*Mortuary Academy*' and, Egad!, Soon a Sequel," *St. Petersburg Times*, July 9, 1988.
85. Patrick Goldstein, "Working Stiffs," *Los Angeles Times*, June 21, 1987.
86. Kevin Jackson, "Film Reviews," *Independent* (London), May 18, 1989.
87. Stephen Holden, "*Out of the Dark*, Phone Sex," *New York Times*, May 5, 1989.
88. Dave Kehr, "Farce Falls Flat in Unfunny *Checking Out*," May 5, 1989.
89. Musto, "La Dolce."
90. Hartl, "Without Compromise."

Chapter 7

1. Hartl, "Without Compromise."
2. Richard Blackburn, in discussion with author, November 11, 2014.
3. Ted Mahar, "Bartel Let *Scenes* Simmer for Years," *Oregonian*, July 18, 1989.
4. Liam Lacey, "Tinseltown Under

the Microscope," *Globe and Mail* (Toronto), November 1, 2014.
5. Andy Meisler, "...And the Shadowy Figure Who Dreamed It Up," *New York Times*, May 16, 1993.
6. Jim Emerson, "Kitsch of the '60s is '80s Chic," *Register* (Orange County), May 14, 1989.
7. John M. Wilson, "Sexual Politics," *Los Angeles Times*, August 17, 1986.
8. Hartl, "Without Compromise."
9. John M. Wilson, "Sexual Politics," *Los Angeles Times*, August 17, 1986.
10. Hartl, "Without Compromise."
11. Patrick Goldstein, "Paul Bartel Sticks It to the Idle Rich," *Los Angeles Times*, September 25, 1988.
12. Paul Bartel, interview for *Fresh Air*.
13. Goldstein, "Idle Rich."
14. Leonard Klady, "Fickle Faye," *Los Angeles Times*, November 29, 1987.
15. Goldstein, "Idle Rich."
16. Kelly, "Bittersweet."
17. Bartel, "Two of a Kind," 69.
18. Hartl, "Without Compromise."
19. Goldstein, "Idle Rich."
20. Rita Zekas, "Arnetia Walker a Movie Star ... at Last," *Toronto Star*, July 13, 1989.
21. Stanley, "Down and Kinky."
22. Kelleher, "Bad Taste."
23. Zane W. Levitt, in discussion with author, May 13, 2015.
24. Kelleher, "Bad Taste."
25. Goldstein, "Idle Rich."
26. Kelleher, "Bad Taste."
27. Kevin Koffler, "Struggling Along with Paul Bartel," *Los Angeles Herald-Examiner*, June 28, 1989.
28. Nikki Finke, "New Rash of Books," *Los Angeles Times*, July 2, 1989.
29. Lance Loud, "Is Director Paul Bartel the First Casualty of *Casualties of War*?" *Los Angeles Times*, June 25, 1989.
30. Anne Thompson, "Adults Only," *L.A. Weekly*, June 16, 1989.
31. Kelleher, "Bad Taste."
32. Anne Kimmel in discussion with author, November 8, 2014.
33. Hartl, "Without Compromise."
34. Kevin Allman, "Into the Night," *Los Angeles Times*, June 8, 1989.
35. Dave Kehr, "*Scenes from the Class Struggle*, a Sour Film," *Chicago Tribune*, July 21, 1989.
36. Frank DeCaro, "Naughty Bawdy Bartel," *Newsday* (Long Island), July 2, 1989.
37. Jay Carr, "Class Struggle: Nothing Succeeds Like Excess," *Boston Globe*, June 16, 1989.
38. Emerson, "'80s Chic."
39. Caryn James, "Social Comment? Wrap It in Laughs," *New York Times*, June 25, 1989.
40. Lawrence Van Gelder, "At the Movies," *New York Times*, July 14, 1989.
41. Howie Movshovitz, "Bartel Acts as Only He Can in *Class Struggle* Comedy," *Denver Post*, July 30, 1989.
42. Claudia Eller, "Bartel Bringing *Shelf* to Movie Life," *Variety*, July 31, 1992.
43. Kelleher, "Bad Taste."
44. Pickrell, "Cult Stories."
45. Kelly, "Bittersweet."
46. Gary Indiana, "Gus Van Sant," *Bomb*, Fall 1993, 36.
47. Paul Bartel, interview for *Fresh Air*.
48. Jon Davison, e-mail message to author, July 28, 2015.
49. Ellis Cashmore, *Martin Scorsese's America* (Malden, MA: Polity Press, 2009), 152.
50. Robert L. Snow, *Stopping a Stalker* (Cambridge, MA: Perseus, 1998), 73–74.
51. Pete Axthelm, "An Innocent Life, a Heartbreaking Death," *People*, July 31, 1989.
52. Michael Kilian, "Daffy Derangement," *Chicago Tribune*, May 31, 1992.
53. Terry Kelleher, "Fine Young Cannibals," *Newsday*, May 15, 1992.
54. Jesse Hamlin "On the *Shelf*," *San Francisco Chronicle*, November 17, 1992.
55. Szatmary, "Bartel Eats."
56. Kelleher, "Cannibals."
57. Kenneth Jones and Peter Szatmary, "Actor-Filmmaker Paul Bartel, of *Eating Raoul*, Dead at 61," *Playbill*, May 18, 2000, accessed December 11, 2014, http://www.playbill.com/article/actor-filmmaker-paul-bartel-of-eating-raoul-dead-at-61-com-89313.
58. Killian, "Daffy."
59. Mel Gussow, "Trying to Be Whimsical with a Bit of Cannibalism," *New York Times*, May 16, 1992.

60. John Simon, "Out of the Wrong Side of the Mouth," *New York*, June 1, 1992, 61.
61. Anne Thompson, "Leap of Faith," *L.A. Weekly*, January 29, 1993.
62. Kathy Henderson, "One View: Daytime's Dickens," *Los Angeles Times*, July 5, 1992.
63. Daniel Neman, "Director's Intention 'To Charm, to Surprise,'" *Richmond Times-Dispatch*, September 8, 1994.
64. Eller, "Movie Life."
65. Thompson, "Faith."
66. Edward Guthmann, "Shelf Life Goes Bad in a Hurry," *San Francisco Chronicle*, August 19, 1994.
67. Eller, "Movie Life."
68. Ibid.
69. Kelly, "Bittersweet."
70. "Reel to Reel—Shelf Life," *Village Voice*, March 15, 1994
71. Todd McCarthy, "*Shelf Life*," *Variety*, February 9, 1993.
72. Liam Lacey, "Film Review: *Shelf Life*," *Globe and Mail* (Toronto), February 24, 1993.
73. Thompson, "Faith."
74. L. M. "Kit" Carson, "4 Rooms, 5 Jokers," *Filmmaker*, Fall 1995, 44.
75. Musto, "La Dolce."
76. See Dorothy Hobson, *Channel 4: The Early Years and the Jeremy Isaacs Legacy* (London: I.B. Tauris, 2008), 118.
77. Barry Dennen to Debra Leschin, 14 July 1983.
78. Anne Kimmel, in discussion with author, November 8, 2014.
79. John Hartl, "Low Budget, Big Impact: This *Kiss* Smacks of L.A. Style," *Seattle Times*, August 2, 1998.
80. Bartel, "Two of a Kind," 69.
81. Morris, "Paul Bartel," 46.
82. John Meyer, e-mail message to author, January 27, 2015.
83. Bartel, "Guilty Pleasures," 60.
84. Christy Slewinski, "Welcome Hollywood to the Small Screen," *New York Daily News*, September 8, 1996.
85. David Chute, "Is 'Secret' *Truman*'s Precursor?" *Los Angeles Times*, June 8, 1998.
86. Finnell in discussion with author, January 11, 2016. See also Derek Elley, "Locarno Fest Wraps, Hands Out Hardware," *Variety*, August 16, 1999.
87. David DeCoteau, interview for "The Importance of Being Paul."
88. Duralde, "Reel," 57.
89. Jon Bowman, "The Projector," *Santa Fe New Mexican*, June 16, 2000.
90. "Bartel Memorial Slated for June 11," *Variety*, June 2, 2000.
91. Jon Davison, e-mail message to author, July 28, 2015.
92. "Paul Bartel Memorial," *New York Times*, June 24, 2000.
93. Paul Sherman, "Bartel Turned Ridicule into Avant-garde Glee," *Boston Sunday Herald*, May 21, 2000.
94. C. Ford, "Cannibalism: Hollywood's New Recipe for Success," *Herald Sun* (Melbourne, Australia), August 1, 1992.

Interviews

1. Joe Dante, in discussion with author, May 13, 2015.
2. Allan Arkush, in discussion with author, November 22, 2014.
3. Roger Corman, in discussion with author, March 16, 2016.
4. Richard Blackburn, in discussion with author, November 11, 2014.
5. John Waters, in discussion with author, March 18, 2015.

An Excrescence of Style

1. Noël Carroll, "The Future of Allusion: Hollywood in the Seventies (and Beyond)," *October*, Spring 1982, 57, 53.
2. Michael Walker, *Hitchcock's Motifs* (Amsterdam: Amsterdam University Press, 2005), 170.
3. Laura Mulvey, "Visual Pleasure and Narrative Cinema," *Screen* 16.3 (1975): 6–18.
4. John Meyer, e-mail message to author, January 27, 2015.
5. Justin Edwards and Rune Graulund, *The Grotesque* (New York: Routledge, 2013), 6.
6. Singer, *Cut Above*, 16.
7. Joe Baltake, "A Comedy That Fails to Fizz," *Philadelphia Daily News*, February 9, 1985.

Bibliography

Abraham, Adam. *When Magoo Flew: The Rise and Fall of Animation Studio UPA.* Middletown, CT: Wesleyan University Press.

Belsito, Peter. "Interview with Jim Jarmusch/1985." *Jim Jarmusch: Interviews*, ed. Ludvig Hertzberg, 21–47. Jackson: University Press of Mississippi, 2001.

Biskind, Peter. *Gods and Monsters: Thirty Years of Writing on Film and Culture from one of America's Most Incisive Writers.* New York: Nation Books, 2004.

Bryant, Wayne M. *Bisexual Characters in Film: from Anaïs to Zee.* New York: Harrington Park Press, 1997.

Carradine, David. *Endless Highway.* Boston: Journey Editions, 1995.

Cashmore, Ellis. *Martin Scorsese's America.* Malden, MA: Polity Press, 2009.

Corman, Roger, with Jim Jerome. *How I Made a Hundred Movies in Hollywood and Never Lost a Dime.* New York: Da Capo Press, 1998.

Crisp, Quentin. *How to Go to the Movies.* New York: St. Martin's Press, 1989.

Deitch, Kim. *Eating Raoul.* From a screenplay by Paul Bartel and Richard Blackburn. New York: Mercury Film Distribution, 1982.

Dixon, Winston Wheeler. *The Exploding Eye: A Re-Visionary History of 1960s American Experimental Cinema.* Albany: SUNY Press, 1997.

———. "Roger Corman." *Contemporary North American Film Directors: A Wallflower Critical Guide*, ed. Yorah Alom, Del Cullen and Hannah Patterson, 104–107. London: Wallflower Press, 2002.

Ebert, Roger. *Great Movies III.* Chicago: University of Chicago Press, 2010.

Edwards, Justin, and Rune Graulund. *The Grotesque* New York: Routledge, 2013.

Feinstein, Michael, with Ian Jackman, *The Gershwins and Me: A Personal History in Twelve Songs.* New York: Simon & Schuster, 2012.

Gray, Beverly. *Roger Corman: An Unauthorized Biography of the Godfather of Indie Filmmaking.* Los Angeles: Renaissance Books, 2000.

Hobson, Dorothy. *Channel 4: The Early Years and the Jeremy Isaacs Legacy.* London: I.B. Tauris, 2008.

Hunter, Tab, with Eddie Muller, *Tab Hunter Confidential.* Chapel Hill: Algonquin Books, 2005

Jay, Bernard. *Not Simply Divine.* New York: Fireside, 1993.

Karney, Robyn. *The Hollywood Who's Who: The Actors and Directors in Today's Hollywood.* New York: Continuum, 1993.

Manning, Martin. *Historical Dictionary of American Propaganda.* Westport, CT: Greenwood, 2004.

McGee, Mark Thomas. *Roger Corman: Best of the Cheap Acts*. Jefferson, NC: McFarland, 1997.
Mikics, David. *A New Handbook of Literary Terms*. New Haven: Yale University Press, 2010.
Morris, Gary. "Paul Bartel." *The Queer Encyclopedia of Film and Television*, ed. Claude Summers, 45–46. San Francisco: Cleis Press, 2012.
Naha, Ed. *The Films of Roger Corman: Brilliance on Budget*. New York: Arco, 1989.
Nashawaty, Chris. *Crab Monsters, Teenage Cavemen, and Candy Stripe Nurses: Roger Corman: King of the B Movie*. New York: Harry N. Abrams, 2013.
Newman, Kim. *Nightmare Movies: Horror on Screen Since the 1960s*. New York: Bloomsbury, 2001.
Petit, Chris and Tony Rayns. "Getting the Show on the Road." *Roger Corman's New World*, ed. Jim Hiller and Aaron Lipstadt, 24–32. London: British Film Institute, 1981.
Petrie, Duncan, and Rod Stoneman. *Educating Film-Makers: Past, Present and Future*. Chicago: Intellect, 2014.
Schelle, Michael. *The Score: Interviews with Film Composers*. Los Angeles: Silman-James Press, 1999.
Singer, Michael. *A Cut Above: 50 Film Directors Talk about their Craft*. Los Angeles: Lone Eagle, 1998.
Snow, Robert L. *Stopping a Stalker*. Cambridge, MA: Perseus, 1998.
Walker, Michael. *Hitchcock's Motifs*. Amsterdam: Amsterdam University Press, 2005.

Index

Numbers in **_bold italics_** indicate pages with photographs.

À nous la liberte 15, 91
Ackerman, Meyer 61, 63
Actors Studio 14
Adam's Rib 143–144
Airplane! 136
Allen, Nancy 71, 72, 180
Allen, Steve 126
Allen, Woody 21, 60, 94
Ally McBeal 119
Almereyda, Michael 107
Almodovar, Pedro 108
Alsobrook, Jane 61
Amarcord 141
Amazing Stories 5, 82–83, 85, 89, 91, 92, 121, 122, 132, 169, 181
Amazon Women on the Moon 94, ***95***
Amblin Entertainment 85, 92
American International Pictures (AIP) 130, 132
An American Werewolf in London 71, 85
Anger, Kenneth 123
Animal House 31
Annie 68, 160
Antonioni, Michelangelo 14
Araki, Gregg 120
Arden, Eve 46, 85, 89
Arkoff, Sam 132
Arkush, Allan 4, 37–38, 42, 45, 46, 47, 62, 96, 119, 121, 129, 134, 136–147, 150, 179
Arrabal, Fernando 23, 133
Arthur, Jean 70
Artists Entertainment Complex 41
Ashman, Howard 112
Astaire, Fred 84

Attack of the 50 ft. Woman 7
Aubrey, James 26
Austen, Jane 120
AVCO 53, 132

Babenco, Hector 100
"Baby, It's Cold Outside" 105
The Bad Seed 68
Balaban, Bob 91
Balaski, Belinda 107, 128, 179
The Band Wagon 84
Bande à part 18
Bardo, Robert John 110–111
Barfly 102
Bartel, Bill 9, 10, 11, 12, 13, 16, 17, 54, 104, 114, 155
Bartel, Jesse 9, 10, 11, 12, 13, 54, 104, 155
Bartel, Lucy 10
Bartel, Paul: acting 1–2, 7, 10, 12–13, 19–20, 37, 39, 45, 50, 54, 66, 68, 85, 89, 91, 92, 94–***95***, 97, 101–102, ***103***, 107, 113, 118, 119–120, 122–123; Army service 15–16; childhood 10–12; death 9–10, 121–122, 146–147; education 11–13, 14–15; family 9–11, 13, 47–49, 52, 54, 55–56, 58–59, 155; film career 15–116, 178–181; sexuality 5, 10, 12, 13, 104, 110, 123, 160; television 5, 82–85, 89, 91–94, 118–119, 120–121, 181–182
Bartel, Peter 10
Bartel, Wendy 9–10, 11, 13, 56, 112, 179, 180
Basquiat 119–120
Beast of the Yellow Night 24

195

Index

Beatty, Warren 100
Beaumarchais, Pierre 67
Begley, Ed, Jr. 102, 179, 181
Bellochio, Marco 14–15
Beltran, Robert 57–58, 59, 102, 106, 107, 156, 165, 179, 181
Benson, Lucille 24, 25, 26, 178
Bergman, Ingmar 137
Berkeley, Busby 70, 113
Berlin Film Festival 51, 80, 154
Bertolucci, Bernardo 14
Beverly Hills Brats 106
Beverly Hills Cop 106
Beverly Hills Vamp 106
Big Bad Mama 4, 27, 38, 45, 125–126, 137, 138, 148
The Billion Dollar Hobo 86
Billy's Hollywood Screen Kiss 120
Bisset, Jaqueline 102–103, 105, 108, 110, 181
Black, Karen 97
Black Panthers 99
Blackburn, Richard 40, 50, 51, 52, 53–54, 56, 58–59, 60, 64, 66, 67, 68, 71, 99–100, 107, 111, 152–163, 167, 173, 179, 180
Bland Ambition 67–68, 94–95, 107, 158, 160–161, 162, 167
Blazing Saddles 78, 81
Bleecker St. Cinema 23
Blood Relations see *Private Parts*
The Blue Lagoon 116
The Blues Brothers 31
Blythe, Gene 57
Bonnie and Clyde 27
"Born in a Trunk" 134
Boxcar Bertha 136
Brackett, Charles 70
The Brady Bunch Movie 117
The Bride Wore Black 109
Bridges, Jeff 67
British Sounds 21
The Brood 139
Brookbank, Loma Lee 55
Brooks, Mel 2, 60, 74
A Bucket of Blood 28, 119
A Bucket of Blood (remake) 119
Buckley, William F. 122
Bundy, Ted 66
Bunuel, Luis 23, 99, 108
Burbank Studios 106–107
Burnett, Carol 88
The Burning Hills 75
Burroughs, William S. 21
Burton, Tim 69

Buzzi, Ruth 71
Bye Bye Birdie 75

Caddyshack II 147
Caged Heat 4, 38, 41, 137
Camp, Hamilton 135, 179
Cannes Film Festival 60–61, 66, 69, 157
Cannonball! 7, 14, 18, 22, 40–44, 107, 123, 127–129, 144–145, 149, 164, 166, 169, 176, 179
Cannonball Baker Sea-to-Shining-Sea Memorial Dash 40–41
Canova, Judy 128
Capra, Frank 70
Car and Driver 41, 145
Carlson, Philip 18, 178
Carlton Hotel 61
Carne, Michel 15
The Carol Burnett Show 86
Carpenter, John 119
Carr, Allan 76
Carradine, David 4, 31, 32, 33, 35, 42, 44, 128–129, 145, 179
Carradine, Free 145
Carradine, Keith 2
Carradine, Robert 179
Carrie 71
Carter, Rick 85
Carver, Steve 27, 148
Castro Theatre 80, 107
Cathay de Grande 155
CBS 17, 110
Cedars-Sinai Medical Center 111
Centro Sperimentale di Cinematagrafia 14
Channel 4 118
Chaplin, Charlie 63, 134
Charlie's Angels 76
Charnin, Martin 112
Chateau Marmont 117
Cheap Trick 137
Chelsea Girls 30
"Cher, Inc." 121, 182
Chihara, Paul 179
Children of Paradise 15
The Children's Corner 106
Chopin, Frederic 67
Chopping Mall 94, 151
Christie, Julie 154
Cinecom 100–101, 102, 106–107, 181
Cinemax 1
Cinerama Releasing Corporation 21
Clair, René 70
The Clash 131

Index

Clay, Stanley 176, 179
Cline, Rick 41
Clouzot, Henri-Georges 15
Clueless (film) 120–121
Clueless (TV series) 120–121
Cockfighter 41, 137
Collins, Courtenay 112, 113
Collins, Joan 109
Collins, Roberta 31, 179
Coltrane, Robbie 118
Columbia, David 67
Comedy Store 58
The Comic Strip 118
The Comic Strip Presents.... 118, 181
Concorde-New Horizons 94, 95, 151
Consolidated Film Industries (CFI) 114, 140
Conway, Tim 86, 87, 88, 89, **90**, 180
Coppola, Francis Ford 60, 136, 152
Corman, Gene 24, 25, 27, 178
Corman, Julie 140
Corman, Roger 4, 24–28, 30–34, 37, 41, 42, 44, 45, 46, 52, 74, 80, 94–95, 105, 111, 119, 121, 125, 126, 127, 129, 130, 131, 133–134, 136, 137, 138–139, 140–141, 148–151, 153, 159, 165, 172, 179
Cornucopia Sexualis see *Does Size Really Count?*
Cort, Bud 97
Cottrell, Mickey 115
Coward, Noël 111
Craven, Wes 97, 100
Crawford, Joan 81
Crews, Harry 2, 45
Cries & Whispers 137
Crisp, Quentin 80
Criterion 56
Cronenberg, David 139
Crtichly, Bruce 114
Cruikshank, Sally 91
Cudney, Dean 130
Cukor, George 143–144
Cullman, Joan 112

Dante, Joe 4, 7, 33, 37–38, 42, 44, 45, 53, 56, 74, 83, 94, 95, 107, 121, 122, 125–135, 136, 144–145, 146, 150, 179
Dark Passage 93
Daves, Delmer 93
Davison, Jon 27, 37–38, 39, 45, 55–56, 110, 121, 122, 133, 136, 139, 145, 146, 180
Day for Night 102–103
Death Race 2000 2, 4, 7, 18, 27–36, 37, 38, 39, 40, 42, 44, 45, 58, 73, 74, 81, 122, 123, 125, 126–127, 129, 137, 138–139, 140, 143, 145, 148–149, 152, 153, 164, 169, 173, 176, 177, 179
Deathsport 4, 146
Debussy, Claude 106
DeCoteau, David 119
Deitch, Gene 62
Deitch, Kim 62
Demme, Jonathan 39, 74, 139
"Demonella" 92, 118, 183
De Niro, Robert 19, 22
Dennen, Barry 2, 12–13, 15, 17, 70, 71, 72, 84, 85, 118, 119, 178, 180, 181
De Palma, Brian 18, 19, 22, 71, 83
Desolation Angels 142
"Devil in a Blue Dress" 155
The Dharma Bums 142
Dickinson, Angie 27
"Digesting Raoul" 66
Directors Guild of America (DGA) 80, 107, 131–132
Dirty Mary, Crazy Larry 31
The Discreet Charm of the Bourgeoisie 99
DistribPix 19
Divine 5, 6, 76, 77, 78–79, 80, **82**, 97–98, 158, 160, 166, 167, 174, 180
Does Size Really Count? 19–20, 22, 37
Donaggio, Pino 53
The Double-Barrelled Detective Story 16, 99
Double Indemnity 93
Downey, Robert 21, 178
Drake, Miller 133
Dressed to Kill 71
Dressler, Marie 26
Drugstore Cowboy 110
Dubin, Al 70
Duel in the Sun 76
Dunaway, Faye 100–101, 102
Dunne, Griffin 85
Dvonch, Russ 45
Dye, Cameron 97

Eat My Dust! 45, 149
Eating Raoul 1–2, 4–5, 7, 17, 18, 50–55, 56–66, **67**, 68, 69, 71, 72, 74, 77, 78, 79, 81, 84, 85, 87, 93, 96, 99, 101, 102, 108, 109, 111, 115, 123, 134–135, 145–146, 150, 153–160, 161, 163, 167, 173, 174, **175**, 176, 177, 179–180
Eating Raoul: The Musical 111–113, 114, 161–162
The Ed Sullivan Show 117

Index

Edinburgh Film Festival 44
Edwards, Blake 28
Egyptian Movie Theater 122
Elias, Alix 85, 179
Elliott, Lang 87, 150
Ellison, Connie 18, 178
Emma 120
"Encore" 12–13
Erotic Cinema Circus 21
Escape from L.A. 119
E.T. 83
Europa Films 60
European Vacation 94, 120
Evergreen Club 21
Exploding Plastic Inevitable 30
Eyes Without a Face 40

Falk, Peter 67
Fame (TV series) 147
The Fast and the Furious 28
Fein, Art 154, 155
Feinstein, Michael 91, 106, 181
Felio, Gordon 18, 178
Fellini, Federico 161
Female Trouble 76
Fern, Bob 152
Feuer, Jed 111
Film Bulletin 125
Film-Makers' Cooperative 14, 178
Film Society of Lincoln Center 15, 23, 62, 122, 146
Filmex *see* Los Angeles International Film Exhibition
Finian's Rainbow 121
Finnell, Mike 53, 121, 130, 179
Fisher, Carrie 94, **95**
Fitzgerald, F. Scott 158
Fleischer, Max 137
Flo & Eddie 62
Fogel, Joe Ann 85
Fonda, Peter 30–31
Footlight Parade 70
42nd Street 70
Four Rooms 117–118
Fox International Classics 61, 179
Fox Run Productions 76, 180
Franju, Georges 40
Frankencar 39–40, 50, 55, 68, 153, 173–174, 176
Frankenheimer, John 2, 28
Frankenweenie 69, 101
Franklyn Theater 10–11
French Film Office 15
Frenzy 169
Fresh Air 110

Friday the 13th 97
Friedhofer, Hugo 26, 178
Friedkin, William 68
Fuller, Sam 55

Gangster Girl 15
Geffen Company 112
Gelfman, Sam 127, 179
Genet, Jean 21, 100
George, Rita 39
George Burns Comedy Week 85
Gershuny, Ted 19, 30
Gershwin, George 91, 92, 93, 94, 105, 108, 111, 181
Gershwin, Ira 92
"Gershwin's Trunk" 91–94
Get Crazy 62, 144
Getting Away with Murder 109
Gibbs, Ann 24
Ginsberg, Allen 142
The Girl Can't Help It 109
Girls' Gym *see* Rock 'n' Roll High School
Glaser, Allan 76, 77, 78, 80, 180
Glatzer, Richard 120
Godard, Jean-Luc 14, 15, 18, 21
Golan, Menahem 109
Golddiggers of 1934 113
Gonzalez, Gonzalez 77
Goodrow, Gary 85, 179, 180
Gordon, Ruth 143–144
Gottlieb, Carl 42, 94, 179
The Graduate 87
Graham, Boyd 111
Graham, Gerrit 22, 179
Grand Prix 28
Grand Theft Auto 45, 149
Grandy, Fred 31, 179
The Great Race 28
The Great Train Robbery 143
Greetings 19, 22
Gremlins 83, 95
Gremlins 2: The New Batch 107, 135
Grief 120
Grier, Rosey 75
Griffith, Charles 28, 32, 127, 148–149, 165, 179, 180
Griffith, Simone 33, 179
Gross, Terry 110
Groundlings 155
Grove Press 21, 165
The Gumball Rally 41, 44
Gunman's Walk 75

Hahn, Archie 128, 179
Hairspray 167, 168

Index

Haller, Ben 56
Halloween 97
Hanna-Barbera 28
Hanson, Curtis 56
Harbor Productions 42, 179
A Hard Day's Night 130
Hayden, Sterling 81
HBO 1
Hearst Metronome News 19, 21
Heartbeeps 144, 145, 147
Heartburn 87
Heckerling, Amy 94, 120–121, 182
Henry, Buck 56–57, 122, 155, 179
Hepburn, Katharine 143, 144
Hi, Mom! 22, 83
High Plains Drifter 76–77
Hill Street Blues 58
Hirsch, Charles 19, 22, 24
Hirsch, Tina 19, 33, 38, 95, 127, 139, 140, 179
Hirschfield, Al 93
Hitchcock, Alfred 22, 25, 122, 169, 170, 171, 173
Hochman, Larry 92
Hof Film Festival 69
Hoffman, Dustin 78
Hogan, Hulk 117, 135
Holahan, Philip 114, 181
Hollywood Boulevard 37–39, 84, 94, 129, 140, 141–144, 146, 147
The Honeymoon Killers 50, 159
The Honeymooners 87
Hooper, Tobe 92
Horizontes 19
Horovitz, Adam 107
The Hot Box 4
Howard, Ron 4, 45, 130
"Howl" 142
The Howling 53, 131–132, 134
Hudson, Rock 133
Hunter, Tab 5, 74, *75*–77, 79–80, 81, 97, 166, 167, 180
Hunter, Tim 133
Huston, John 68, 160
Hynes, Kevin 54

I Am Curious (Yellow) 165
Ice-T 88
In the Boom Boom Room 30
Inspector Clouseau 2
Into the Night 94, 101

Jack Rabin & Associates 137, 139
Jaguar Prey 119
Jamaica Inn 171

Jarmusch, Jim 7, 69, 72
Jaws 45, 130
Jewison, Norman 35–36
Johnny Guitar 81
Jones, O-Lan 113
Jones, Tommy Lee 4

Kanin, Garson 143–144
Kaplan, Jonathan 129, 136, 142, 179
Karloff, Boris 150
Katz, Jim 76, 77, 78, 100, 107, 180, 181
Katzin, Lee H. 28
Kaylan, Howard 62 **90**
Kazan, Lainie 5, 77, **82**, 91, 97, 180
Keach, James 127, 179
Kearney, Phil 24
Keaton, Buster 134
Kellman, William F. 95, 96
Kennedy, John F. 114
Kent State University 123
Kern, Jerome 111
Kerouac, Jack 142
Kimmel, Anne 54, 56, 58, 61, 71–72, 107, 114, 119, 135, 154, 179, 180, 181
Kind Hearts and Coronets 50, 63, 68
Kirkland, Sally 2, 107
Kissinger, Henry 123
Korbich, Eddie 112
Korman, Harvey 87, 88, **90**, 180
Kotite, Toni 112
Kovacs, Ernie 126
Krippendorf's Tribe 162
Kuchar brothers 123
Kung Fu 31

The Lady Eve 63
The Ladykillers 63, 159
The Lair of the White Worm 107
Landis, John 31, 50–51, 53, 56, 71, 83, 85, 94, 101, 146, 179, 189
Lane, Stewart F. 112
Lang, Fritz 39
Laughton, Charles 112
The Lavender Hill Gang 91
Lay, Carol 62
Le Mans 28
Le Millions 15
Lemora: A Child's Tale of the Supernatural 40, 152
"Let's Misbehave" 106
Leustig, Elizabeth 102
Levitt, Zane W. 95, 96–97, 105, 181
Lewis, Geoffrey 76, 97, 180
Lewis, Joseph H. 56
Lex Theatre 113

Lightning Over Water 69
Limelight 134
Lindbergh, Charles 92
Lindeman, Doug 115
Little Shop of Horrors (Frank Oz film) 112
Little Shop of Horrors (musical) 111
The Little Shop of Horrors (Roger Corman film) 28, 111
The Living End 120
Livingston, Stanley 26, 178
Locarno Film Festival 121
London Film Festival 18
The Longshot 5, 53, 86–89, **90**, 95, 123, 132, 146, 176, 180
Los Angeles International Film Exposition (Filmex) 56, 90, 100
Los Lobos 155
Love and Death 94
The Love Boat 31, 76
Love Kill 125
Love Me Tonight 70
The Lovers 18
Loy, Nanni 14
Lubitsch, Ernst 70
Lucas, Gail 12, 13
Luckinbill, Laurence 71, 180
Luddy, Tom 60
Lugosi, Bela 142
Lust in the Dust 2, 5, 6, 53, 74–**82**, 88, 95, 96, 97, 100, 107, 122, 132, 146, 160, 166–167, 169, 174, 176, 180
Luxury Liner 158, 160

Mackendrick, Alexander 50, 91, 109, 159
Mad 108, 126
Mailer, Norman 45
Majors, Lee 31
Malin, Amir 106
Malle, Louis 18, 101, 109
Mamet, David 45
Mamoulian, Rouben 56
The Man Who Knew Too Much 169
Margolyes, Miriam 118
Marnie 169
Married ... with Children 167
Martin, Steve 60
Marx, Groucho 100
Marx Brothers 108
Maslansky, Judd 114
Massey, Edith 77–78, 166
Masters, George 78–79
Maupin, Armistead 119
Maxim 149

May, Jack 41
Mayall, Rik 189
Mazursky, Paul 101, 106, 181
McBride, Joseph 45
McCambridge, Mercedes 81
McCook, John 91
McDowall, Roddy 133
McHale's Navy 86
McNamara, Robert 123
McNichol, Kristy 55
Mekas, Adolfas 14, 16
Mekas, Jonas 14, 15, 17
Melchior, Ib 27, 179
Melrose Hotel 71
Mencken, Alan 112
Menjou, Adolphe 77
Mexico City Olympics 19
Meyer, John 70, 71, 72, 91, 92, 93, 120, 158, 169, 173, 180
MGM 25, 26, 107, 140–141, 148
Miller, Dick 38, 42, 62, 121, 128, 179
Miller, Henry 21, 100
Million Dollar Mermaid 107
Minelli, Vincente 84
The Miracle of Morgan's Creek 163
Miramax 117
"Miss Stardust" 92
Mr. Billion 45
Mr. Deeds 70
Modern Marriage 109–110
The Monolith Monster 137
Monsieur Verdoux 63
Moonlight and Pretzels 70
More Tales from the City 119
Moreno, Frank 25
Moritz, Louisa 31, 179
Morrissey, Paul 78, 165
Mortuary Academy 95–96
Motion Picture Academy of Arts & Sciences 83
MTV 1
Munchies 95, 151
Murder à la Mod 18
Murder by Television 142
My Dinner with Andre 101
My Sister Sam 110

The Naked Truth 63
National Public Radio 110
Naughton, David 71, 72, 92, 180
"Naughty Nurse" 63, 81, 85, 103, 104, 117, 126, 165, 178
NBC Entertainment 82, 83, 181
"The New World" see *Stranger Than Paradise*

Index

New World Pictures 4, 24, 25, 27–28, 33, 37–38, 39, 41, 42, 44, 45, 49, 52, 53, 56, 62, 69, 80, 94, 119, 121, 125–126, 128, 131, 132, 136–143, 145, 146, 148, 149–150, 179, 180
New York Film Festival 18, 60, 61, 62, 121, 157
New York University (NYU) 2, 37, 136
Niccol, Andrew 121
Nichols, Mike 85, 87, 88, 112, 156, 180
Nicholson, Jack 87
Nicholson, James H. 132
Night Call Nurses 136
A Nightmare on Elm Street 3: The Dream Warriors 100
North by Northwest 169
Norton, Richard 112
Not for Publication 5, 7, 18, 53, 69–74, 77, 91, 92, 132, 135, 146, 150, 158, 159, 170, 174, 177, 180
Nothing Sacred 70
Notorious 169

Of Thee I Sing 12
O'Haver, Tommy 120
Oliver, Barret 69, 101, 181
On the Road 142
One Life to Live 113
One Step Beyond 118
Opatoshu, Danny 38, 62, 142
Open Season 31
Orion Pictures 53
Oswald, Lee Harvey 114
The Other Side of the Wind 134
Our Miss Brooks 46
Out of the Dark 96–98
Oz, Frank 112

Pacific Film Archive 60
Paragon, John 156
Paramount Pictures 15, 53, 56
The Party at Kitty and Stud's 31
Paul, Richard 71, 180
Peck, Gregory 76
Peckinpah, Sam 76, 79
Pee Wee Herman *see* Reubens, Paul
Pee Wee's Big Adventure 156
Peters, Bernadette 70
Petri, Elio 14
Peyser, Penny 85, 89
The Philadelphia Story 2
Pink Flamingos 76
Pinocchio 11, 40
Piranha 4, 45, 129–130, 131
Pixote 100

Planer, Nigel 118
Plaza Hotel 17
Police Academy 96
Pollack, Sydney 78
Polyester 76, 77, 166
Pop, Iggy 2
The Pope Must Diet 118
Porter, Cole 43, 105, 106, 111
"Preludio Olimpico" 19
Preminger, Otto 39
Prince 98
The Private Eyes 86
Private Parts 2, 5, 7, 18, 23–27, 28, 35, 37, 40, 70, 73, 81, 110, 123, 125, 126, 140, 148, 152, 164, 165, 169, 170–171, 175, 177, 178–179
The Prize Fighter 86
Progetti 14–15, 117
Psycho 25, 170–171, 172
Putney Swope 21

Quartet/Films, Inc. 61, 63, 179
The Queen 165
Queen Kong vs. the Devil Dykes 19
Quinn, Aileen 68, 160

Rabid 139
Rabin, Jack 137, 139, 140
"The Racer" 27
Radio City Music Hall 16
Radio Werewolf 96
Raiders of the Lost Ark 83
Ramones 1, 45, 46, 47, 131, 134
Raul's Key Service 154
Ray, Nicholas 69, 81
Reagan, Nancy 65
Reagan, Ronald 65, 93
Rear Window 22, 170, 172
Rebecca 118, 171
"Reckless Youth" 94, **95**
Red Ball Garage 41
Redd, Mary-Robin 152, 161
Reed, Lou 2, 62
Rendelstein, Les 24, 178
Renoir, Jean 99
Reubens, Paul 155–156
The Reverend and Rosie 75–76
Rialson, Candice 38, 142
Richardson, Peter 118, 119, 181
Rio Bravo 77
Rivers, Joan 77
RKO Pictures 100
Rock 'n' Roll High School (film) 1, 45–49, 59, 85, 96, 129–131, 134, 144, 146, 150

Index

"Rock 'n' Roll High School" (song) 130
Rocketship X-M 137
Rockwell, Alexandre 117
Rocky 31, 52
The Rocky and Bullwinkle Show 144
The Rocky Horror Picture Show 52, 167
Rodgers and Hart 105, 111
Rohmer, Eric 67
"Roll Over Beethoven" 144
Rollerball 27, 36
Romero, Cesar 75, 76, 96, 180
Roosevelt, Eleanor 98
Rose-Magwood Productions 16, 17, 19
Roud, Richard 60–61, 158
Rudolph, Alan 117
Ruhm, Jane 30
The Rules of the Game 99, 100
Russell, Ken 107
Ruymen, Ayn 24, 25, 178

Saiger, Susan 58, 62, 85, 102, 156, 180, 181
St. Elsewhere 147
St. John, Chris 20, 178
St. Mark's Theatre 23
Sarte, Jean-Paul 176
Saunders, Jennifer 118
Sayles, John 139
Scenes from a Marriage 99
Scenes from the Class Struggle in Beverly Hills 2, 6, 7, 9, 18, 53, 67, 69, 92, 96, 99–109, 110–111, 121, 123, 158, 160, 165, 174, 181
Scenes from the Class Struggle in Portugal 99
Schaefer, Rebecca 102, 110–111, 181
Schlossberg, Julian 61
Schnabel, Julian 119
Schroeder, Michael 88, 95, 96-r97
Schulenberg, Bob 2, 12, 13, 16, 17, 55, 88, 93, 154, 178
Schwab's Pharmacy 40, 41, 50, 101, 128, 153
Schwartz, Teri 139
Scorsese, Martin 40, 42, **43**, 44, 83, 85, 136, 179
Scott, Helen G. 15
Scream 97
Screw 21
Seattle Film Festival 61
"The Secret Cinema" (short film) 15, 16–19, 20, 21, 24, 52, 58, 71, 81, 82, 83, 84, 92, 117, 121, 126, 164, 165, 170, 173, 176, 177, 178

"Secret Cinema" (TV program) 83–85, 89–91
"The Secret Ingredient" *see* "Demonella"
Seven Beauties 144
Sex Pistols 153
Sgt. Rutledge 76
Sharkey, Ray 104, 111, 165, 181
Shatner, William 27
Shaw Brothers 127, 149
Shawn, Wallace 101, 103, 105, 113, 121, 181
Shelf Life (film) 2, 18, 109, 114–117, 119, 123, 167, 176, 177, 181
Shelf Life (play) 113–114, 115, 116
Sight & Sound 60
Silent Night, Bloody Night 30
Silver, Joan Micklin 66
Silverman, Elinor 23, 15, 16, 17
Simon, John 113
Simpson, Don 40–41, 42, 44, 128, 149, 179
Singer, Bryan 119
The Six Million Dollar Man 40
68th Street Playhouse 21
Skeletons 119
Skerritt, Tom 27
The Slams 132
Smiles of a Summer Night 100
Snoops 119, 147
Soles, P.J. 46, 130
Solondz, Todd 2
Some Like It Hot 96
Sondheim, Stephen 112–113
Spheeris, Penelope 4
Spielberg, Steven 5, 45, 82–84, 85, 89, 92, 135, 181
Stallone, Sylvester 4, 31–32, 33, 42, **43**, 52, 138, 179
A Star Is Born 134
Steele, Don 56, 127, 179
Stein, Andrea 113, 115, 181
Stein, Andy 143
Stevens, George, Jr. 19
Stevens, Robert 85
Stoler, Shirley 144
Stone, David C. 99
Stone, Robert 66
Stranger Than Paradise 69, 72
Streep, Meryl 87
Strode, Woody 76
Stud, Big John 7
The Student Nurses 24
The Student Teachers 136
Sturges, Preston 63

Sugar Cookies 30
Sundance Film Festival 74, 115
Sweeney Todd 112, 159
Synapse 152

Take Me Out to the Ball Game 107
Take the Money and Run 21, 63
Tambellini's Gate 18
Tarantino, Quentin 117
Tartikoff, Brandon 83
Tavoularis, Alex 114
Tavoularis, Dean 114
Taylor, Philip John 76, 180
Teague, Lewis 38, 127, 139
Tedesco, Denny 55, 56
The Terror 150
Theatre of the Ridiculous 18, 30
"These Foolish Things" 106
Thom, Robert 28, 32, 148–149, 179
Thomas, Betty 58
Thompson, Marshall 56
Thorn EMI 70, 72, 132, 180
Thunder and Lightning 4
To Catch a Thief 2
To Sir, with Love 46
Tony Rome 153
Toomayan, Alan 2, 53, 60, 88, 106, 179, 180, 181
Tootsie 78
Torn Curtain 169
Toronto International Film Festival 115
Tracey, Spencer 143, 144
Trailers from Hell 143
The Trip 31
Troop Beverly Hills 106
Truck Turner 137
Truffaut, François 15, 102
The Truman Show 121
Tubor, Mort 42, 128
Turner, Lana 153
Turner, Jim 113, 114, 115, 181
Twentieth Century-Fox 41, 45, 61
21st Century Entertainment 109
The Twilight Zone (TV show) 83, 85
Twister 107

UCLA Theater Arts *see* University of California at Los Angeles
Un Chien Andalou 23
Under the Yum Yum Tree 75
Underground Aces 44
Union Square Theater 112
United Artists (UA) 27, 50, 131
United Productions of America (UPA) 11, 62

United States Film Festival 74, 80
U.S. Information Agency (USIA) 19
Universal Pictures 53, 133
University of California 60
University of California at Los Angeles (UCLA) 12–13, 14, 17, 24, 40, 60, 139, 152
University of Southern California (USC) 60
Upstairs,Downstairs 108
The Usual Suspects 119

Valdez, Luiz 57
Vane, Amy 17, 178
Van Sant, Gus 110
Vanya on 42nd Street 101
Ventantonio, John 24, 26, 125, 178
Vera Cruz 76
Vertigo 171
Vestron Pictures 107
The Viking Women and the Sea Serpent 137
Village Voice 15, 51
Villalonga, José 153
Ving, Lee 62
Viva La Muerte 23, 25, 133
Vogue Theatre 135
Volz, Nedra 78, 96, 180
von Stroheim, Erich 39

Wacky Races 28
Wagner, Bruce 96, 99–100, 103, 104, 105, 107, 109, 122, 158, 181
Waiting for Godot 87
Waits, Tom 2
Wakely, Mike 125
Walker, Arnetia **103**, 105, 106, 107, 181
Walt Disney Studio 11, 40, 69, 88
Walter, Tracey 97
Warhol, Andy 30, 64, 110, 119, 165, 168
Warner Bros. Pictures 11, 41, 112, 134
Warren, Harry 70
Wass, Ted 87, **90**, 180
Waters, John 2, 7, 64, 68, 76, 77–78, 81, 108, 123, 160–161, 164–168
"We Shall Overpack" 121, 182
Weir, Peter 121
Weiss, Franz 15
Weiss, Robert K. 94
Weitzenhofer, Max 112
Wenders, Wim 69
Werner, Oskar 15
Weston, Jack 87, **90**, 180
White, Michael 52

White Dog 55–56
Whiting, Margaret 70
Whitley, Richard 45
Who Killed Bambi? 153
Who's Afraid of Virginia Woolf? 87
The Wild Angels 31
The Wild Bunch 76
Wilde, Oscar 2–3, 12, 118, 119
Wilder, Billy 70, 93, 96
Williams, Esther 107
Williams, Gigi 144
Williams, Robin 68
Winfield, Paul 55
Women in Cages 24, 38
Woronov, Mary 1, 18, 30, 31, 35, 38–39, 42, 46, 47, 50, 52, 53, *57*, 58, 59, 62, 64, 66, *67*, 71, 81–82, 84–85, 89, 94, 96, 101, 102, 105, 106, 110, 121, 127, 134, 140, 142, 143, 144, 146, 147, 150–151, 153, 156, 164, 165, 166, 167, 168, *175*, 179, 181
Writers Guild of America 130
Wynorski, Jim 94

Yates, Brock 41

Zanuck, Daryl 133
Zemeckis, Robert 83
Zmed, Adrian 112, 113
Zoetrope Studios 60
Zoot Suit 57

www.ingramcontent.com/pod-product-compliance
Ingram Content Group UK Ltd.
Pitfield, Milton Keynes, MK11 3LW, UK
UKHW042002140426
5217IPUK00015B/946